INTRIGUE THROUGH TIME
INTRIGUE THROUGHT TIME

I0160652

FREDERICK MONDERSON

SUMON PUBLISHERS

1

FREDERICK MONDERSON

SuMon Publishers
PO Box 160586
Brooklyn, New York 11216

fredsegypt.com@fredsegypt.com
sumonpublishers.com@sumonpublishers.com
blackfolksbooks.com@blackfolksbooks.com
blackegyptbooks.com@blackegyptbooks.com

ISBN – 978-1-61023-017-9
LCCN – 2010918491

In the "**Tribute to Professor George Simmonds**," '**Unsung Hero**,' Dr. Fred Monderson sat at the feet of his heroes, Brother X, Michael Carter, Dr. Leonard Jeffries, Elombe Brathe, Dr. Lewis, Prof. George Simmonds, Dr. ben-Jochannan, Sister Camille Yarbrough, among others.

Dr. Frederick Monderson is a retired college professor and school teacher who taught African History in the City University of New York and American History and Government in the New York public schools. He has written more than 1000 articles in the New York Black Press, *Daily Challenge, Afro Times* and *New American* newspapers. In this venture, Monderson lends his expertise as a

INTRIGUE THROUGH TIME

historian, Egyptologist, journalist and author of several books including *Michael Jackson: The Last Dance*; *Barack Obama: Ready- Fit to Lead*, *Barack Obama: Master of Washington, DC*, *Obama: Master and Commander*, and *Obama: The Journey Completed*; *Sonny Carson: The Final Triumph* (5 volumes); *Black Nationalism: Alive and Well*, *Black Nationalism: Still Alive and Well*; *African Nationalist Poetry and Prose*; *Black History – Part One* and *Black History – Part Two*; and on **Ancient Egypt** *Seven Letters to Mike Tyson on Egyptian Temples* and *10 Poems Praising Great Blacks for Mike Tyson*; *Where are the Kamite Kings?*; *Medinet Habu: Mortuary Temple of Rameses III*; *The Holy Land: (A* Novel on Egypt); *Intrigue Through Time* (A Novel about Egypt); *Hatshepsut's Temple at Deir el Bahari*; *The Majesty of Egyptian Gods and Temples* (a book of Egyptian Poems); *Research Essays on Ancient Egypt*; *Egypt Essays on Ancient Kemet*; *The Ramesseum: Mortuary Temple of Rameses II*; *The Colonnade: Then and Now*; *Reflections on Ancient Kemet and Glory of the Ancestors: 19 Letters to O.J. Simpson on Ancient African History*; *Celebrating Dr. Ben-Jochannan, Black History Extravaganza: Praising Dr. Ben-Jochannan* and *Let's Liberate the Temple*; *Ethiopians in Egypt*; *Ancient Egypt: Synthesis*. A student of the esteemed Dr. Yosef ben-Jochannan, Dr. Monderson conducts tours to Egypt. For Tour information, please contact Orleane Brooks-Williams at Nostrand Travel, 730 Nostrand Avenue, Brooklyn, New York 11216. Phone Number 718-756-5300.

Necklaces of the type our hero's father made for him and his love.

FREDERICK MONDERSON

1.   The Happening

The sun rose on the eastern horizon at *Waset* (Thebes) on the morning of the 12th day of the First Month of the Spring Season.

It was a normal day like any other day during the reign of Queen Hatshepsut of the 18th Thutmosid dynasty. The Queen had come into prominence as ruler of the "Throne of the Two Lands."

The night before there was a celebratory banquet at the palace. Many Nobles, Lords and Ladies were in attendance and the customary festivities had unfolded. Ministers of the government and members of the military and sacerdotal orders were there. Ambassadors from Palestine, Crete, Libya, Ethiopia, and as far away as Kadesh and Syria were among the revelers.

The Vizier Puyemre, his wife Cheraisha, and son Lord Mentuhotep and his sister Kasheisha, were at a table being served wine, beer and food by servant girls. Two orchestras provided the entertainment. Both had twelve pieces each in their musical repertoire. The band presently playing had two harps, one castanet, and a couple of other instruments.

The Nubian and Syrian Ambassadors presented the Vizier two chests with gold and jewels as tribute from their respective states. Puyemre asked Lord Mentuhotep to safeguard the treasure so he could have it transported to the treasury of the Queen the next day.

Since everyone was in a festive mood, the young prince had the treasure moved from the banquet hall by two of his assistants. The chariots transported the wealth to the river where the Vizier's craft was moored. Resting just beside this was the prince's own vessel, and he had the chests loaded aboard and set sail for the vicinity of *Djeser-djeseru,* the *Holy of Holies,* (Deir el Bahari). However, instead of delivering the riches to the temple, he had a plan that the two servants move the chests to a secret hiding place high upon the cliffs of the north side of Deir el Bahari where he secreted them away. He then had them swear an oath upon death, that they would never reveal the secret hiding place of the treasure.

INTRIGUE THROUGH TIME

On the way back across the river, there was a collision with another vessel. Both servants were knocked overboard and drowned; only to have their bodies washed ashore two days later. Mentuhotep was able to be rescued by the offending vessel, as his own ship sank. Coming ashore, he hurried by chariot to his residence, changed and returned to the banquet. As he joined his father, Vizier Puyemre, the Lady Nekajai approached.

What a beautiful maiden! Olive complexioned like he, she had stunning features. Her lips were as soft as milk with traces of pink color. Her cheeks were highly colored with shades of red and yellow. Long flowing hair to her shoulders was accentuated by golden earrings.

A necklace of gold with inlaid stones fell between her young, firm breasts lifted by the dress' halter that fell just below the globes. Her balanced walk is captivating, bedazzling, for it stuns the onlooker, transfigured by her magnetism. Drawing closer, as she extends her soft, silky hands, the aroma of her perfume magnified her qualities and just makes the mouth water.

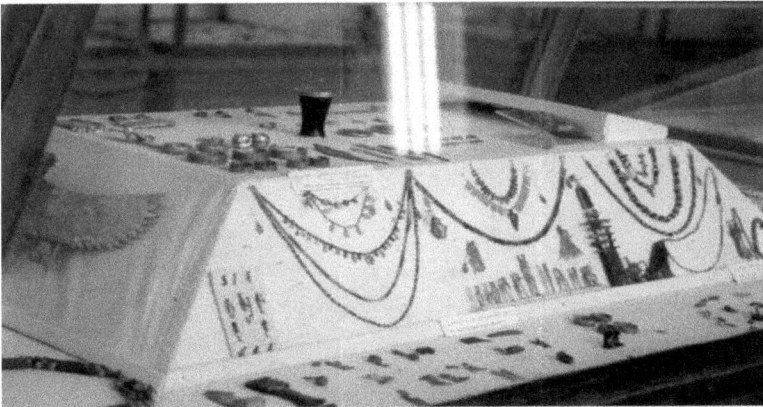

A wide assortment of gold and precious stone jewelry in the Cairo Museum of Egyptian Antiquities.

Puyemre notices the magnetic attraction between the two young people, and whispers to his son:
Puyemre: "Mentuhotep, you must marry Lady Nekajai so I can have grandchildren before it's too late."

5

FREDERICK MONDERSON

Mentuhotep: "Will do, father. I am so captivated by her beauty; I feel lost when I'm not in her presence."

Puyemre: "Lady Nekajai, do sit with us for I am sure you are aware of how you affect my son."

Nekajai: "Yes, My Lord, I am sure you realize this is the way I feel about him too."

Puyemre: "As today is my birthday, I would like to present you this wonderful necklace of gold inlaid with turquoise, obsidian, carnelian, lapis lazuli, feldspar and jasper. It is part of a-his-and-her set. I got one for Mentuhotep too."

Nekajai: "Thank you, Lord Puyemre. I will forever wear this wonderfully beautiful necklace, and keep Mentuhotep ever closer to my heart."

Puyemre: "Thank you, my dear." Turning to Mentuhotep he said: "Son, did you take care of that business I asked of you?"

Mentuhotep: "Yes, father. My two trusted servants have taken the chests to a safe place for me."

Puyemre: "Then here is your necklace, treasure it as you should treasure Lady Nekajai."

Mentuhotep: "Thank you, father. I shall always love it, you and Nekajai."

Puyemre: "Well, tonight is a wonderful night to celebrate with Nekajai here. My family is now complete with my wife Cheraisha, my daughter Kasheisha and now you two. However, I will have to cut short my celebration for I have an audience with Her Majesty very early tomorrow."

Necklaces of goddesses that protect the person as an amulet.

INTRIGUE THROUGH TIME

What a beautiful portrait of Queen Hatshepsut, Mentuhotep thought as he wept for his beloved mistress.

Two days later, the servants' bodies were recovered from the Nile River. Showing his grief, Mentuhotep first took their bodies to the temple morticians who dressed and prepared them for burial. The next day the two companions were buried in simple graves at the rear of the family estate. He never had a chance to explain to his father about their deaths. Puyemre, who had sailed to Memphis for an audience with the Pharaoh, had no knowledge of these events.

Meanwhile the young Lord had tried to return to the normal routine of his daily activities. As junior architect in charge of public works, he had returned to erecting the Temple of Mut in Asher under the direction of Senmut, the Queen's Chief Architect.

At the end of his first day back at work, while driving his chariot, he stops at the marketplace and orders a bouquet of flowers sent to his beloved Nekajai.

Two days later, at the end of the day's work, the young Lord Mentuhotep drives his chariot at a terrific speed, as he headed to meet his wonderful young love. The horses are startled by an asp. They rise frighteningly. Young Lord Mentuhotep is thrown from his chariot, hits his head and breaks his neck. What a calamity!

Word is dispatched to his father Vizier Puyemre in Memphis: "Come, My Lord, your son Mentuhotep has had a terrible accident. He has been killed."

Puyemre: "Oh my goodness! I must leave immediately. Steward, please arrange for a hurried audience with Her Majesty. O, I must beg leave of her."
Steward: "Very well, My Lordship."

Puyemre, with all the customary court platitudes and practices completed, says to Her Majesty: "My revered Majesty, my eldest son Mentuhotep has been killed in a riding accident at *Waset* (Thebes). I must offer a humble apology and beg leave of Your August Majesty to attend to this matter in this time of tragedy."

The Temple as Mentuhotep envisioned it back in his day.

Pharaoh: "Without doubt, my trusted Vizier Puyemre. The Crown will put at your disposal a contingent of soldiers and a second contingent of workers, quarrymen, artisans and a ship. They will sail to Aswan and hew a most splendid Sarcophagus to house your most beloved son."

INTRIGUE THROUGH TIME

"There is, I am told, a tomb nearing completion in the Valley of the Nobles. We
shall expropriate this and have your beloved son buried within. The Crown will compensate the owner of that tomb with all the customary apologies for all the inconveniences caused as a result of this untimely tragedy. The Pharaoh has spoken, so let it be done."
Puyemre: "Your Majesty has always been a most loving, considerate and just divinity, among us mere mortals. I will forever sing praises to Your August Majesty."

Her Majesty Himself, Queen Hatshepsut, *Ma'at-Ka-Ra* revered by her subjects and our Hero.

FREDERICK MONDERSON

Puyemre buried his son with all the customary trappings and accoutrements consistent with New Kingdom burial practices. He had a special *Book of the Dead* made for him with an eye to the challenges of the Judgment. It was his duty and intention that his son survives the judgment and attains everlasting life through immortality.

The body was taken to the embalming house at Thebes where it was prepared with great care, and after the customary waiting period, it was wrapped in the best linen. His jewelry as personal belongings were affixed on the body. Puyemre thought, 'I must remember to place his dagger and necklace on the body.' He personally inspected the *Book of the Dead*, or *Book of Going Forth by Day*, to make sure the pitfalls were pointed out clearly. He was prepared to leave nothing to chance. He did for his son, as he as son would have done for his father. He made sure the *Negative Confessions* were included because his son had been a good person, a loving son, and a model citizen. He was to recite them in the Judgment.

THE NEGATIVE CONFESSIONS

1. I have not done Iniquity
2. I have not robbed with violence
3. I have not done violence to any man
4. I have not committed theft
5. I have not slain man or woman
6. I have not made light the bushel
7. I have not acted deceitfully
8. I have not purloined the things which belong to God
9. I have not uttered falsehood
10. I have not carried away food
11. I have not uttered evil words
12. I have not attacked any man
13. I have not killed the beasts that are the property of God
14. I have not acted deceitfully
15. I have not laid waste the land which has been ploughed
16. I have never pried into matters to make mischief
17. I have not set my mouth in motion against any man
18. I have not given away to wrath concerning myself without a cause

INTRIGUE THROUGH TIME

19. I have not defiled the wife of a man
20. I have not committed any sin against purity
21. I have not struck fear into any man
22. I have not encroached upon sacred times and seasons
23. I have not been a man of anger
24. I have not made myself deaf to the words of right and truth
25. I have not stirred up strife
26. I have made no man to weep
27. I have not committed acts of impurity, neither have I lain with men
28. I have not eaten my heart
29. I have abused no man
30. I have not acted with violence
31. I have not judged hastily
32. I have not taken vengeance upon the god
33. I have not multiplied my speech over much
34. I have not acted with deceit, and I have not worked wickedness
35. I have not uttered curses on the king
36. I have not fouled water
37. I have not made haughty my voice
38. I have not cursed the god
39. I have not behaved with insolence
40. I have not sought for distinctions
41. I have not increased my wealth, except with such things as are justly mine own possessions
42. I have not thought scorn of the god who is in my city.

Once everything was properly done, he personally led the funeral procession to *Abtu* (Abydos) so his son could receive the blessings of Osiris. He thought to himself, 'Even though we worship Amun-Ra, I just want to make sure I touch all the bases. After all, my son shall live again!' Then they returned to *Waset* for burial in the Valley of the Nobles. Even further, to ensure everything was done, he visited her shrine at *Djeser-djeseru* (Deir el Bahari) and besieged the Goddess Hathor, patron of the western Necropolis, to have pity and provide safe passage for his son, Mentuhotep. Just above her shrine there at *Djeser-djeseru*, he made sacrifices at the portal where the soul on its journey into the land beyond, entered in through that cavern. Truly it was said Puyemre loved his son and did everything for his resurrection. At the burial, his mother Cheraisha, sister Kasheisha, and sweetheart Nekajai could not contain themselves. Their grief seemed uncontrollable. Everyone who came to the funeral, from far and wide, agreed Mentuhotep was a wonderful person. His passing was indeed a great loss not simply to his family, but to *Waset*, the Monarchy and *Kemet* (Egypt) as a whole.

Standing before an Osiride Figure of Queen Hatshepsut, Erik Monderson assumes a "Royal Position" on the Upper Terrace.

INTRIGUE THROUGH TIME

At a sleepy antique dealer's store, **GHAFOOR'S ANTIQUES**, 1968 Fifth Avenue, between 48th and 49th Streets, a cat pursues a rat one night in mid-June, 1985, in a back room in the basement. A small obscure case is knocked over, causing a puff of smoke, out of which a tall thin man appears standing in a sort of Osiride figure position. His hands, the right on top of the left, are crossed against his chest. He opens his eyes, looks around at very unfamiliar surroundings. Frightened, he touches his side and is reassured in the safety of his dagger being there. This was his favorite weapon and knowing it's at his side he beams in confidence. He opens his eyes, looks around and thinks out loud: 'Where am I?' 'How did I get here?' 'What day is this?' Then he notices a calendar that reads Wednesday June 12, 1985.

Yet, he begins to think of 1000 questions. Then reasons: 'I have awoken in a different time and place.' Looking around further, he notices unfamiliar objects, many old and dusty. Then his gaze catches a glimpse of an old wooden coffin lying in a corner. He moves to investigate and notices familiar Egyptian markings on the exterior. He looks further and notices a set of stairs. As he moves in that direction, he catches a glance of himself in a mirror on the wall. He was a startling figure, 6 feet 4 inches, and 190 pounds; olive-complexioned, very handsome, about 30 years old, wearing a long flowing brown robe over bandages, and leather sandals.

His necklace was there, placed on his neck and, in an instant, he had recollections of his beautiful Nekajai. 'Will I ever see her again?' he thought. The gold rings on both his fingers on each hand sparkled in the mirror as he clasped his face in his hands. There were bracelets and armbands on both hands noticed in the cutaway of both sleeves. He also wore one anklet on each leg.

His memory began to clear. He could now remember some events of that fateful day. He remembered finishing work, getting in his chariot and riding at a fast speed for he had a date with his beloved Lady Nekajai. Just then as asp spooked his horses, he remembers falling, the pain of striking his head, then nothing. He grasped his head and his neck. There was a bump on his head from a healed cut of some sort. He could remember nothing else!

FREDERICK MONDERSON

The right "Eye of Horus" is also an amulet of protection.

Both right and left "Eyes of Horus" studded in precious stones.

INTRIGUE THROUGH TIME
3.   Coming Forth by Day

Mentuhotep ascended the stairs and emerged in a bazaar with beautiful artifacts scattered in display cases and on counters. Looking through the glass window, he instantly saw unfamiliar surroundings.

First, he could not see the Nile River. The buildings were unfamiliar. There were no chariots but some sort of contraption with four wheels that moves about. The clothing people wore was equally unfamiliar.

People were looking through the glass window at the strangely dressed man in the store. Just then he moved to explore other parts of the store. In a back room he found a complete wardrobe.

Finally, he reasoned to himself, 'Clearly, I'm in a strange place, the people are certainly dressed differently; and if changing my clothes will make me blend in, then for expediency's sake, I must now wear what these people wear.'

A photograph on the wall is of a well-dressed gentleman in a dark suit, shirt and shoes with a handkerchief in his left breast pocket. Our Hero searches the closet, chooses an outfit and duplicates the attire of the figure in the photograph. He relaxes the rest of the night. By 10:00 am the morning of Thursday, June 13, 1985, the owner arrives, opens his "Bazaar;" and by 11:00 am, there are more than a dozen persons in the store, pursuing, admiring, and purchasing antiques. He listens to the pattern of speech. He also notices they use paper to purchase.

From the wardrobe room the Hero moves stealthily to the bathroom, as the owner is busily engaged with customers. No one notices that Mentuhotep did not come through the entrance door, though he has appeared on the floor of the Antiques store. He first stops to admire a painting on the wall. Meanwhile he listens to the discussions on the floor and, being a man of great intelligence, possessing and certain observing or perceptive, hearing and thinking characteristics

15

FREDERICK MONDERSON

taught by his father, he easily fits in with use of the new language. Just then the owner notices the well-dressed gentleman who seems so imposingly out of place in his store. 'Somehow I did not notice when he came in,' Ghafoor thinks. The Hero then approaches the main counter and Mr. Ghafoor asks: "May I help you, Sir?"

Mentuhotep: "I'm just admiring some of your jewelry."

Ghafoor: "Well, we sell, buy or trade, all types of valuable items. We pay in cash money"

Mentuhotep: Realizing he needs cash money to function in this new society, he says: "I am actually looking to sell a few pieces of family heirlooms."

Ghafoor: "I will be glad to take a look at your pieces and give an appraisal of their value."

Mentuhotep removes two of his rings and the two bracelets and places them on the counter. Ghafoor's eyes light up because these items seem authentic and uniquely ancient. He had seen these types of items in the Metropolitan Museum of Art. Just then he catches a glimpse of the handle of the dagger in the gentleman's waist. The jewels of the handle seem to sparkle. Not only do his eyes do a double-take, but Ghafoor's heart begins to pound.

Ghafoor was 53 years old. He had been an antiques dealer for more than 30 years. He inherited the business from his father who passed away more than 15 years ago. He himself had lost his wife some years ago and his only daughter Angeline, 33 years old, lives in Los Angeles, California. She is a writer, studies art at Berkley and manages her own art gallery there. She fits comfortably in the young Hollywood set.

Nevertheless, Ghafoor had traveled extensively in Europe and the East, securing antique items and making deals. Therefore, he had seen items, developed a trained eye for authentic and unusual pieces; and he had an excellent list of *Who's Who* clients who are collectors and would purchase such items at short notice. He realized these were unusual pieces in front of him and kept running his hands over the bracelets. Then he picks them up. Next, he cups the lot and in a transfixed gaze seems to savor the antiquity of the pieces within his grasp.

INTRIGUE THROUGH TIME

While he could not precisely place the pieces, he did realize they seemed like ancient Egyptian. Even more, his eyes kept returning to the sparkling dagger in the gentleman's waist.

Ghafoor: "May I ask the origin of these pieces and how you came into possession of them?"
Mentuhotep: "Oh, they're Egyptian, family heirlooms and that sort of thing. Personal property, you know what I mean?"

Ghafoor keeps thinking, 'This must be my lucky day!' But his eyes kept returning to the dagger. Then he asks:
Ghafoor: "Is the dagger for sale?"
Mentuhotep: "No, not really, I feel naked without it."

Ghafoor thinks, 'He feels naked without his dagger!' 'What manner of man is this,' he thought further. Then he looks at Mentuhotep again. He now begins to study the fellow. The gentleman is well dressed. He wears suits similar to mine. He is about 6 feet 4 inches tall, my height. He weighs anywhere from 185 to 192 pounds. He has an interesting face and olive colored skin, an Egyptian nose, and not a sign of gray in his hair. He must be no more than 30-31 years old. 'Why did he come to my store?' he thought. 'Is this really my lucky day?'

Mentuhotep: "I may have two additional pieces for sale if the price is right."
Ghafoor: "I will contact some potential buyers and if you will return within two hours, I may have some news for you. The Metropolitan Museum of Art is a few blocks from here. It offers one of the most enlightening displays in all of Manhattan, actually in New York City. Perhaps you may want to view their Egyptian collection, while I make the contacts. Here is a complimentary ticket that will get you into the museum. If you will allow me to take a photograph of these pieces, then you can retain them until we are able to make whatever arrangements."

Ghafoor then produces a camera and takes a series of photographs of the pieces together and individually.

Mentuhotep: "That is ok with me. Thank you for your time and the ticket. I will see you in two hours."

FREDERICK MONDERSON

Walking him to the door Ghafoor points towards uptown and says: "The Museum is on this Fifth Avenue at 81st Street. You could walk along the park and get there in 15 minutes." Thus, the Hero makes his way uptown as he admires the names of the stores, and observes the architectural features of the buildings lining the avenue, the hotels and the various people. He equally attracts more than an occasional glance from women who are attracted by his princely demeanor, handsome features and his seeming mysterious personality. Along the way he notices the Parks Department Building and the Monument to New York Veterans around 67th Street. A few steps later he sees what appears to be the upper reaches of a *Tekhen* or an obelisk. That's strange he thought! Soon he arrives at the Met and as an architect, takes a minute to admire the external façade of the building.

This is the first building he notices that significantly displays columns at its entrance. Columns in front of this building create an instant flashback for our Hero who remembers the prodigious use of columns in his home city *Waset* (Thebes).

Erik Monderson stands beside the *in situ* 10-step altar in the Court of Ra-Horakhty, the Sun God, where the ritual is performed in the Open Air for instant communication with the deity.

INTRIGUE THROUGH TIME
4.   The Sighting

Meanwhile, Ring, Ring, Ring!

"Hello!"

Ghafoor: "This is Ghafoor. I have a piece you may be interested in. While I don't have it presently, I have seen it and felt it and have a photograph of it. The owner will be back in my shop within two hours. I just wanted to give you a heads-up on this set. It comes from ancient Egypt."

Somerset: "That is very kind of you. Have you alerted anyone to its availability?"

Ghafoor: "As you know, I'm under obligation to also inform three of your associates, Mr. Wisenthal, Mr. Gray and Senator Williams. Lord Stanhope is flying in from London this evening, and I will try to get his expert opinion on the authenticity of the pieces and their potential value based on his determination on the particular age from which the pieces seem to have come."

Somersett: "Good work! However, I wish to remind you of my interest in ancient Egyptian jewelry. Equally, I must remind you, I have been more generous to you than most of your other clients. I am also aware of how delightfully ecstatic you are about being the conduit of jewelry of such exquisite quality and age. I remember how delightful and pleased you were to simply touch the last piece I bought. I may extend the same privilege if I successfully acquire it."

Ghafoor: "Thank you, Sir. I should also inform you, there is a dagger I observed in the gentleman's waist under his jacket. While I neither had a good look at it, nor touched it, I did see the sparkle of the jewelry encrusted on its handle."

Somersett: "That's great! However, since this is not an official sighting or offer, there is a $10,000 reward for not sharing that particular information with your other clients."

Ghafoor: "Well, Sir, I know you have always been generous to me for all services rendered. That is why you are the first person I called with the inside track in this respect."

Somersett: "Thank you."

FREDERICK MONDERSON

As our Hero ascends the stairs to the entrance at the Met, they create a flashback in his memory to the times he visited temples at *On* (Heliopolis) and various sites at *Waset* accompanying his father, the Vizier Puyemre. At the top of the stairs he pauses, mindful of the people coming and going and whispering about the Egyptian collection.

Entering through the door he approaches the desk, hands in his ticket and passes into the Hall of Egyptian Antiquities. Our Hero is instantly amazed at the collection, and how it is arranged chronologically from the Prehistoric, through the Old and Middle Kingdoms. He is particularly amazed at the events of the early New Kingdom and the trauma his nation experienced in the subsequent periods. As he perused and took in the entire collection, the Hero experienced multiple flashbacks reflecting on the destiny of his nation as it dealt with the changing circumstances then emerging in the region.

What an experience! If someone tracked Mr. Mentuhotep as he moved from showcase to showcase, they would notice contortions, infusion of energy, and highs and lows as he reflected on the experiences of his nation. Some things he was familiar with and others followed his demise that startled him to find out about these developments.

Like a yo-yo he rode the highs and lows of the Egyptian experience with an effect different from the average visitor, so detached from the cases, while he explored the dynamics of his own cultural history.

Finally, he comes to the end of the exhibit and seeks a place in which to rest and recuperate.

A desire to psychologically relieve himself takes our Hero to the rear of the Met. Just then the odor of the Cafeteria hits him, as if he did not experience enough. Seeking a table to recoup, our Hero notices two females sitting together, enjoying a meal. Not paying much attention to them, he simply sought to recoup from the dynamics of his nation's history he had just experienced. He thought reasonably, so much has happened to my country!

INTRIGUE THROUGH TIME

Further, he wondered 'Whatever happened to my mother and my father, the Vizier Puyemre?' 'What happened to my sister Kasheisha?' 'Whatever happened to my beloved Nekajai?' Just then he felt for the necklace on his neck. So many memories were contained therein. He wondered whatever happened to that wonderful experiment in human experience. He thought of her beauty, gentleness, wonderful aura, aroma, perfume, potential, what a woman! 'How I miss her,' he exclaimed silently.

He thought of Puyemre expecting grandchildren!

The man stood there experiencing power surges from north, south, east and west. Fortunately, he was young and strong, before his fateful experience. The extraordinary individual he was, he was charged both negatively and positively. Standing strong, he absorbed it all, good and bad. But, like any vessel, having experienced the activity, he needed to recharge. Then he sat again!

As if he had not experienced enough, he noticed the two women still sitting at a table staring at him. At first, he thought nothing of this. Then, when the "dust settled" speaking metaphorically; he received a jolt, so to speak!

The woman on the left, there was a familiarity about her. He then did a double-take. She was really familiar. It was as if he had seen a woman from his past. His chest thumped! He grabbed it. In doing so, he made contact with the necklace around his neck and under his shirt. Just then her name and face came back to him. That face was Nekajai. He remembered now. There were two necklaces. It was as if in an instant he had been transported back to his homeland; back to *Waset* (Thebes), back to the banquet at the palace with his father, mother, sister and the beautiful Nekajai. Yes! His father gave both of them necklaces.

Everything seemed to come back to him in the flashback. His father. The banquet. Nekajai. The servants. Their death. The treasure. Oh, yes, the treasure! He remembered he had buried the two chests of treasure at Thebes on the hills above *Djeser-djeseru*, Temple of Queen Hatshepsut.

21

FREDERICK MONDERSON

All these events happening within his head had created an enormous weight on his shoulders, on his person. He sat there as calm as ever, while the dynamo of events was occurring within his head. He realized people were staring at him. Transfixed as he was, they knew something was happening, yet the man sat there with a quiet dignity, stately, as if with a royal demeanor.

After a while he got up to leave. He noticed the two women again. They were watching him with a sort of approving smile. The one on the right had the approving look with soft lips that seemed to invite him, but he just walked on because it was almost two hours since he left the antiques shop and he had to return. Out the door, he headed downtown for his appointment.

On the way, his mind began to wander. Quickly it flashed back across time into antiquity, thinking of Nekajai. Then back to the faces he saw at the Museum. For an instant he thought wickedly, 'Has Nekajai come back into my life? She meant so much to me.' Nevertheless, he fought to suppress that thought, for a most pressing business lay at hand.

World War II Memorial on 5th Avenue on way to Metropolitan Museum of Art.

INTRIGUE THROUGH TIME

Coming to the end of Central Park at 59th Street and Fifth Avenue, he noticed the Plaza Hotel that seemed so ideally situated. It seemed 5-star at least. In need of accommodations, he thought of seeking residence there. However, that must wait upon conclusion of the business of the appointment.

As an architect himself, he began to take note of the special features of the buildings lining Fifth Avenue and the names and nature of businesses located there. He passed the huge Cathedral reminding him of some temples of his ancient land. It seems he is transported back and forth through time in an instant, reflecting on his ancient past, with recollections of his family, love, work, and pastime, boating on the river, hunting in the marshes, riding in his chariot at a terrific speed. Wow! He stopped dead in his tracks. He realized he is a perfect example of speed kills. This he dismisses! He thinks of the wonderful face he saw in the Museum. Just then he crossed 49th Street and the antiques shop came into view. Before entering, he paused for a moment and composed himself. Now he must secure the best deal for his treasure. While in the Museum he removed the two arm bands adding to his small cache. For an instant he thought of the larger cache he had hidden at *Waset*. Smiling, he thought 'I must devise a means to retrieve my treasure.' One thing he has come to realize, great pride and price is placed on antiquities from his ancient land. He heard enough comments in the Museum to realize he may be a very wealthy man. That is, if he could secure his treasure.

As he walked into Ghafoor's Antiquities this Thursday afternoon about 4:00 pm, there were about a dozen people in the store. Unlike his previous appearance in the store when he was hardly noticed, the proprietor spotted him immediately. Ghafoor seemed nervous, almost biting his lip, wondering if the tall, cultured, olive-skinned gentleman would return with his antique jewelry.

He approached him immediately.

Ghafoor: "I hope you had a pleasant afternoon, Sir," he said.
Mentuhotep: "Oh, yes," he replied. "It was very eventful. Thanks again for the ticket to the Museum. I was really fascinated with the Egyptian display. Some of it I was aware of, but other parts are

relatively new to me, so I was happy to fill in the gaps in my knowledge and memory."

A Memorial on 5th Avenue along the way to the Metropolitan Museum of Art at 5th Avenue and 82nd Street.

Ghafoor: "You will be pleased to know I have contacted a collector who may be interested in your cache. In fact, I contacted at least three potential buyers who may be interested. However, I am expecting an antiques expert, an English Gentleman, Lord Samuel Milford Stanhope, who is flying in from London tonight. Within a few days we should be able to conclude the entire matter."

Mentuhotep: "Well, such a delay may force me to make other arrangements because I have to address a financial matter by the end of the day. Not being able to attend to that may cost me a substantial sum. More importantly, my credibility may be at stake in terms of my ability to deliver."

Ghafoor: "My good Sir, I have a proposition for you."
Mentuhotep: "And what is that?"
Ghafoor: "I would like to propose a partnership in this matter. Let me advance you the sum of $100,000.00 on the collection to show you I am acting in good faith. I will provide you with the cash; you deposit the jewels in my vault. Upon conclusion of the transaction, you will receive the full value of your merchandise minus the advance."

24

INTRIGUE THROUGH TIME

Mentuhotep: "I am a pretty good judge of character and believe you are acting in good faith. Therefore, I will deposit my jewels in your vault. However, I do have one question for you."
Ghafoor: "What is it?"
Mentuhotep: "Do you keep that type of cash on hand?"
Ghafoor: "Yes, My Lord. It is to be able to transact and complete such an opportune transaction as the one you just presented."

Our Hero thinks to himself, 'How does he know I am a Lord, the son of Lord Puyemre, Vizier of the Kingdom of Upper and Lower *Kemet* (Egypt), residing at *Waset*, the Scepter, the Throne of the Two Lands?'

Ghafoor motions him into a side room, opens a wall safe, produces the sum of $100,000.00 and lays it before the seated gentleman. Mentuhotep reaches into his breast pocket and removes a pouch containing four rings, two bracelets and two armbands. He hands over the jewel cache to Ghafoor and retrieves the sum of money. With this transaction completed, Ghafoor places the jewels in his vault, closes his safe and says: "Thank you, partner."

Mentuhotep thanks him and leaves the premises. He heads uptown to the hotel by the Park. Crossing the street, he noticed a parked van, Los Angeles, California Moving, delivering furniture at the curb. Noticing, yet not noticing the vehicle, he kept heading uptown, his mind working overtime.

Our Hero thought of the "Partnership" Ghafoor offered him; the Museum; the ladies he noticed, especially the one with the familiar face; the cache of jewels in the old country; and the Museum experience. He thought about his family. He wondered how his father, the Vizier Puyemre, had fared after his untimely death. Whatever happened to his younger sister and his mother? The Lady Nekajai, did she stay celibate? Did she marry again? Who was the lucky person to win her soft, gentle, but wonderfully stimulating heart?

25

FREDERICK MONDERSON

Metropolitan Museum of Art on 5th Avenue and 82nd Street where our hero began his modern education and the experiences that would shape his life into the future.

He remembered telling his father he would be 'lost without Nekajai,' and that was tantamount to being dead! Now dead and resurrected, in a new time and place, he has to start over. He must build a life in this new land. His skills as an architect may not be as useful because the type of buildings constructed in this new city is so different than his Nile River country. Then his mind came back to the "Partnership." Perhaps he could add the anklets to the cache in Ghafoor's office. This may certainly add to the settlement he will receive. Then he felt his chest, the necklace was there. He again wondered about the second necklace belonging to Nekajai. He wondered if she kept it; 'Whether she was buried with it. Is it still attached to her body, soul, spirit, through the timeless void of eternity? Is it still hanging around that soft, strong and beautiful neck? Is it still resting on that beautiful and warm olive-complexioned chest, gently caressing the firm and inviting breasts, where he so frequently and gently rested his head feeling he stood at the gates of paradise? Oh, darn, there's the hotel,' he thought even more.

INTRIGUE THROUGH TIME

The Plaza Hotel where our Hero stayed and launched his expedition to create ancient and modern memories, recover his buried treasure and where he met and fell in love with the woman of his dreams and past life.

The doorman eyed him, noticing he had no luggage but there was an air of nobility, self-confidence, self-assured leadership about this gentleman. 'I wonder if he is a good tipper,' the doorman thought.

Amulets and pendants of all sorts in gold and precious stones.

5. Contact

He walked through the door, glancing right and left, picking up details, noticing people and movements with that trained eye. Even more important, as a Commander of the Imperial Guard, he was always very keen-eyed as he conducted daily inspections. He was Assistant to Lord Senmut, Chief Architect of the Queen and builder of the Temple of Mut in Asher. In this position, he trained himself to pick up architectural and artistic details on the highest points of the pylon or on the architrave and cornice overhead. He also kept a keen eye on workmen so his projects would be completed on schedule.

He approached the reception desk. The pretty young lady asked: "Can I help you, Sir?"

Mentuhotep: "Certainly. I would like some accommodations."

Clerk: "We have rooms of all sizes. Those on the higher floors are more luxurious, and more expensive. What would you like?"

Mentuhotep: "Not top of the line, but comfortable."

Clerk: "We have rooms from three hundred, five, six and eight hundred per night. They're a little less if you book multiple nights."

Mentuhotep: "The six hundred will be fine. I will be here for 10 days. Hopefully by that time I will be able to conclude my business."

Clerk: "If you stay 10 days, I can give you the six hundred for five. If, however, you stay real long term, we can make better arrangements. This includes meals served in our restaurant across the lobby. It does not include beverages."

Mentuhotep: "Good."

Clerk: "Great. Name?"

Mentuhotep: "What name?"

Clerk: "Your name, Sir."

Mentuhotep: "Michael Mentuhotep."

Clerk: "Address? Any luggage?"

Mentuhotep: "Los Angeles, California. No!"

Clerk: "Good. How will you pay? Will that be Cash, Check or Credit Card?"

Mentuhotep: "Cash. Here's $10,000.00 in cash, in case I stay beyond the 10 days. Here's $200.00 for you being so kind and professional."

INTRIGUE THROUGH TIME

Clerk: "Why thank you, Sir. William, please show this gentleman to his room, number 1825. Thank you again, Sir. Please call on me if you need any assistance. We begin serving dinner at six. Cocktails are extra, as I indicated. Thank you, again."

William: "This way, Sir. You're on the eighteenth floor. The elevator is waiting." To the elevator operator he says: "18."

In a minute the Elevator Operator says: "Here we are on the 18th floor."

William: "This way, Sir. I'm familiar with your room. You have an excellent view of the Park. Here we are." He opens the door exposing the luxury of the guest's accommodations. Next, he moves to the door at the balcony and motions his guest to follow. "You have an excellent view here. You could see the Great Lawn and there's Cleopatra's Needle."

Mentuhotep: "Cleopatra's needle?"

William: "Yes. The Obelisk!"

"Hmm" Mentuhotep muttered, 'he means the *Tekhen.*' "Thank you," he said to William, slipping him a $100.00 bill.

William: "Thank you, Sir. My name is William. If you need anything please don't hesitate to call me. I will alert the Maître D that you will be down for dinner later."

Mentuhotep says: "Thank you." William leaving, he is once again alone. He removes his jacket, shirt and tie then flops down on the bed. The necklace seemed plastered to his smooth, muscular chest. Before you know it, he was asleep.

The ringing of the phone woke him.

Mentuhotep: "Hello!"

William: "Sir, this is William the Valet. I just thought I would give you a call to remind you that dinner is being served."

Mentuhotep: "Thank you, William. What time is it?"

William: "Its 8:00 o'clock, Sir.

Mentuhotep: "Good. I shall be down shortly." He reflects upon his day since arrival and considers it a really eventful day and feels pleased how he has held up.

Fully dressed, our Hero leaves his room and moves towards the elevator. He begins to construct a mental "to-do List." 1. Need

29

FREDERICK MONDERSON

additional clothing; 2. Luggage; 3. Must take a day trip around Manhattan, New York City, to become familiar with its layout and some of its landmarks; 4. Must devise a means to return to Egypt to find the treasure; 5. Perhaps William can be really helpful; 6. Must return to the Museum to revisit the display; 7. Need to determine the value of Egyptian antiques.

"Here we are, Sir" said the elevator operator. Stepping out, he walks across the lobby following his nose to the restaurant. He opens the door and steps in. A male and a female waiter approached him. It's as if he was expected. As he follows them, he surveys the room. People are busy eating. There's chatter. Soft, but titillating, music fills the ear. As he was being seated, across the room someone said softly, "Look! A sight for sore eyes!"

Two women sitting at a table sipping cocktails and waiting on their dinner were surprised to see the tall gentleman from the Museum.

First Lady: "Isn't that the gentleman from the Museum?"
Second Lady: "Yes. It is the handsome devil. He looks and moves with such self-confidence, as if he has been around."
First Lady: "There is such an air of nobility about him. I wonder if he's married." A strange feeling came over her. It's as if she's blushing.
"Are you alright, darling?" her companion enquired: "You can tell me."
First Lady: "Strange, but I felt a kind of jolt as I thought about the perspective of him being married."
Second Lady: "Jealous?"
First Lady: "Ha. Ha."
Second Lady: "Let's invite him over."
First Lady: "Waiter!"
Waiter answers: "Yes, Madam."
First Lady: "I wonder if you can do me a very special favor."
Waiter: "Anything, Madam."
First Lady: "I would like you to go over and convince that gentleman over there to join us," she said slipping him a ten-spot.
Waiter: "Thank you, Madam. I will do my best."
Sarlinda: "Go for it."

INTRIGUE THROUGH TIME

The waiter walks over to where the gentleman is sitting, reading the Menu. He says to the gentleman: "Sir, those two beautiful Ladies over there request the pleasure of your company. They wish if you could join them for dinner."

Looking over at them, the women waved at him. He is jolted. "Thank you. Tell them I will be delighted." And the waiter was off to deliver the news.

Collecting himself and rising from his seat, Mentuhotep felt as if charged by a bolt of electricity. It's as if he had made "contact." Moving across the dining hall, this man of extraordinary poise and confidence had heads turning. As he moved closer to the women, he thought, 'Did Nekajai also make the journey through time?" Then he was there!

Mentuhotep: "Good evening, Ladies. Thank you for inviting me to join you for dinner. I thought for sure this would have been a boring evening, but within the company of such stunning and distinguished beauty, that thought is farthest from the truth. My name is Michael Mentuhotep."

"Mr. Mentuhotep, please do sit down. My name is Fantegla Somersett. My companion is Sarlinda Wisenthal. We're very pleased to meet you."

"I think the pleasure is really mine," said Mentuhotep as he sat down
Sarlinda signaled the waiter.
Waiter: "May I help you, Madam?"
Sarlinda: "We'll have the same!"
Waiter: "And you, Sir?"
Mentuhotep: "It's been quite a day! Perhaps I need a rather stiff drink, to make me fully realize how fortunate I am to be in such wonderful company of not one but two beautiful ladies." However, he still has not looked closely at the ladies. What do you have, perhaps you could recommend something?"
Waiter: "Well, Sir, we have Johnny Walker Black Whiskey, Royal Crown Whiskey, Irish Scotch Whiskey, Hennessy Brandy, Russian Vodka, and other special drinks that are concoctions we make."
Mentuhotep: "Did you say Royal Crown?"

FREDERICK MONDERSON

Waiter: "Yes Sir."

Mentuhotep, musing, said: "I always liked Royal Crown." No one really understood that statement!

Waiter: "Will that be all, Sir?"

Mentuhotep: "In addition, I'll have, did you say, Hennessy Brandy?"

Waiter: "Coming right up, folks."

While all this was going on, the women's gazes were glued taking in every contour of the face of this handsome, young, poised gentleman. The light played tantalizingly on the smooth, spotless olive colored skin. The lips were sexually inviting, a little full, falling just below the characteristic Egyptian nose. His eyes were dark brown, hazelish, confident, and inviting! Perhaps it was the two drinks they each had previously that created that starry-eyed, questioning, 'I would run away with you' look, as the waiter arrived with their drinks.

As if recharging himself and not uttering a word, he looking intently at the towering beauty of a twin-dish in his company, Mentuhotep's mind flashed back to the last such occasion he sat in beautiful company. It was the banquet at the palace with his father, mother, sister, and the woman who meant so much to him. The wonderful Nekajai, 'Oh, how I miss her,' he thought.

Waiter: "Here you are, folks! The same for you, Ladies. Royal Crown and Hennessy's for you, Sir. Your meal will be here shortly, Ladies. Have you ordered dinner as yet, Sir?"
Mentuhotep: "Actually, no. I have not ordered dinner as yet. I will have broiled salmon, with onions and garlic, salad, two vegetables and a pinch of lemon. Make the vegetables potatoes and squash."
Waiter: "Yes, Sir, coming right up."
Mentuhotep: "Well, ladies, Fantegla and Sarlinda, let me toast you for allowing me the pleasure of enjoying your charming company this wonderful evening."
Sarlinda responded, "You certainly have not said much but you do remember our names. So, tell us, what do you do other than break women's hearts?"

INTRIGUE THROUGH TIME

Mentuhotep: "Pardon me!"

Sarlinda: "What type of work do you do?"

Meanwhile Fantegla has not relaxed her gaze, searching his facial contours and confessing, thinking, 'I must have you.'

Mentuhotep: "Well, I'm an antiques dealer and I travel a great deal. In fact, I'm in town to conclude an important business transaction."

Sarlinda: "Did we not see you at the Museum this afternoon?"

Mentuhotep: "Oh, yes! Quite an interesting collection."

Sarlinda: "Which one did you enjoy?"

Mentuhotep: "Oh, the Egyptian collection. I prided myself with knowing something about Egyptian culture, but was surprised to find out how much I did not know. Then again, I was fortunate to see you two."

Fantegla: "We were fortunate to see you." Scheming she thought, 'I am fortunate to get to hit on you and I won't miss. I will keep my eyes on the ball and go the distance.'

Waiter: "Here's dinner. For you Madam, salad, steak with carrots, potatoes and peas. The chef's steak sauce is heated to a boil with garlic, onions, mustard and a pinch of hot sauce. And for you, Madam, salad, lamb roasted with potatoes, broccoli and spinach, sautéed in butter with a pinch of lemon, garlic, salad, two vegetables and a pinch of lemon. The chef has recommended his steak sauce for you too. Here's warm bread and also butter. We serve custard pie and coffee for dessert. Here is my companion with your meal, Sir. Enjoy! If there's anything else, please don't hesitate to call."

Mentuhotep: "Thank you very much. The aroma promises a great deal. I must confess it has been a while since I sat down to enjoy a sumptuous meal with a Lady, much more two beautiful Ladies."

Fantegla: "Are you married, Mr. Mentuhotep?"

Mentuhotep: "No, I'm not."

Sarlinda: "Is there a Lady in your life?"

Mentuhotep: "Not at this time!"

Fantegla: "What happened?"

Mentuhotep: "Well it's a long story of a long time ago. And I have been so busy with my work I must confess I have not had time to think along these lines."

They both thought, 'Well, open season.' The question is who will get the first crack at him. They both thought 'I don't want to compete with my good friend over any man, but then again this is not any man. He certainly is a prize worth pursuing.'

FREDERICK MONDERSON

At the conclusion of their meal, another round of drinks was ordered.

Mentuhotep: "Waiter, how much do I owe you for the drinks?"
Waiter: "Well, Sir, you do not have to pay now. You can simply charge it to your room number. What is it?"
Mentuhotep: "I'm in room 1825."
Thereafter everyone made a mental note of room 1825.

Sarlinda: "Mr. Mentuhotep, do you have an engagement for tomorrow evening?"
Mentuhotep: "You can call me Michael. This is what my friends call me."
Fantegla: "Well, Michael, are you engaged for tomorrow evening?"
Mentuhotep: "I don't have any commitments after six, tomorrow evening."
Sarlinda: "We do have a social function tomorrow evening, and would greatly appreciate the pleasure of your company."
Mentuhotep: "I'll be delighted to join you. To enjoy the company of one Lady for an evening is quite an experience. Two such beautiful creatures, is food from the Gods."
Sarlinda: "There will be a chauffeured car here to pick you up at about 7:00 pm."
Mentuhotep: "Ok."
Waiter: "Ladies and Sir, can I serve the coffee and custard pie now?"
Mentuhotep: "Go right ahead."
Sarlinda: "Well, I must get to Queens and it's already 9:30." Turning to Fantegla she says: "My friend, can I beg that you take care of our friend until our engagement tomorrow?"
Fantegla: "For sure. Get home safely. Have a good evening." Soon she was gone and Mentuhotep found himself staring in the face of the extraordinarily beautiful woman. 'This is Nekajai reincarnated,' he thought as she too was quietly staring. They both got up and he walked toward the door, as if to see her out, and she followed.

Myth meets reality on Fifth Avenue, in New York City.

6.   The Walk

Not knowing what to say, he hoped she would relieve him of the awkward position of not knowing what to do with her, since she showed no desire to leave. So, he stepped out into the night saying: "I'm going to take a walk alongside the Park."

Fantegla: "I guess I'll come along with you," and as he offered no objection, she placed her right arm in his left, around the elbows, and they moved off. They approached the corner and crossed the street onto the side of the park.

He hesitated, thinking of which direction to go. He knew the path uptown is where he traveled earlier on his way to the Museum. He was not sure about the other, so why not stay with the familiar.

FREDERICK MONDERSON

Fantegla on the other hand, once across the street, now gripping his arm more firmly, seemed to feel the hesitation of him deciding which way to go. Seeing he's from out of town, she thought, 'Why don't I give him a walking tour?' Turning left, they began walking down 59th Street along the southern end of the Park, towards Columbus Circle.

Rockefeller Center Plaza with its wonderfully inviting Rink ambiance, a place thought to be the "Center of Christmas!"

INTRIGUE THROUGH TIME

FIVE ELEVEN FIFTH AVENUE

Michael paused to admire the wonderful artwork of this entrance way.

Silently they walked, not too brisk steps, and each in their own thoughts. Fantegla cannot remember when last she felt such at ease with a man. She felt calm in being in company of a remarkable man brimming with confidence; and also, a quiet excitement of being this close to him, arms locked, body touching, their strides matching. She felt her heart pounding. The cauldron within her begins to boil. Sure, it's a warm summer night and it certainly did not help her. She felt warmth. A trickle of perspiration had formed on her neck and it began to run down her body. She started fanning herself, while glancing at him looking straight ahead engrossed in his thoughts. She then thought, 'Has he noticed what is happening to me?'

That drip of perspiration, now departed from her neck, cast an eye at both globes, as it headed south. Circumventing the clothing she wore, minding its own business, that busy drop of perspiration picked up speed and fell over heading south, as if chased by a pounding heart.

The woman could pass out; she had never felt this titillatingly wonderfully excited, weak. She leaned firmly on the strong arm of Michael as the perspiration continued its chaotic path. Speeding, it hit a bump, a depression, her navel. It exited the lisp with greater

37

speed, its decision to enter the park. 'Oh, my goodness!' she thought.

Rockefeller Center Rink Plaque reads: "I believe in the supreme worth of the individual and in his right to life, liberty and the pursuit of happiness."

Mentuhotep on the other hand, once he had crossed the street did not have park on his mind. Since he did not go in the direction of the Met, he thought about the collection and insisted on making a revisit. More importantly, he thought about the gold in Ghafoor's vault. 'He, Ghafoor,' thought Mentuhotep, 'seemed a reasonable man, really excited about being involved in an important deal.' Next it was the places he had to visit in the city to get a broader perspective of his new time and place. 'I must get a good guide. Perhaps William will be glad to help. Who are these people Ghafoor has contacted?' And on and on, his mind raced! However, he was not unmindful of the beautiful, warm and exciting companion whose body was in contact with his. It was as if he felt a sort of trembling. As he continued to walk, he paid no attention to it, just glad to be in her company.

His mind next flashed back across time to his ancient homeland. So different, yet so sweet, because it's what he knew. On a night like this the cloudless sky would be littered with stars. From the heavens there would be enough light for him to find the location of his buried treasure. He must devise a means to retrieve it and also to get it to his new home. Perhaps Ghafoor could be useful in more ways than one.

INTRIGUE THROUGH TIME

The full view of the entrance to the Rink at Rockefeller Center that some have called the "Heart of Christmas!"

FREDERICK MONDERSON

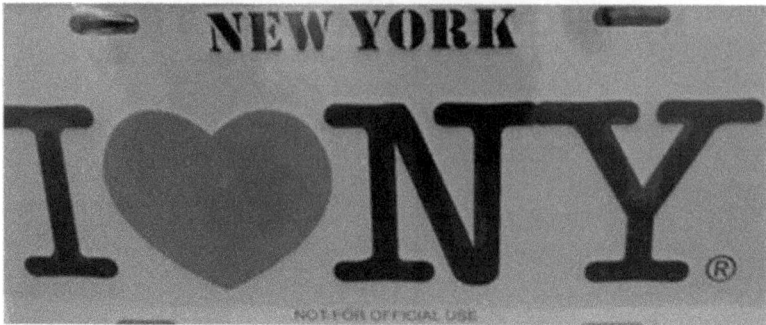

The sign that says it all and this made our hero more pleased to be in such a wonderful city.

As it was a warm night, he felt a trickle of perspiration and, touching his shirt as if to fan himself, he touched his necklace and instantly thought of the other around the neck of Nekajai. 'Oh, Nekajai,' somehow there seemed to be a resemblance between Nekajai and Fantegla and he turned to look at her and suddenly stopped, smiling. She on the other hand with the perspiration at work, in the park, was startled and seeming to fall in his arms, planted a passionate kiss on his startled lips. It was as if soft lips meeting soft lips in a hard and sensual explosion. They embraced awkwardly then broke it off and came to the end of the park at Columbus Circle.

Mentuhotep: "That was some walk," he told her, expecting to turn back.
Fantegla: "It certainly was!" she exclaimed. Sensing his desire to turn back, the modern American woman she is, this was not going to happen. 'This is a God-given opportunity,' she thought, and 'I'm not going to give it up easily. Equipped as I am, I could walk to Jericho, Jericho Turnpike, that is,' she thought further.

An ice cream vendor was plying his "wares" in the Circle and they crossed the street, arms more firmly locked. "Give me two Klondike Bars," she ordered and paid. Opening the first, she handed it to him, and took the second. Opening it she began to suck it, and he, looking at her, followed suit. Savoring the sweet, cool taste on a warm summer night, following a rather stimulating walking experience, he told her: "This is so good."

Fantegla, turning and looking down Eighth Avenue, told him, "Let's walk!" Then they took off like school kids, giggling, arm in arm, walking down Eighth Avenue in the most jovial embrace imaginable. She, happy to have found someone of this caliber, and he, thankful to the Gods for having transplanted Nekajai across the millennia and planting her here beside him, and merrily along they went.

Down Eighth Avenue, she commented on some 'sights under the lights,' never realizing he had never before seen any of this. Yet, he took it all in with a nod and a smile. Soon they made Forty-Second Street, turned into it and moved across town. This time they moved slower, taking in both sides of this famous street, often designated "Red Light!" When they got to Seventh Avenue and Forty-Second Street at Times Square, they paused to view the lights back up the "Great White Way" of Broadway. Next, they headed towards Sixth Avenue and then Fifth Avenue.

Bryant Park, and further on, New York Public Library across the street, some stores and the curiously skewed white Grace building next to the City University of New York were all sites that came to his attention. Soon they hit Fifth Avenue, turned from Forty-Second Street and headed back up-town.

Along this great "Visitor's Way," she paused to view pieces of clothing in different show-windows. He, on the other hand, was amused to see "statues wearing clothes." He not saying anything, silently supporting her preference for this outfit and that one; meanwhile she thought 'this was normal for him.' He, on the way, was impressed by the "columns" at Morgan Stanley between Forty-Third and Forty-Fourth Streets along Fifth Avenue. At the Bank of New York, between Forty-Fourth and Forty-Fifth, the plaque read, it was founded in 1874 and stands a block away from Barnes and Noble between Forty-Fifth and Forty-Sixth.

As they continued uptown, they soon crossed Forty-Eighth Street, and she said: "There's Ghafoor's. They always carry interesting antiques."
Mentuhotep: "I did not know you are interested in antiques?"
Fantegla: "Oh, I'm not really, but my father is a collector and he has often shown me some of his newest additions. In fact, he called me this afternoon very excited about the prospects of acquiring a new piece. These things really make his day."

FREDERICK MONDERSON

Plaque of The University Club Building erected in 1957

Mentuhotep thought: 'Her father is a collector!' 'Was he probably contacted by Ghafoor?' 'Is he interested in my pieces?' 'Who is this woman really?' 'She has hardly unhooked herself from me since we left the hotel, and I have not enquired of her person.' Lingering further at Ghafoor's, she turned and looked deep within his eyes and planted another passionate kiss on his lips. Momentarily he held her firmly and he liked it. Then they moved on.

Passing Saks Fifth Avenue between Forth-Ninth and Fiftieth Streets, they crossed the road to look at Atlas holding up the world in front of Rockefeller Center between Fiftieth and Fifty-First Streets, opposite St. Patrick's Cathedral. Seeming to not notice the busy activity in the Plaza, she enquired: "Do you skate?" to which he replied: "Actually no, but I have always wanted to take up the sport." He lied! Then continued, "But I have been so busy with my work there has been no time."
"I will be delighted to teach you," she laughed.

INTRIGUE THROUGH TIME

St. Patrick's Cathedral opposite Rockefeller Center.

They moved on past Fortunoff between Fifty-Third and Fifty-Fourth Streets; the Peninsula Hotel at Fifty-Fifth Street; and World of Disney opposite Fifth Avenue Presbyterian Church.

FREDERICK MONDERSON

Fifth Avenue Presbyterian Church at 55th Street.

Opposite Tiffany and Co., at 727 Fifth Ave, Atlas was again holding up the Globe. Next was Bergdorf-Goodman on both sides of the avenue between Fifty-Seventh and Fifty-Eighth Streets, that caught her eye. She was what you call an avid shopper! Our Hero stood right beside all her stops, being supportive, being there. She on the other hand, was enjoying being in his company and did not want it to end; and, that is probably why she seemed to want to take it slow looking at all the stores along Fifth Avenue.

It was nearly 11:00 pm, when they returned to the Plaza Hotel. He thought for sure she would be off now that they returned.

"Old Glory" adorns the Fifth Avenue Corridor where Michael so frequently traveled.

INTRIGUE THROUGH TIME

He hesitated in front of the hotel, and then moved to enter and she was still there. "Can I call you a cab or take you home?" he said. "No," she replied, "I live here. I'm two floors above you in 2005." "I see," he responded, "no wonder you seemed so relaxed in this environment," as they walked to the elevator.

The Elevator Operator said: "Good evening, Ms. Somersett, Sir." Glancing, Mentuhotep noticed his name tag read, Viberto Gibsoni. "Good evening," said Mentuhotep, "Eighteenth floor."

Within a minute they were there, and stepping out he said to Fantegla: "Thank you for a wonderful evening, my dear." "You're welcome," she responded and the elevator door closed.

On the way to his room, our Hero began reflecting on the events of his day, and indeed it was a hectic one. He cannot remember having as eventful a day as this one. Perhaps it was that day when he led a force under General Ptahotep-Ra to pacify the rebels who had massed north of the Lebanon. The logistics of that operation, preparation of their forces, descent of the river from *Waset* (Thebes, Luxor), and overland march of a day and night, enabled their deployment very early that morning to catch the rebels unprepared, and they were routed. The exemplary leadership of his forces caught the General's attention who reported it to the Pharaoh, who in turn promoted him to Commander of the Imperial Guard. That was the only time he was that "busy." Still, that was on his turf and the events here are of an altogether different experience.

After he exited the elevator and as Fantegla continued to her floor, she was beaming, heart pounding, excited at how her day and night, had turned out. Even the elevator operator could notice her joy as he said "Here you are, Ms. Somersett." "Thank you, Mr. Gibsoni." 'She must be extremely happy,' he thought, 'this is one of the very few times she has called me by my name.'

On way to her room she thought, "A hot bath is what I need," realizing the perspiration was still at work in the park! Entering her door, she had never before been this happy!

Thinking that William could be of assistance to him early in the day tomorrow, our Hero left his room and returned to the elevator.

FREDERICK MONDERSON

When the door opened, he asked the operator: "Can you tell me if William is at work?"

"No, Sir," he answered, but thought: 'William! This man said good night to the most beautiful woman in the world who seemed very happy and willing. What does he want with William? Is there something wrong with him?' Even further he thought, 'I did not realize that was William's preference.'

'Well,' Mentuhotep thought, 'perhaps a bath will help to relax me.' As he returned to his room, he began to undress; having removed his jacket, tie and shirt, the doorbell rang. 'Who could that be?' he thought. So, slipping back into his unbuttoned shirt he opened the door. There she was! Slipping past him she said, "I could not sleep and thought I may view the park from your balcony." In her hands she held a bottle of Hennessy and two glasses!

7'What do I do now?' he thought. This part of events was certainly unexpected, as she opened the bottle and poured two drinks. She quickly downed one of the drinks while he tried to tidy up his shirt. Just then she noticed the necklace on his chest.

"Oh, my goodness," she exclaimed, "I have never seen anything so beautiful," moving for a closer inspection. Within inches from him, she moved her arms to open the shirt and slipped them around his waist and held him in a tight grip, with her face against the necklace on his smooth, muscular, hairless chest. 'This is so heavenly,' she thought.

Utterly dumbfounded, our Hero doesn't know what to do. He does feel a tingling sensation caused by the night's events and the hard grip she has him in. With that he embraces her and they kiss. She then proposes a toast to "The most beautiful man I have ever known," and downs her second drink and he followed with his first.

Clearly the woman has hit on him, but not wise to the ways of the modern world, he is not thinking like that.

Mentuhotep: "I was just about to take a bath," he said.

Fantegla: "Go right ahead," she murmured. As he headed into the bathroom, she took a third drink and entering his bedroom, undressed and slipped between his sheets in the skimpiest underwear.

INTRIGUE THROUGH TIME

When he came out of the shower dressed in the complimentary pajamas provided by the hotel, he looked but could not see her. He searched the balcony to no avail and looking in the bedroom noticed a bulge and movement under the sheet. Just then he thought, 'I had better have that drink to calm my nerves.'

Holding Aba Scepter and in Osiris Crown, Queen Hatshepsut – *Ma'at-Ka-Ra*, raises her arms in praise of Deity while Thutmose III - *Men-Khepper-Ra* stands behind her incensing the resident god, Amon-Ra.

Life, Stability, Dominion from the "Red Chapel" of Queen Hatshepsut.

FREDERICK MONDERSON

7.　　　The Expert

Earlier, at 10:00 pm, Ghafoor stood at the Customs exit of the main terminal at JFK International Airport, awaiting the arrival of his friend, a visitor, Lord Stanhope of London, England. He had heard the announcement, "We would like to announce the arrival of British Airways BA 815, from London."

As he waited on Lord Stanhope who was to authenticate his holdings, Ghafoor began to think of his "Partner," the cache, and whether there was more gold! 'How fortunate I am to be in this position,' he thought. Before he left for the airport, he removed the jewels from his safe and examined them again, trying to determine whether he was in fact holding a dud. More importantly, however, he wanted to touch them, bask in their aura, and enjoy the satisfaction of being the conduit through whose hands they had passed. His collector clients will most certainly come to hold him in even greater regard, for he could deliver!

The passengers now began to emerge from the doors of Customs. There is Lord Stanhope rolling a wheeled suitcase and scanning the waiting crowd of people expecting friends and relatives coming through those doors. Lord Stanhope soon made out his waving hands as they made eye contact and he said, "Ghafoor."
"How are you, My Lord," Ghafoor replied: "How was your flight?"
"Very smooth flight. I'm as well as to be expected," he responded.
"My chauffeur is waiting outside to take us into the city."

With the luggage packed away in the trunk and both seated in the back, Ghafoor rolls up the partition between himself and the driver.

"What's this all about?" asked Lord Stanhope. "You sounded excited, but puzzled on the phone."
Ghafoor: "Well, Sir, this gentleman came into my shop, he seemed to appear from nowhere, and offered me four rings, two bracelets and two arm bands, claiming they are ancient Egyptian."
Stanhope: "OK."
Ghafoor: "He needed to make a quick sale so I contacted some of my clients. Interestingly enough, I caught a glimpse of a dagger in his waist under his jacket. It was of gold but the handle seemed to sparkle with encrusted gems. Though not a part of the lot, but with

48

the thought of eventually brokering it, I offered him an advance of $100,000.00. So, he handed over the jewels and they're now in my vault, awaiting your inspection. We're headed there now."

Stanhope: "Good. I will certainly be delighted to get a look at his lot. That was smooth of you to make the advance for it practically assures you the deal."

Ghafoor: "Well, here we are, **GAFOOR'S ANTIQUES**." To the chauffeur he says: "Lord Stanhope will be here for a while but he needs transportation to the hotel he will be staying in."

"Yes, Sir," replied his driver.

As they entered the door, Lord Stanhope noticed some small improvement in the store; generally well-kept, however, with pieces of gold and other jewels in cases here and there, and other antiques more visibly exposed. They passed through a side room and entered the room with the vault.   Then Ghafoor brought the pieces Mentuhotep had deposited with him. He seemed to hesitate as he handed each piece to the expert. It was as if he were savoring the aura of the antiquity of each piece.

Lord Stanhope, paying no attention to Ghafoor's actions, reached into his bag and brought out a magnifying glass to examine each piece and then he comes up with the same conclusion. Authentic gold jewelry. Early 18th Dynasty. 'To any collector, these have a substantial value,' he thought. 'I wonder how this fellow came into possession of these royal gems,' he continued.

"Well, My Lord" Ghafoor asked, "What do you think?" "Excellent. Excellent! Authentic! Early 18th Dynasty! Egyptian. 16th Century B.C. I think you have done well, Ghafoor. When will you see this fellow again? I will love to examine the dagger you mentioned."

Ghafoor: "My Lord, he never said anything about it being for sale."

Stanhope: "My good man, the mere fact he offered these pieces for sale, that piece will also be available. These are the bait to hook you with the bigger piece."

Ghafoor: "What do you think they're worth?"

Stanhope: "It is hard to tell about collectors. They have a tendency to cut each other's throats in bidding. However, because of the age, early 18th Dynasty and being fairly new, no scratches and so on, conservatively I'll say they're worth about $350,000.00. But, like I said, you can't tell about collectors' desires to own these things. Well, my work is done here. I must get to my lodgings for the night."

Ghafoor: "Well done, Sir, I expect my man to be here sometime tomorrow. I will call as soon as he arrives." To his driver, waiting outside, he says: "Please take Lord Stanhope to his hotel, the Plaza at 59th and 5th Avenue.
"Yes, Sir" he responded and sped away with the Lord.

At the hotel, the night clerk who had been alerted about the arrival greeted him, "Good evening, Lord Stanhope. The usual?"
Stanhope: "Yes," he replied. "I think that is 1717."
Clerk: "Yes, Sir. We were expecting you. As usual, the view of the park is excellent. Will there be anything else, Sir? Here are your keys. I'm sure you know the way."
Stanhope: "No. Thank you. I have to get some rest and prepare for tomorrow. I'll find my way."

View of the Pyramids from Mena House Garden Hotel.

Golden pendants in form of heads and scarabs, part of the treasure.

INTRIGUE THROUGH TIME

8. The Talk

Ring. Ring. Ring.

Sarlinda dialed her friend to discuss how her evening went and plans for the next evening's social event. Getting no response, she thought, 'Fantegla's still out. I wonder if she is making headway on my time.' However, knowing her companion all she could say is: 'Good luck to her. My time will come.' She dialed another friend Lynaudra. This time she got a response.

"Hello."
Sarlinda: "Hello, darling. How are you?"
Lynaudra: "Sarlinda. How have you been? I hope to see you at tomorrow's function. I've just got off the phone with Mrs. Edwards. Their daughter Michele has come home from college and they plan to make her birthday memorable. They reminded me to make sure you and Fantegla are there. So, what's new with you?"
Sarlinda: "Girl, if I only told, you won't believe."
Lynaudra: "Try me."
Sarlinda: "Honey, we were at the Museum today and saw this handsome and exciting gentleman. Would you believe he was having dinner at the Plaza so we invited him over to join us? Unfortunately, I had to come home to Queens and my driver got caught in a traffic jam; that's why I'm calling you so late."
Lynaudra: "That's OK. You can call me anytime."
Sarlinda: "Anyway, I had to leave them having dinner. I tried calling her room and no answer. She is probably out with him now."
Lynaudra: "The hussy."
Sarlinda: "Well, I don't want to read anything into it as yet."
Lynaudra: "Did you invite him to the event?"
Sarlinda: "I certainly did. I'm telling you girl, you will fall for him, but don't try to make headway on my time."
Lynaudra: "Let me tell you something you little hussy, you're not married to him, so he's fair game."
Sarlinda: "Let me say I saw him first, but let the best man, I mean woman, win."
Lynaudra: "Anyway, so what's new?

Sarlinda: "Nothing. Same old, same old! I can't find a decent man despite my social standing and wealth. I'm so often sleeping alone at nights."

Lynaudra: "Anyway, like you said, this one may be the one to fry your fish. Hold on. I'm getting an incoming call."

"Hello."

Mrs. Edwards: "Hello, honey. It's me again. I have a few questions for you."

Lynaudra: "Hold on. Hello. Yes. It's Ilene Edwards. She wants to go over some last-minute issues with me. Her daughter's here. I'll call you early tomorrow. 'Night."

Sarlinda: "'Night." Hanging up she tried Fantegla again and the phone just kept ringing. She thought: 'My best friend and she's out having a whale of a time with my man.'

Mrs. Edwards asked, "By the way, honey, have you invited anyone?"

Lynaudra: "Oh, yes, Fantegla and Sarlinda."

Edwards: "Not them. The regulars! I mean any new men!"

Lynaudra: "I'm glad you asked. Sarlinda mentioned this new man she and Fantegla met in the Museum and were having dinner with."

Edwards: "They're moving fast. That's good. Did they invite him to the party?"

Lynaudra: "I think they did. By the way, how's your Mr. Edwards?"

Edwards: "He's as sweet as ever, out there making all that money."

Lynaudra: "So who's on the guest list?"

Edwards: "Many of the regulars. Of course, you and your fiancé, Fantegla, Sarlinda, their parents, Mr. and Mrs. Edwards and Mr. and Mrs. Wisenthal, Senator Jonathan and Mrs. Williams, the art dealer Richard Gray and his wife. There are a few others I can't think of right now. Oh, yes, the English Lord, Stanhope. I hear he is coming in this evening. News along the grapevine does travel fast. I'm not sure if any of these people invited others. Nevertheless, we have the makings of great company and should have a wonderful time. Oh, yes. My daughter Michele Cheryl-Ann said she invited a few college friends. We've got to have some of the younger set, you know."

Lynaudra: "You have quite a list there. How will the evening unfold?"

Edwards: "Well, cocktails, dinner, dancing, live entertainment by the pool. You know, then the women get together and talk about the men and the men get together and talk about money, collectibles,

INTRIGUE THROUGH TIME

sports, power, and also women. Nevertheless, all this makes for a wonderful evening."

Lynaudra: "Great. I'll tell the others. Anything I should bring?"

Edwards: "Yes, bring your pretty self, your beau, and that interesting gentleman the girls seem so excited about. I want to meet him."

Lynaudra: "Ok. Consider it done. What can I say about the gentleman, they both seem taken by him? Ok. See you tomorrow night."

"Night," Mrs. Edwards responded and they both hung up.

With glass in hand, Mentuhotep sat on the sofa beginning to sip his drink. Just then he thought, 'I need to make a "to-do-list" for tomorrow's events starting with the meeting with Ghafoor.' Pulling the coffee table near the sofa, he leaned over and began to make notes on the pad. Being off his feet as the day's events began to catch up with him, he started feeling tired. He began to feel sleepy and in the midst of his writing, he fell fast asleep on the sofa.

"Khufu Gleams," the "Great Pyramid," as seen from the desert at Ghizeh; a sight Michael was familiar with having visited with his beloved Queen Hatshepsut.

53

FREDERICK MONDERSON

View of the Mena House Garden Hotel where Mentuhotep stayed on his first trip.

9.   Party Frame of Mind

Meanwhile the sun over the Plaza has awakened the sleeping beauty. She reaches over for her companion only to realize she is alone. 'H'mm. He is an early riser,' she thought. Collecting herself, she realizes also, her 'night clothing' is unruffled and intact. Getting out of bed she searches for her companion, only to realize he is asleep on the sofa in the living room. 'What, he did not want it?' she thought. Then she realized he was doing some writing and fell asleep and never came to bed. 'Poor fellow,' she murmured. 'He must have had some kind of day and night.'

Not discounting the effectiveness of her full-court press, reflecting, she imagined, 'maybe I did overwhelm him and perhaps that late night visit did put him over the edge. I only wish he had gone there with me.' He, on one hand, was in that dream mode and seemed to be remembering the warm and exciting embrace of the beautiful young woman with whom he had such fond memories. This was his first full night, and he kept squirming in his sleep, smiling, while reflecting and living out his dream. She, on the other hand, sensing something was going on in his dream, returned to the bedroom, grabbed the covers, returned and snuggled up next to him, asleep on the couch. Somehow, she fit comfortably well in the little crook opening of his bent body warmth, and, as if, reality was a dream, he embraced her. Like a dancing partner she followed on the floor, he

54

living in a dream, she dreaming in reality, for this is what he had been dreaming of.

While that warm, intimate, exciting and exhilarating experience only lasted for a brief period before he awoke, in her mind's eye, it lasted a long time. With all her wealth, beauty, playfulness, social encounters, she had long been searching, while deep down, her life had been empty. Even her father, the Wall Street tycoon, had cause to wonder in one of those rare intimate moments when a father and daughter would confer about such matters. She simply confessed she had not met anyone who really moved her to have a serious relationship. That is until now! Just then he began to stir and she began to be annoyed for he was interrupting her heaven on earth.

Opening his eyes and realizing his position, he said: "Good morning," and held her tightly. Expecting him to rise startled instead of holding her tight, she barely managed a croak. "Good morning," as her butter began to melt. They stayed embraced like this for a while, just enjoying the warmth of each other.

Her active mind, even from down under, began to scheme. 'What a wonderful way to start the day.' Never before had she felt this way. If she started her day this way, who knows about the evening's events? Maybe her dad will finally see how happy she really was. Wickedly she thought, 'Maybe that speeding drop of perspiration in the garden may finally find a bush in which to hide.' After what seemed a lengthy snuggle, they both got up and began to prepare for the day's activities.

Now fully awake, Mentuhotep began to wonder what to do with this wonderful dilemma. Here is a very beautiful woman who seems to do to him what Nekajai did, and quite obviously, he too has had an effect on her. However, she knows nothing about him. He knows nothing about her. What if by some stroke of the imagination she should find out he's from another era, who knows what may happen. He prays that all the gods, Ra, Amun, Mut, Selkis, Isis, Osiris, Horus, Ma'at, Seshat, Thoth, Anubis, Bes and Hathor, all bless and endow his every action, for he truly deserves a chance at happiness; having been deprived of experiencing the warmth and tenderness of his beloved Nekajai.

FREDERICK MONDERSON

Mentuhotep: "My beautiful Fantegla," he said, "There's so much I have to do today. What time do you go to work? When will we meet again?"

Fantegla: "I do not really work. I volunteer with my friend Sarlinda on Tuesdays at the Marcus Garvey Nursing Home in Brooklyn and on Thursdays at the Veterans Hospital in Manhattan. We spend four hours per week at each site. Come to me as soon as you can. Have no fear, I'll be here."

Holding her in a warm embrace and looking deep into her brown eyes, he said: "Have no fear my sweet, your time will come, and it will be wonderful."

If her butter was melting it now turned to oil, olive oil, that is. Breathtakingly she kissed him saying "Good bye," and was glad he was leaving for she was shaking uncontrollably, but what a wonderful feeling. She remembered earlier while lying on the couch beside him, she felt as if she was indeed flying. Now she thought 'I'd better anchor myself for like a balloon, I might fly away.'

Out the door he went, leaving her in his apartment. Taking the elevator down to breakfast, he noticed another operator on duty. Since there were three other riders in the elevator, he was not able to read the operator's name tag.

Entering the dining hall, he was seated, the waiter brought coffee and offered him a menu from which he chose scrambled eggs, sausages, toast, fruit and marmalade.

He took out his pad and began to scribble "things to do."

1. Meet with Ghafoor at 11:00 am
2. Purchase a new wardrobe
3. Contact William for some pointers
4. Revisit the Metropolitan Museum of Art
5. Devise a plan of action to return to Egypt

The waiter brought his breakfast along with *The New York Times* newspaper for Friday June 14, 1985. The front page made for interesting reading.

Lead: "Reagan deferring arms for Jordan as Economic Aid"

INTRIGUE THROUGH TIME

International: "Gandhi in a Speech to Congress calls for a Non-Aligned Afghanistan"
National: "Senate 98-0 Rebuffs Reagan on Water Fund."

Nevertheless, he began to devise a strategy to deal with Ghafoor. He thought, 'the collector already has the four rings, two bracelets, two armlets, so now I will throw in the two anklets and dangle the necklace before him. As a last resort, I will offer the dagger, but not right now.'

After all, he can't go around naked and feels he needs it for protection.

At 11:00 am, Mentuhotep walks into Ghafoor. The proprietor spots him instantly and gets on the phone to call Lord Stanhope, informing him the car will be in front of the hotel in 15 minutes. Then he dispatches his chauffeur to bring the Lord to the shop. With that taken care of, he approached our Hero: "Good morning, Mr. Mentuhotep, I trust you had an interesting time after you left the shop yesterday."
Mentuhotep: "Wonderfully exciting. In fact, I met some people who showed me around the city last night. I realize this is a city that never sleeps."
Ghafoor: "Indeed. There is always something going on."

By this time, about eight people were in the store talking about looking and purchasing pieces of jewelry, but two of Ghafoor's assistants were handling this very well. Mentuhotep thought, 'Perhaps it's the location that causes a steady stream of customers to come into this store.' He wondered further, 'If I am able to retrieve the treasure in Egypt and get it here, where would be the best place to sell it? Perhaps this spot will do.'

Just then a gentleman walked into the store. There was an air of confidence about him. He had a noble posture. Not strange, one Lord recognizing another Lord!

Ghafoor said: "Pardon me," and got up from his desk to greet the gentleman. "Good morning, Lord Stanhope, please, let me introduce you to Mr. Michael Mentuhotep."

FREDERICK MONDERSON

Stanhope: "Pleased to meet you, Sir."

Mentuhotep: "It's a pleasure to make your acquaintance," and, shaking Stanhope's hands, looked deep into that experienced face.

Ghafoor: "This is the gentleman I told you about, Lord Stanhope of London. He came to examine and authenticate the jewelry. You must realize buyers want expert opinion before they will buy."

Mentuhotep: "I understand. Well, what did you find, Sir?"

Stanhope explained: "Authentic jewelry. Egyptian. 18th Dynasty. Very likely early Thutmosid period. Either Thutmose I or Hatshepsut's reign. Theban School of Art."

Mentuhotep: "Are you sure?"

Stanhope: "Positive."

Mentuhotep thought, 'This man is indeed an expert on the jewelry and period. He hit the mark. He is good!'

Mentuhotep: "In that case, let me add two other pieces, anklets, to the collection."

Reaching into his bag and removing his magnifying glass the Lord begins to examine the anklets with the same methodological precision. After giving them the "Acid Test," he stopped, removed his glasses and said: "These belong to the same class as the others." Then he looked enquiringly, fishing, at Mentuhotep as if to say: 'Where did you get these?'

Mentuhotep answered: "That is correct."

Ghafoor looked intently at the drama unfolding in his shop as the two men exchanged glances and said a great deal without saying anything. Just then Mentuhotep reached into his breast pocket and brought out a cloth handkerchief containing the necklace!

Lord Stanhope glanced at it and turning to Ghafoor asked if he could have a cup of coffee. Then he looked again at the necklace, then at the gentleman across from him. He said nothing. No one spoke! But their looks said a great deal.

Again, without touching the jewelry, but simply looking at it, Lord Stanhope had a great realization. 'I have seen this necklace before.' He looked again at Mentuhotep without saying a word. Ghafoor, producing a tray with the makings, said: "Coffee." That simple and single word sounded like an explosion. They all had a cup. Lord

INTRIGUE THROUGH TIME

Stanhope held his in the traditional English fashion with the pinky out. Meanwhile, over the brim of his cup he looked enquiring at the man in front of him.

Ghafoor noticed the tension and electricity. He did not understand it all, but he did realize something was up. Lord Stanhope began to think, was his mind playing tricks on him. Finishing his coffee, he gave a cursory glance to the necklace. Since it was not a part of the collection he concentrated on the cache. He did know; however, he had seen this necklace before in the Cairo Museum. Human nature forced him to silently question the man, wondering, 'Did he steal this beautiful work of art?' However, etiquette and protocol dictated he not ask such a question out loud.

Well, thrusting that thought aside, he concentrated more on the now expanded cache of 4 rings, 2 anklets, 2 bracelets and 2 armbands.

"Well, Sir, what do you think?" asked Ghafoor. "How much is it worth?"
Stanhope looked at both of them and said, "$1,200.000.00"

Ghafoor's eyes lit up as he contemplated his percentage of the finder's fee.

Without dwelling further on the necklace, thinking he must investigate this further, he asked of Mentuhotep, "I hear you have a dagger."
"It's not for sale," he replied, "I feel naked without it." That was a strange reply, Stanhope thought. 'I feel naked without it.' Ghafoor had said he took off the rings and bracelets as he laid them before him. How strange indeed, this man is acting as if these are actually his jewels! He laid it to rest.

Ghafoor broke the silence. "I will contact my buyers and see what they have to say and offer. I will be in touch with you later Mr. Mentuhotep."

Realizing this portion of the transaction was complete, Mentuhotep picked up the necklace, wrapped it in the handkerchief, placed it back in his breast pocket and said, extending his hand for a shake: "Gentlemen, I will see you later." To the English Lord he said,

"Thank you for a thorough and professional appraisal." Then he walked out of the store.

Mrs. Edwards was up early. Even her husband noticed, but did not realize what was driving her. She knew she was expecting the new gentleman, and based on what she was told so far, only "the best silver ware will do." By midday she was nearly exhausted from fussing with the servants, calling the caterers, lining up her guest list, this must be one of her best parties. The live band agreed to be there on time. She ordered new chairs and tables for the pool. She had a long talk with both Mrs. Samuels and Mrs. Gray about the party, local gossip, the bridge club, etc. Long in planning her summer party, they had planned to follow with one each on successive Fridays. So now she had this surge, but not telling them about the new guest. She needed an edge to best them in this first round of parties. Having taken care of all that, she called Lynaudra and enquired if her fiancée would also be there, and whether there was anything new and exciting. Hearing 'yes' to the boyfriend coming and 'no' to new news, the busybody moved on to Sarlinda.

Ring. Ring. Ring.

Sarlinda: "Hello."
Mrs. Edwards: "Hello, my darling. How are you this good Friday?"
Sarlinda: "Good, but not like you."
Mrs. Edwards: "How so?"
Sarlinda: "Well, you're not a spring chicken but, at least you have a man, even if you stopped doing it."
Mrs. Edwards: "Ha. Ha. Ha. How could you. That old goat I have, he still gets it up, and as long as he's happy, I'm happy."
Sarlinda; "See what I mean? At least you're doing it."
Mrs. Edwards: "You're young. Don't despair, honey. This may be a little dry spell, but your rainy season is coming."
Sarlinda: "I can't wait for the rainy season; I could use a little wetting right now."
Mrs. Edwards: "Well the world is full of surprises. Who knows you may luck out? Anyhow, see you later."
Sarlinda: "OK. Bye."

Next, she called Fantegla who answered as if expecting a call.
Fantegla: "Hello."

INTRIGUE THROUGH TIME

Mrs. Edwards: "This is Mrs. Edwards. Hope to see you at the party tonight."

Fantegla: "Without a doubt. I may even have a surprise for you."

Mrs. Edwards: "A gift. Great! I'm so tired of those expensive presents my husband keeps giving me."

Fantegla: "Well, it's not that kind of gift."

Mrs. Edwards: "Whatever, honey. It is always better to give than to receive and I know everything you do is heart-felt. We'll see you later. Bye."

Fantegla: "Bye."

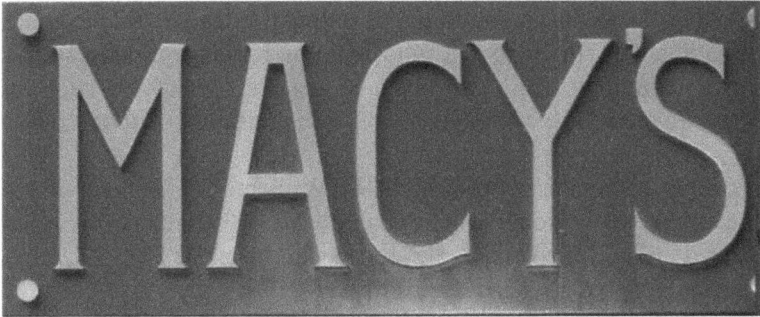

Macy's, the "world's largest store" whose window displays Michael stopped to admire as he started his whirlwind tour to begin creating a modern memory of his new homeland.

High end gold and precious jewelry same as Mentuhotep owned.

10. The Whirlwind

Mentuhotep left the antique shop and headed back to his hotel, with the intent of putting William to work. He needed a new suit for the event this evening, but he kept thinking about Lord Stanhope. 'He has enormous knowledge and with great precision he pinpointed the place and time of my origin. He seemed a bit puzzled though. While he was able to place the jewels, he certainly cannot place me there. Therefore, he has to wonder how I came into possession of these wonderful pieces. The price he gives as the value represents a substantial sum.' Mentuhotep wondered how much the necklace would bring. He had no intention of selling the dagger, but he would wave it tantalizingly to see who was interested, and whether he could manipulate their interests and desires, to possess such an exquisite piece of jewelry. He also had to consider Ghafoor's offer.

Arriving at the Plaza he thought of William. As he entered the lobby, his "man Friday" had kept a steady stare on the door. So, he noticed him immediately. He approached the Bell-Hop saying: "William, I need some advice from you."
William: "How can I help you, Sir?"
Mentuhotep: "I need a couple of suits and wonder if you can recommend some place, I could get them today."
William: "I would recommend Lloyd's on Broadway. They give good and special service. If you want, I could take you there when I get off at two o'clock. That's an hour and fifteen minutes from now.
Mentuhotep: "I have to get some things done in my apartment, so perhaps you can call for a taxi at 2:10, and I'll meet you up front."
William: "Very good, Sir, consider it done."

Mentuhotep approached the elevator, pushed the button and as the door opened it was Viberto Gibsoni on duty.
Mentuhotep: "18th floor."
Gibsoni: "Yes, Sir." But apparently, he saw this gentleman talking to William. Mischievously he wondered, 'Is something going on with these two? I'll have to keep my eyes open and focused on these two.' "18th floor" he announced.

INTRIGUE THROUGH TIME

Our Hero exited and headed for his room. Arriving, he poured himself a shot of Hennessy and wondered about his lady friend. He moved to the balcony with a drink in hand, took a seat and gazed at the park, on a bright and sunny Friday afternoon. He took out his "to-do-list" and checked off the first: Meet with Ghafoor to discuss the antiques. Second – the clothing. Third - meet with William. Fourth - the Museum. Etc.

While sitting enjoying the greenery of the park the doorbell rang. Getting up to answer, it was Fantegla.
"Hello," she whispered, slipping past him. Closing the door, he had a good view of her from the rear as she moved through the open door of the balcony.
"How was your day?" she continued.
Joining her on the balcony, she noticed his glass of brandy.
Fantegla: "I could use a stiff drink," she exclaimed, and moved to find a glass and pour herself one.
He kept admiring her, feeling confidently this is a carbon copy of Nekajai, with a few differences. With drink in hand, she approached to toast. Up close and personal she started examining, admiring, appreciating this man who suddenly appeared and turned her world upside down. Something happens to her, in his presence. Yes, she feels good in his presence.

After their drink she took his glass, placed it on the table and grasped his palms. Ducking under, she was within his embrace and pressed her body close to his. Then she kissed him passionately. Just then he checked the clock. It was 2:05. He had to go. "Honey, I must leave now."

Not wanting to appear annoyed, bossy or too forward, she eked out an "OK," not realizing this was a clothes hunt to appear with her at the affair later. Looks like 'he doesn't want it,' she thought. 'Perhaps I have to try harder. I will be a bombshell this evening,' she continued. And, out the door he went. He did turn and blow her a kiss, however; and she scrambled to grab it feeling a sense of relief, but full of joy because he seemed really pleased with her.

Lord Stanhope appeared at Ghafoor's just before 2:00 pm. He wanted to have another look at the cache of jewels to make sure he had not overlooked anything.

FREDERICK MONDERSON

Ghafoor: "My Lord, what brings you here now?"
Stanhope: "Well, Ghafoor, I wanted to have another look at the cache of jewels."
Ghafoor: "But of course, My Lord. You have a track record of excellence, and we don't want to get this wrong because others are involved." He took him to the vault room and retrieved the jewels.

Lord Stanhope conducted the same meticulous examination he had performed earlier. He came up with essentially the same results in terms of time, place, reign, school and again the lingering question bothered him. 'Where did this gentleman get these jewels?" It's a pity he did not have the necklace to give it one more examination. Even though he was essentially correct with these pieces, he had to rely on that initial perhaps incomplete, examination. One thing he was absolutely sure about, he had seen that necklace in the Cairo Museum. Again, the nagging question is: 'How did he get that necklace?' Nevertheless, everything he knew told him the necklace was genuine.

Nonetheless, he was more concerned about those pieces in Ghafoor's possession. He knew the top list of Ghafoor's clients were friends of his, and believed firmly that more than likely they would end up with the pieces, since they were collectors of that same genre of jewelry. That is why he had to get it right. In fact, he thought further, 'I am meeting with some of those people this evening at the affair the Edwards' is having for their daughter.' Still the necklace puzzled him.

Ghafoor, on the other hand, kept a watchful eye on him. He was familiar with the thorough nature of Lord Stanhope's work. He had observed him at work for almost two decades and he never seems to get it wrong. 'That is why he is my authenticator of first resort,' Ghafoor thought. He also thought about the percentage he would acquire, 5 percent, finder's fee. Oftentimes grateful clients gave him a handsome reward for not only finding a piece, but for giving them the heads-up on it.

All day Mrs. Edwards had been trying to stay on top of preparations. She called practically everyone. She called guests, caterers, musicians, deliverymen, some of her gossip partners, everyone. The new poolside furniture gave the place a different, look compared to the last affair. The color was no longer blue matching the pool tiles.

INTRIGUE THROUGH TIME

She chose white this time. Even the umbrellas showed a brighter and more colorful décor. The caterers agreed to be ready to serve by 7:00 pm, at which time the guests should be arriving.

The musicians too agreed to begin playing at that time. Everything has to be perfect for this special evening. It's going to be red carpet treatment, all night long.

Sarlinda telephoned Fantegla and could not reach her. Then she called Lynaudra to find out if she had heard from Fantegla. No word. She thought, 'my friend must be having a terrific time with the wonderful gentleman. At least I'm glad for her. We have both traveled the same road; two rich girls, unlucky in love. How people often think because you may be pretty and have lots of money, your love life should be wonderful. Unfortunately, this is not the case especially for me. That is why I feel good about the new joy descending on Fantegla.'

When Mentuhotep walked out the door of the Plaza, William was there with the taxi. He sat next to the driver and gave instructions to their destination. They arrived at Lloyd's on Broadway. Entering the store with Mr. Mentuhotep, he took him to the exclusively men's section. He got him a knowledgeable attendant and withdrew to the taxi, saying: "I will be outside, Sir. They will give you the most courteous and efficient service here."

"Thank you," Mentuhotep replied.

"My name is Leonardo, Sir, how may I help you?"
Mentuhotep: "I need a collection of suits, shirts, under-clothing, ties, socks, shoes and so on."
Leonardo: "You need a complete wardrobe, Sir."
Mentuhotep: "Yes."
Leonardo: "That's no problem. It would be easier if I took some measurements," which he did and then began making notations on his pad.
The two men seemed to work very well together. Leonardo chose some of the best outfits in the store, outfitting this gentleman as he would a prince. He chose 10 suits with matching accoutrements down to shoes for each outfit. Then he chose an extra dozen shirts,

socks, vests, underwear, handkerchiefs, and ties. He added pajamas, bathrobes, slippers, etc. Then he moved his client over to the men's toiletries where he chose perfume, toothbrushes, soaps, powder, and shaving apparatus, both mechanical and practical. Everything imaginable for a gentleman was gotten in the store with Leonardo's help.

The total cost was nearly $20,000.00 and he wondered how the gentleman would pay. To his surprise he paid all in cash and gave him a $500.00 tip. Leonardo was elated.

Mentuhotep: "I would like these delivered to my hotel, the Plaza, by 5:00 pm. I will not be there but please, ask the Desk to have this delivered to Room 1825?"

Leonardo: "Yes, Mr. Mentuhotep, consider it done. I will attend to it personally, to see it's delivered to your room." The business concluded and Mentuhotep left the store at 4:00.

William: "Is everything OK, Sir?"

Mentuhotep: "Yes. Everything's fine. As you know I'm from out of town and would like to see a few landmarks that would help to orient me, while I'm in the city."

William: "That can be easily arranged. I'll have the taxi drive us around, and we will see some of the landmarks and note their location for later reference."

Mentuhotep: "Let me inform you I must be back by 6:00 pm."

William: "I think we can get a lot done in two hours."

Mentuhotep: "What is the driver's name?"

"My name is Omarishaba, Sir."

Mentuhotep: "Where are you from?"

Omarishaba: "I'm from the Sudan, Sir. That's in Africa."

Mentuhotep: "I've heard of it."

William: To the driver: "Let us take Broadway down through Times Square, left on Forty-Second Street to Fifth Avenue, then down to Thirty-Fourth Street to see the Empire State Building and Macy's. Then you swing back to Madison Square Garden on Seventh Avenue and Thirty-First Street." After that they were off and running.

All along the gentleman's keen eyes picked up landmarks, locations, advertisements, on both sides of the street. His observatory skills from days of old came in handy. At Forty-Second Street and Fifth

INTRIGUE THROUGH TIME

Avenue, William pointed out the New York Public Library next to Bryant Park. He remembered it from the walk with Fantegla.

He was intrigued by Macy's, the world's largest store, across from the Empire State Building. This very tall building had him stop, get out, and look at its height. He had never seen anything like it.

William: "Sir, Macy's also puts on a terrific balloon extravaganza in the Macy's Thanksgiving Day Parade in November."

Mentuhotep: "I would certainly like to be there to see it."

Madison Square Garden from the 7th Avenue entrance where Michael attended the Ali/Frazier Heavyweight Title fight.

As they turned into Seventh Avenue, William said: "Madison Square Garden is famous for some of the most exciting sports events"

Mentuhotep: "I have seen some of them," he remarked, but actually lied about such events at Madison Square Garden.

He did remember sports in his time. Beni Hasan was famous for wrestling. There were water sports, hunting in the desert and in the marshes, fishing, and there were tournaments. Once he had taken part in a chariot race. Of course, the chariot was his favorite vehicle.

FREDERICK MONDERSON

The sign at Madison Square Garden said: "Ali-Frazier," Return Bout on Saturday.

William: "You should see it, Sir."
Mentuhotep: "I'll have to think about it, depending on my schedule."

Then they turned down Thirty-First Street to reach Eighth Avenue, for a turn on Thirty-Fourth Street; to reach the West Side Highway, on the way past the World Trade Center.

As they passed the large Midtown Post Office opposite Madison Square Garden on Eighth Avenue and Thirty-Third Street, he said, "Stop," and the driver pulled over.

The General Post Office on 8th Avenue with its massive colonnade.

The colonnade of columns in front of the Post Office attracted his attention. He got out looking at them. He counted 20 columns. Neither William nor Omarishaba could understand what caught his attention.

He was instantly transported back "home." The type of columns here reminded him of Beni Hasan and *Djeser djeseru* (Deir el Bahari). The thought of *Djeser* got him to thinking about his

INTRIGUE THROUGH TIME

treasure. Even more, he remembered some of the columns he installed in the Temple of Mut in Asher. These here and at *Djeser* were different from those of the Queen's father Thutmose I, at Karnak. After this reflection, he returned to the taxi and they headed towards 34th Street, turned left and rode out past 12th Avenue, where they joined the West Side Highway, heading south.

With the Hudson River to their right, they headed downtown. Our Hero remembered his beloved Nile. He also remembered the accident on the river that took the life of his two trusted servants. He did right by making sure they had a proper burial, but with them also went knowledge of his secret cache of jewelry.

William: "This is Canal Street and ¼ mile away is the entrance to the Hudson Tunnel that takes you to New Jersey, the New Jersey Turnpike and points south along Interstate or I-95."

Soon they were passing the World Trade Center.

Mentuhotep remarked: "These are certainly very tall buildings."
William: "They are called the Twin Towers of the World Trade Center, Sir. They are more than 110 floors. There is an Observation Tower that enables a view for miles on a clear day." Passing the Twin Towers within two minutes they enter a small tunnel that brings them to the Franklin Delano Roosevelt Highway (FDR) North.
On the way, William mentions: "This is the South Street Seaport on the right, and that is the Brooklyn Bridge ahead that takes us to Brooklyn across the river."
Mentuhotep noticed there was another river. 'Two Niles,' he thought and enquired: "What is the name of this river?"
"This is the East River, Sir" William responded, and then he turned to the driver, "Take the Exit for the Brooklyn Bridge." After a while as they were coming off, he said, "Stay left, and don't go on the bridge. Let's get a view of City Hall."

Signs indicating locations along the route towards Brooklyn Bridge.

Coming out of that exit, City Hall is located on the right. Mentuhotep again noticed columns at City Hall. Just then he said: "Stop." The driver pulled over to the left and Mentuhotep got out. William followed. He told the driver: "Circle. You may have to go as far as Church Street, but come around so we can get back on the bridge."
"OK. No problem," responded Omarishaba.

Front entrance to New York City Hall with its colonnade that impressed our hero.

INTRIGUE THROUGH TIME

As Mentuhotep crossed the street to view City Hall and its columns; his eye caught an even more interesting sight farther on. As he walked, William followed. Facing him were the elevated columns of the Probate Court, and to the right the magnificent columns of the New York Municipal Building, Office of the City Clerk. Even further, he noticed both the State Court of Appeals and the Federal District Court were fronted by colonnades.

New York Municipal Building with its colonnade of massive columns.

The highest New York State Court has engraved on its cornice, "The true administration of justice is the firmest pillar of good government."

FREDERICK MONDERSON

The Thurgood Marshall United States Court House, in downtown Manhattan, New York City.

Lost in the memory of the significance of the colonnade, he was revived by William who was shaking his arm and saying: "Sir, we must return to the car." William glanced at his watch; it was now 5:00 pm. They returned to the car parked in an awkward site and headed to the Bridge. He looked keenly at this magnificent creation that spanned the river, and wondered if his country had ever spanned the Nile.

A scene along Fifth Avenue where Mentuhotep often strolled.

INTRIGUE THROUGH TIME

Mentuhotep stopped to admire the elevated columns of the Surrogates Court.

View of the entrance to Manhattan Municipal Building with its massive columns. To the left is the Surrogates Court building (end).

View of the heart of downtown Manhattan with City Council to the right behind the green fence; buildings of the financial districts further on; and entrance to the Brooklyn Bridge to the left.

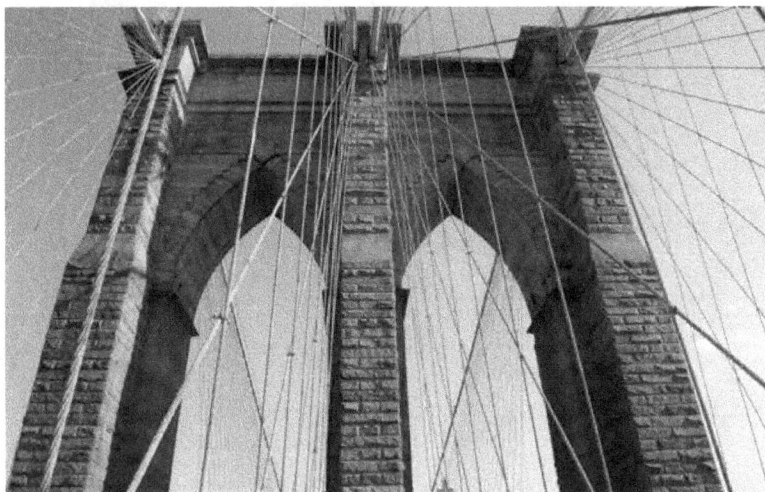

Summit of Brooklyn Bridge as seen from the New York side.

Plaque erected by the Brooklyn Engineers Club honoring builders of the bridge, Colonel Washington A. Roebling and his son John Roebling, who were ALSO influenced by Emily Warren Roebling, wife and mother, as they worked at the arduous task of finishing the project.

NYC Dept. Public Works Brooklyn Bridge Reconstruction plaque.

FREDERICK MONDERSON

Close-up of the emblem of New York City College of Technology.

They crossed the river, arriving, a sign read: "Welcome to Brooklyn," with Howard Golden as Borough President. From the ramparts they passed the Post Office on the right; New York City Technical College, the Family Court, and Board of Elections, on the left. Down from the Post Office on the right is the New York State Court. As they continued along Adams Street, William pointed out the Brooklyn Borough Hall and Brooklyn Law School on the right. The Municipal Building with its colonnade lay further down on Joralemon Street. Mentuhotep thought further, 'They certainly seem to like columns in this culture.' Even further, William pointed out the Transit Building and behind that the Brooklyn Criminal Court Building also on the left. Further on, the Brooklyn House of Detention still on the left. They continued and then turned on to Atlantic Avenue, getting a better view from the front of the multitude of windows in the Brooklyn House of Detention. Several blocks later on, they saw the Flatbush Avenue Clock and Tower of the Williamsburg Bank Building, and the driver turned left, then headed back to the Bridge.

INTRIGUE THROUGH TIME

Brooklyn Municipal Building with its columns on Joralemon Street.

Brooklyn Boro Hall on right opposite the Municipal Building.

Brooklyn Law School

FREDERICK MONDERSON

Brooklyn House of Detention (center), Brooklyn Criminal Court (left) and way in back, the Flatbush Tower building.

Winding their way through the local streets, they entered the entrance to the Brooklyn Bridge and reversed their way across. Off to the right, parallel with the Brooklyn Bridge, they noticed the other bridge, the Manhattan Bridge. Exiting the Brooklyn Bridge, they headed uptown, via, the FDR North. Soon they passed the Williamsburg Bridge and a sign for New York University on the left. Approaching Forty-Second Street, William pointed out the United Nations Building and finally Fifty-Ninth Street Bridge. They exited the FDR at Sixty-First Street, and headed across town to arrive back at the Plaza.

He exited the taxi saying: "Thank you, gentlemen," and gave $200.00 to William and $200.00 to the taxi Driver, Omarishaba. They were very grateful.

As he entered the lobby, the Front Desk informed him a package had been delivered to his room. He then thanked them and headed upstairs and flopped down on the now familiar sofa. It was 6:00 pm. Reaching over he poured himself a shot of Hennessy, took a sip and after a long sigh, he began to reflect on some of the events of his day.

INTRIGUE THROUGH TIME

View of the top of the Municipal Building as seen from New York side of the Brooklyn Bridge ramparts.

The first thing that came to mind is the fact twice this day he had to pull himself away from the arms of his beautiful Fantegla. If only she knew how he felt about her. Love and inspiration are one thing, but he has to be careful she does not affect him totally, as Nekajai did. Of course, they had grown up as childhood playmates but she affected him tremendously. He seemed to remember telling his father at the banquet how, he 'feels lost when she is not beside him.'

FREDERICK MONDERSON

Here, however, in this new and challenging time, he cannot afford to be 'lost;' he must remember to remain ever vigilant, focused, alert, controlled, as the players in this environment are equally challenging, but faster paced. 'Yet,' he thought, 'I'm equipped for this journey.'

Pinnacle and back of the United States Courthouse as seen from New York side of Brooklyn Bridge as our hero headed to the FDR Drive back uptown.

William was excellent! 'In his whirlwind tour he expanded my horizons tremendously,' allowing a greater view of the new terrain. 'When time permits,' he thought further, 'I must re-visit some of these landmarks to get a better view of the dynamics of their operation. Of course, I must revisit the Museum to re-orient myself with my cultural history, especially the period after my experience.'

The colonnade had the greatest impact on his consciousness. They brought back the memories of the erection and decoration of these sacred features. He wondered if his "name was ever written in the colonnade." He knew for sure his father, Puyemre the Vizier, had earned such a distinction, for there was talk of such an honor

80

INTRIGUE THROUGH TIME

considering he had served both King Thutmose and his daughter Queen Hatshepsut. Importantly, however, there was one thing he noticed about the colonnade, particularly those fronting the Municipal Buildings in Manhattan and Brooklyn. They were seamless and not as disjointed as his columns when they were erected, treated and decorated. Also, these were not decorated as in some cases in his experience.

Here there are two rivers as opposed to his Nile. These rivers also flow north to south into the ocean, as opposed to the Nile that flows south to north, into the great sea. They seem to remind him of his father's descriptions of the rivers in Syria he observed when he traveled there with King Thutmose. These rivers of *Mesa Potamos* ran north to south also. His Egyptian countrymen who were on the military expedition described them as the "rivers that go up-river when going down river." He found the pitched roads were numerous. The vehicles have conquered the land as "We" had conquered the Nile for transport. Still thinking about the Nile, he wondered if his ancient countrymen had bridged it as he further reflected on the technological might of the Brooklyn Bridge. He thought the Twin Towers of the World Trade Center are monumental accomplishments. Further he felt, "the technology of this society by far out-distances ours!"

Ghafoor and his associate Lord Stanhope have raised the stakes. 'I wonder how soon I'll be able to conclude a deal with them,' he thought. Looking around the room he realized he did not see his package. Moving into the bedroom he opened the closet. His suits and shoes were neatly hung and put away. The shirts were also hung. The other things were neatly put away in drawers. 'Wow,' he thought, 'Leonardo certainly did a good job. I must remember to thank him. Perhaps he too can be useful.'

FREDERICK MONDERSON

Queen Hatshepsut, *Ma'at-Ka-Ra*, along with Thutmose III, *Men-Khepper-Ra*, offer flowers, a plant and jars of ointment to Amon's sacred bark.

In Hatshepsut's "Red Chapel," Thoth writes and Amon-Min stands firm.

INTRIGUE THROUGH TIME

11.   The Life of the Party

At 6:30 pm, his doorbell rang. It was the seductively beautiful Fantegla Somersett. She was stunningly captivating in a long-flowing black gown. She just stood there, as opposed to previous times when she brushed past him and entered. He begged her: "Please enter, my angel." She flashed him a big smile and walked in.

He was flabbergasted at the beauty, poise, captivating smile and confidence bordering on daring of this wonderful woman who had lit up his life. "Well, my dear," he said, "how beautiful you look this evening. You'll be the belle of the ball. I was just going to get ready. I was momentarily delayed reflecting on my busy day. I haven't even had a chance to decide on my wardrobe for this evening. But let me get my bath, first." With that he entered the bedroom, then bath, disrobed and entered the shower to wash his-self.

Having poured herself a drink, she wandered into the bedroom and noticed the bathroom door slightly ajar. Mischievously she crept over and forced the door open wider. Now she could see his silhouette through the glass curtain in the shower. Her mind began to play tricks on her, as she wondered how he would be as a lover in bed. As an activated busybody she decided to choose his outfit for the evening and opened the clothes closet. 'Wow!' she thought, 'I did not notice this earlier. I wonder if this is why he rushed off so suddenly this afternoon.' She thought further, 'Perhaps I acted immaturely by thinking he was not in the mood then. I must just chill and go along for the ride, trusting him to make his move when he's ready. Anyway, let me set out his attire for the evening.' She chose a black pinstripe suit, blue shirt, red tie with blue dots, blue handkerchief with white dots, underwear and black Bruno Magneli shoes.

When he came out the shower in his robe, expecting to do these things, he was surprised she had done them for him. He said to her, "Come here," which she did. Then in a warm embrace he kissed her and said "Thank you, honey." Equally, he thought, 'she's acting like a wife, already.' Then she left the room and moved to the

83

balcony so he could get dressed. A tantalizing smile pursed her lips as she sipped her drink. 'Looks like I'm in like Flint,' she thought.

Unlike most women, within minutes he was dressed and ready to go. "Shall we, my dear," he whispered and her face lit-up. Approvingly, she thought, 'That's my man. He is the apple of my eye. We're going to knock them out tonight.' They left the room and headed for the elevator. When the door opened, they walked in arm-in-arm. Gibsoni was the operator and his jaw dropped seeing them linked up arm-in-arm. 'What a fool I must have been to think this man would choose William over this beautiful woman.'

"Here we are, Sir, Madam, have a wonderful evening."
"Thank you, Mr. Gibsoni," she responded.
'She called me by my name,' he thought, 'Things are looking up.' With that they were out the door.

The party got off to a prompt start at 7:00 pm. The band began playing on time and most of the guests had arrived. The *Maître D* gave a final inspection of the food, drinks, glasses, plates, silverware, mints, seating around the pool, on the lawn, and also his special liqueur in case there was to be a toast of any sort. Then he inspected the staff for the little nuances that make or break a party, viz., nails, hair, uniform, head-cover, shoes, and when he was satisfied, he commented: "All is well. Let the games begin." And, they were off to the races.

The first guests to arrive filling the Edwards' driveway were the ladies from her Bridge Club, with their husbands in tow. Then arrived Mr. and Mrs. Somersett and their younger daughter Kasheisha Valencia, Fantegla's sister. Senator Eugene Williams and Mrs. Williams came along with Admiral Barry Reynolds, whose ship was in port as part of "Fleet Week." Also accompanying them was Colonel Sanderson, just back from a Middle Eastern assignment, as an attaché to an Embassy delegation.

Next were Mr. and Mrs. Charles Wisenthal, the banker and wife, who had been touring the capitals of Europe, and had so much to gossip about. The Missus could not wait to tell all she had seen. A little while later her daughter Sarlinda Wisenthal arrived, and the first person she asked for was Fantegla Somersett, who had not arrived as yet.

INTRIGUE THROUGH TIME

The next arrival was the art dealer and his wife, Mr. and Mrs. Gray. Behind these were two new neighbors opposite the Edwards, the Sapps who ran a Publishing firm, and the Samuels who owned a nationwide furniture chain.

After that came Lynaudra Drummond, and a friend she had dated over the years, Michael Bramwell, the attorney. Pulling right behind her was the Englishman Lord Stanhope, always an interesting fellow; there was much he had seen since his appearance at the last shindig given here.

Meanwhile, Fantegla's personal limousine had arrived. Waiting outside, as she descended the stairs, her chauffeur, Sidney, opened the door and she slid into the back seat. Mentuhotep followed, seated then they were off. "This is my personal limousine and my driver Sidney," she told him. 'Hmm,' he thought, 'a personal limousine, does not work at a regular job, an apartment on a higher floor than mine in a posh hotel. Who is this woman?' That is the question that kept coming back to him, as she snuggled and rested comfortably against him.

Just then he caught the chauffeur eyeing them through the rear-view mirror. Sidney himself had thought 'Who is he? I had never seen him before; yet, I certainly cannot remember Madam being as joyfully happy as at this moment.'

Nonetheless, Fantegla had been prepping herself for the grand appearance where everyone would meet her new and dynamic friend. Her parents will certainly be alarmed, wondering about him. However, 'his calm and professional as well as sociable demeanor will soon win them over.' Our Hero on the other hand, has no idea where he's going, who he is going to meet, and what will be the outcome. One thing he is confident of, his beautiful lady knows what time it is and all he has to do is be cool and let her play her hand.

He seemed to remember his father, Vizier Puyemre, telling him: 'Let leaders lead,' and he intends to do that.

85

FREDERICK MONDERSON

Just then they arrived at their destination, the limousine door opened and 'Sister Girl stepped out,' then her handsome companion followed. At the door they were greeted by a familiar face. "Good evening, Ms. Fantegla, welcome." "Good evening, Jonathan, this is Mr. Mentuhotep. Michael this is Jonathan, the butler. He held me as a baby and practically raised me." "Good evening, Jonathan," he responded. "Good evening, Sir."

"They are at poolside, Madam." "Thank you." Meanwhile she clung to Michael tenaciously, stuck to him like glue.

Jonathan seemed transfixed by the sight of this gentleman who moved with grace and confidence of nobility. After all, some of the best had passed through these doors and he had a chance to study them. 'There seemed to be something unusual about him, he moved with such grace and compelling demeanor. He is an individual who on entering lights up a room. No wonder Ms. Fantegla is stuck on him,' he thought further.

Then the belle of the ball stepped into the limelight of the poolside environment. The festivities were well on the way. Eyes began to turn and the spotlight began to shift to her companion escort. After all, she had made this entrance before but not with the same quiet yet thundering fanfare; beaming, brimming with expressions of joy and happiness. In their dance, our man was just following confidently, allowing her to lead.

Fantegla purposely chose his right side, grasping his right hand with her left. As she advanced into the midst of the party, table after table, she shook hands with her right hand and pulled her date along with her left. "This is Michael Mentuhotep," she kept saying while moving deeper and deeper into the gathering. The first significant introduction was with Mrs. Edwards who kissed her approvingly. "Hello, honey, I was wondering when you would get here."
Fantegla: "Hello, Mrs. Edwards, some party you've got going. This is Michael Mentuhotep." Turning to him she said, "My sweet, this is Mrs. Edwards, our host."
Mentuhotep: "Hello, Mrs. Edwards," he said.
Edwards: "Well, congratulations my dear. He certainly is a handsome devil. So, this is what all the chatter is about."

INTRIGUE THROUGH TIME

Fantegla thought, 'The cat's out of the bag. I'll kill Sarlinda for spreading rumors about me.'

He knew what the word devil meant. It referred to Seth-Typhon the evil god. When Mrs. Edwards turned away momentarily, he whispered to her: "Honey, what's a handsome devil?" "Oh, that's just a compliment she paid you," she responded.

"Your parents are at the end of the pool," Mrs. Edwards continued, when her focus returned to them. "Enjoy, and I need to see more of this gentleman."

"Without a doubt," she responded, moving further, trying to get to her parents. Reaching for a drink from a passing waiter, she would not let go of the man, as he too grabbed a drink. On they kept pushing, until they reached the end of the pool and there was her parents' table. Apparently wondering when she would get there, they kept peering at the pool entrance and were more than relieved when she showed up. However, they did notice she was with a gentleman. Her mother especially noticed how she grabbed his hand and despite hand shaking introductions and welcomes, she would not let go, as if leading a lamb to the slaughter.

"Hello, mother, dad, Lord Stanhope, Kasheisha. How are you all tonight? This is Michael. Honey, these are my parents, the Somersetts, a dear friend, and my sister, Kasheisha."
"Good evening, Mrs. Somersett, Mr. Somersett. Lord Stanhope, I think we've met, Kasheisha. This is a wonderful party." To the parents he said, "I'm very pleased to be here with your daughter. This is indeed a wonderful specimen of a human being you have produced. Her beauty is unmatched, her personality is bubblingly titillating, and it's a delightful pleasure to be in her company."
Her mother turned to Fantegla and said laughingly: "Way to go darling, you've hit the jackpot. Where did you get him? He's a knockout." With that she grabbed his other arm, snuggling close, realizing, 'We've got a winner here.'

Our Hero now faced his first dilemma. Yet, with ladies right and left, he still reached for Mr. Somersett's hand. "Pardon me, Sir," he said. "That's all right, my boy, we're pleased to meet you," Somersett said. His years on Wall Street made him a good judge of

FREDERICK MONDERSON

character. From their entrance into the pool area, he had been observing the young man with his daughter. However, while he paid attention to him, he had also been observing his daughter and noticed an aura about her he had not seen in a good while. He noticed how firmly she stayed attached to him, and when they got up close, he floored her mother with the best compliment a dad could hear of his beloved daughter.

Even Kasheisha looked at her older sister's date with an interestedly approving eye. Thus, for the most part, our Hero had arrived! However, before he could sit with the Somersetts, Fantegla dragged him off to another table with her friends Lynaudra and Sarlinda. Sarlinda was the one Michael had met at the dinner, and, in fact, she had first extended the invitation for tonight's affair. Lynaudra he had not met. Nevertheless, Fantegla proudly introduced her big catch to both her friends. "Honey," she said, "this is Sarlinda whom you met, and Lynaudra, whom you have not. These are my very best friends. We go back a very long way, through thick and thin, to early school days."

"I'm happy to make both your acquaintances. Sorry you had to leave the dinner," he said. "Perhaps we can finish it some time, all of us, that is." And to Lynaudra he said, "You're always invited to join us."

When Fantegla and Michael moved away and Mr. Somersett took his seat, Lord Stanhope whispered to him: "How interesting. That is the young man I told you about. Not only does he have those collectibles, but there is something extraordinary about him. He has some kind of noble upbringing, as well as a military and leadership deportment."
Somersett: "My old friend, when I look at my daughter, I see the man. I have never seen her like this before. If he does that to her; the apple of my eye; he's got my vote. I will give $2,000,000.00 for the collection, to sort of 'keep it in the family.'"

Stanhope: "I believe you made an excellent choice. I should say when I examined the jewels, I scheduled a second inspection because I thought you may secure it. So, I wanted to get it right. How right I actually was. However, there are two other pieces. One is of exquisite workmanship and the other is provocatively intriguing."

INTRIGUE THROUGH TIME

Somersett: "Is that so? Tell me more!"

Stanhope: "He has in his possession a dagger with a sparkling handle that he says makes him feel naked when he's not wearing it. Then there's the necklace with inlaid jewelry."

Next Fantegla had dragged Michael to the table of Senator Eugene Williams and his wife, accompanied by Admiral Barry Reynolds and Colonel Frederick Sanderson. While Senator Williams and wife rose to greet their "Little Fantegla," the two military men could detect a military background in this man's deportment. Nevertheless, they were sidetracked by the vivacious and smiling beauty leading the strange yet interesting gentleman. The Admiral, commander of a battleship, and then an aircraft carrier, on the seven seas, was a good judge of men. He seemed to detect in that "tag along," the notion of the cart leading the horse!

"Honey," she said, "This is Senator and Mrs. Williams, my parents' friends for many years. This is Admiral Reynolds and the other gentleman I've never met," as she finished the introductions.

Senator Williams then said: "Of course, this is Admiral Barry Reynolds and Colonel Frederick Sanderson."

Fantegla: "This is Mr. Michael Mentuhotep."

Mentuhotep: "Pleased to meet you gentlemen, and you too, Mrs. Williams."

Mrs. Williams responded: "Any friend of our 'Little Fantegla,' is a welcomed friend of ours."

Somehow, she was off, heading to the Gray's table. "Hello, Mr. and Mrs. Gray. How are you? This is Michael. Honey, these are the Grays, old friends of our family."

Mentuhotep: "Pleased to meet you folks."

Having made all the introductions, Fantegla grabbed a drink, so too did Michael. Then they walked toward an empty table. Having paraded her prize, she needed a little time for herself to also admire her possession.

On the other hand, amidst the sounds of music, chattering voices, sounds of glass and dishes; Mentuhotep began to reflect further on events since he left his hotel. Yes, personal limousine, no work, apartment in upscale hotel, parents are high society, perhaps

FREDERICK MONDERSON

Fantegla is wealthy, but his mind quickly changed to other things. He wondered about meeting Lord Stanhope here. 'Has he told her parents about me?' He needed to know more about the old guy's thinking. 'Perhaps he can be of assistance to help recover my treasure.' Just then he seemed to get a jolt. What if the treasure had been discovered? What if the secret location had been discovered with new developments?

The thought was too frightening. Luckily, he was rescued by Fantegla who said: "Honey, let's dance," and grabbed his hands and moved him closer poolside.

Perhaps it had been a request but the band began playing a slow oldie, "For Your Precious Love, I Would Do Anything." He had not heard it before, naturally. The beat was soft and melodious, yet the lyrics were clear and couples were hooking up to enjoy. Holding his beloved tightly, he started swaying gently as she did, and in the embrace, he wondered: 'About the beautiful and sensuous Nekajai. I wanted to get married to her. Did she ever,' he thought.

However, the sweet smelling and warm embrace of Fantegla brought him back to reality. In their close embrace he not only felt the warmth of her body, but could hear her heart pounding, thump, thump, thump! He just held her closer, looked in her eyes and kissed her, right there on Main Street, oblivious to the staring eyes, as the song ended. He was not sure whether the loud applause was for the band, the song or for them. Meanwhile Fantegla appeared on platforms, she was flying very high and Sarlinda noticed. She thought to herself, 'Friend or no friend, this woman is having a field day with my man.'

The couple of the evening moved to the buffet layout. They collected plates of sumptuous portions of the sweet-smelling delicacies served by smiling staff. Then they walked back to the Somersett table. Lord Stanhope busily had the ear of Mr. Somersett and Mrs. Somersett welcomed them with "Hello Honeys." Smiling, they began to compare goodies on each other's plate, eat a morsel and even put an occasional spoon in the other's mouth. Oblivious, yet he noticed and could see the two gentlemen not only talking, but smoking an object.

INTRIGUE THROUGH TIME

Somersett: "Have you ever tried one of these Cuban cigars, my son?"

Mentuhotep: "No, Sir."

Somersett: "These were given me by Lord Stanhope who got them when he was in Europe last year. Here try one."

Mentuhotep: "Thank you, Sir, I'll try it later."

After Fantegla finished eating her mother said: "Let's go powder our faces, my dear."

Fantegla: "OK, mother," and they were off.

Somersett: "Where did you meet this wonderful gentleman?"

Fantegla: "Actually, I met him at the Metropolitan Museum of Art."

Somersett: "Cultured, I see."

Fantegla: "Well, passingly, that is. I actually and formally met him when he came to dinner at the Plaza. He is from out of town and is staying there. He's Egyptian."

Somersett: "I noticed his olive-colored skin and his rich bronze tan as if baked by the Egyptian sun. How long is he staying?"

Fantegla: "Initially he said ten days, because he has some business to conduct."

Somersett: "There is a magnetic attraction about him, a sense of nobility about him, in the way he walks, and talks and even looks. His eyes seem gentle yet penetrating. His hands are warm and soft, but he has a firm grip."

Fantegla: "Yes, mother," she said, "and that bit about magnetic attraction, I don't intend to let him go."

Somersett: "Why should you?"

Fantegla: "In a way, both Sarlinda and I met and saw him at the Met, which meant it was open season. We were at dinner last night when he came in. Midway she had to leave. As a result, she feels 'I have stolen her man.' We haven't talked much since but I don't think this will affect our relationship. We have too much in common and have known each other too long."

Somersett: "Well, I certainly noticed how she looked at you both." Still, she thought, 'only two days, and this man has lit such a fire under my daughter. Oh, my goodness!' Still, she continued, 'there is something about him that does something to people. Nonetheless, all I'm concerned about is my daughter's happiness, and she has not been this happy in ages.' Giving herself more liberty, she thought further, 'I wonder if grandchildren are involved.'

"Nevertheless," she said to her, "any breach of the friendship can be worked out later. What is important is how you feel now and in the future. What does Michael think of you?"

Fantegla: "He thinks I'm an angel. Strange, he does not feel threatened by an assertive, modern woman."

Somersett: "Have you told him anything about yourself? I mean really told him about you?"

Fantegla: "No! You mean if I have told him, I may be worth $500 million dollars. No! I have not, and he has never brought it up. He does not seem to care about money. There is something else that drives him. Oh, yes, he wears a pretty gold necklace encrusted with pretty stones. It seems rather antique. However, I did tell him I work as a volunteer at the Veterans Hospital and at a Nursing Home."

Somersett: "That's good. Anyway, the jewelry is your father's area. Well, do you think he may be returning to Egypt? When will he?"

Fantegla: "I don't know. We have not talked about that."

Somersett: "We must be getting back, before they miss us. One thing I can say, I'm so happy to see you happy. You must bring him to the house."

Fantegla: "Thank you, mother. I knew he would make an impression on you, and I knew you would like him."

One of the Bridge Club ladies asked Mrs. Edwards: "Who is that young man I saw with Fantegla Somersett?"

Edwards: "Oh, as far as I could tell, he's just a date."

Lady: "He does look foreign, Mediterranean. Is he Italian?"

Edwards: "No, he's Egyptian, I'm told."

Lady: "He has certainly made an impression on everyone here this evening. Do you know what type of business he's in?"

Edwards: "You are certainly right about the noticeable impression. However, I don't know anything about his line of work. Excuse me I have to consult with the *Maître D.*"

Maître D. "Madam, are you still going to make a toast? I kept the champagne chilled, just in case."

Edwards: "Thank you for reminding me, Arthur darling. Yes, we will make a toast. Pour the bubbly." Then she signaled the band, took the Mike and announced: "Ladies and Gentlemen. Ladies and Gentlemen! I want to thank you for coming and making our first summer party such a success. While it's good to see each and every

INTRIGUE THROUGH TIME

one of you, I am extremely happy to announce my daughter, Michele Cheryl-Ann, now in her third year in college, will be doing an internship in Washington, D.C., beginning in September. The year she will spend there will constitute her senior year. She has agreed to move on from Duke University to do Graduate Studies, a Masters and perhaps a Ph. D. at Columbia, closer to home."

"You know Senator Williams, our power hitter, he brings home the bacon. He has been gracious and made the introductions and connections for the Internship. I would also like to thank the Senator for being a dear and long-standing friend and supporter of the Edwards family. So, let us thank the Senator and toast our beautiful Michele Cheryl-Ann for her hard work, dedication and commitment to complete this portion of her studies. May our toast be the engine that generates fair wind for her sails, to complete the next portion of her academic growth."

Hear. Hear. Hear. Hear. Glasses clinking! A drum roll and a rustle of congratulatory sounds were heard.

Edwards: "I would also like to congratulate my 'Second Daughter' Fantegla and her companion for gracing us with their wonderful presence. Clearly, we see a happy couple, brimming with effervescent joy, evidently well-liked by all, and, if I could speak for the gathering, I would say, Good Luck to you both."

Hear. Hear. Hear. Hear. Glasses clinking and another drum roll, then more congratulatory sounds were heard.

Edwards: "While I would not like to take up more of your time this evening, I would like to implore you to try a piece of the beautiful cake the Maître D, Arthur, designed for this wonderful occasion. Well, enjoy and thank you so very much. Maestro. Music! Please!"

Mrs. Gray: "You know, my dear," she said to Mr. Gray, "Mrs. Edwards' toast was so moving. She is so lucky. Her daughter has achieved so much. They are both so lucky. They have so much to be proud of."

93

FREDERICK MONDERSON

Mr. Gray: "You are so absolutely right my dear. Young people must grasp the opportunity to get a good education that should train the mind to better the lot of humanity."

Sarlinda: "Do you remember your senior year? Where did you go? Was it Penn State?"

Lynaudra: "Yes, but I did my masters at Stamford. I remember you got into trouble in your senior year, sowing your wild oats."

Sarlinda: "Don't ever mention it. If my father had not stepped in, I would probably be married to one of those two boys, Cleveland Roberts or Stephen Sinclair."

Lynaudra: "Whatever happened to those two anyway?"

Sarlinda: "Cleveland became a Navy-man and Stephen a lawyer. I hear they are both successful."

Williams: "How was your tour, Admiral? Where did you sail?"

Admiral Reynolds: "Pretty good, Senator. From the Atlantic we moved to the Eastern Mediterranean. We suspect trouble is brewing in the Lebanon. One of my flights went down, not from hostile fire, but from mechanical problems."

Williams: "In discussions with Senator Scott of the Armed Services Committee, he thought, rightly, we must maintain an active presence in that location. I think Lebanon is fragmenting. The Israelis may be hard pressed, and I think our government may have to have men on the ground."

Reynolds: "We suspected trouble was on the horizon, but since I was in rotation, the destroyer *Frederick Douglass* and the Carrier *Abraham Lincoln* replaced me. By the way, I want to thank you for passing the word that got me this new command."

Williams: "No problem. Well, Colonel what did you learn from your attaché assignment?"

Sanderson: "There are foreign governments fermenting trouble in Lebanon. Of course, I can't go into details. You will have to get it through official channels, and, as you know, the big budget fight looming, we all have to be tight-lipped."

Reynolds: "You're preaching to the choir, Colonel. Senator Williams pulls no punches. He has been an effective advocate for a strong military and a champion of the welfare of servicemen. He is one of our strongest allies, a clutch hitter from start to finish."

Sanderson: "You are more familiar with the Senator than I am, Admiral, and could speak more freely being on his level more so than I. You're both connected like pipes, more than I am. Hence,

94

I'm rather cautious in discussions with my superior for fear of being branded a blabbermouth."

Reynolds: "I agree with you. Rest assured you're among friends."

Williams: "Well-spoken, young man. Admiral, we must watch this young man's back and have him groomed for his next promotion. Waiter, another round for these gentlemen, please!"

"Will you gentlemen join me in toasting our wonderful country and servicemen such as yourself, who keep us safe and free?"

Reynolds: "I'll drink to that, Senator."

Sanderson: "Not to be outdone, I always listen to and respect my elders. It is an honor to be in the company of brilliant minds as yours."

Reynolds: "Thank you."

Williams: "Thank you."

Mr. Gray: "I'm told there's some new jewelry on the horizon. Yet, no one pulled my coat about it."

Stanhope: "Well, since you're principally an art dealer and collector, no one bothered to include you in the loop as its being shopped around."

Gray: "Gentlemen!"

Somersett: "I have agreed to purchase the lot, offering much more than it's worth, believing these are family heirlooms and feeling they should be preserved as a single collection."

Gray: "My brother, if you do secure the collection; please do me the honor of at least viewing the pieces, and basking in the aura of their esoteric or historical significance."

Somersett: "Consider it done, my good friend."

Stanhope: "Do not despair, my good man. You may indeed get your chance for there are two other pieces that may be available. One is a necklace; the other is a dagger. I heard about it from my contact, but I also had a glimpse of it."

Gray: "Who is that, Ghafoor?"

Stanhope: "Yes."

Gray: "How come he does not give me heads-up on these things?"

Somersett: "You must grease the wheel. If you grease the wheel, you would be as high up on the totem pole notification list, as I am."

FREDERICK MONDERSON

Gray: "It's as you said, I'm primarily an art dealer and not an antiques dealer. I am at least glad you're acquiring this. It couldn't happen to a better man."
Somersett: "Thank you. You're so kind."

Arthur: "Now that the major portion of the party has gone off like clockwork, I want to be able to pull the rest off. I need to see the guests' glasses full. Tell the musicians I would like to hear some classics from the 1970s. While they are different age groups among our guests, the 1970s is an important and pivotal period in American contemporary music. Let me say, finally, our host Mrs. Edwards whispered in my ear she was very pleased with our performance. The guests are comfortable, enjoying our hospitality. Personally, I think bonuses may be in order. So, let's go out in a blaze of glory."

Sarlinda: "So tell me, Sister Girl, what's going on with you and Michael? You're hugging him so tight; air can't pass between you. You have him tied to your apron. After all, I spotted him first while we were together, therefore I have a legitimate claim on him, and you don't want to share."
Fantegla: "First of all, let me tell you, this is not a democratic free-for-all. Second, you can't win them all. Some you win and some you lose. Third, while I don't believe he's that type, I have enough confidence in myself that the best man, I mean, woman will win. If you think you can budge him, then you can try."
Lynaudra: "Oh, Sarlinda, you're just jealous that Fantegla has got the man all wrapped up, and you're trying to play spoiler. You know the ropes. Fantegla bowled him over. That's the way the ball bounces."
Sarlinda: "It's not that I'm jealous, but we just met the guy yesterday and you haven't even given him a chance to play the field. I do not mind having a one-night-stand with him. In fact, I would give my eye tooth to hit him one time."
Fantegla: "Even if that were so, and tomorrow is another day, tonight I intend to make him mine. And further, I can't deal with any sour grape's mentality. You know, we should live and let live."
Sarlinda: "That's exactly what I'm trying tell you."

Mrs. Edwards: "Well ladies, are you having a good time? I see your glasses are empty. Shall I order you something?"

INTRIGUE THROUGH TIME

Mrs. Gray: "I will not speak for the rest, but I'm having that dish with the curry, I think. I might get the recipe from you so I can serve it at my next party."

Edwards: "I'll get it from Arthur. He considers it one of his specialties. As for me, I liked the sautéed duck in that wonderful sauce."

Mrs. Griffith: "Let me congratulate you for the wonderful job you have done raising your daughter into such a fine young woman. I'm a firm believer, that, if given the proper guidance young people can become useful members of the society, no matter what their social standing."

Edwards: "Oh, darling, you're so kind. No wonder I have such high regard for your compassion, ethics and a keen sense of being able to see where others refuse."

Griffith: "Though you may be a little younger than we are, we still hold you in high regard because of your kindness and generosity."

Mrs. Charles: "Let us not forget her charity work and willingness to volunteer for social causes. This is what sets you apart from some of the social snobs we meet at the club."

Mrs. Farrell: "All that is well said and you certainly deserve all the praise you get. However, let's not forget next Thursday's club meeting and the quarterly report from the Executive Board."

Lord Stanhope joined Senator Williams, Admiral Reynolds, and Colonel Sanderson. Instantly, he was asked whether his government had any different information on conditions in the Middle East. Whether there was the possibility of British forces to the region. In such matters he was generally tight-lipped. However, being in such familiar company his lips cracked and he said, 'Her Majesty's Government had noticed the interference of foreign elements in Lebanon. Equally, too, the government had been contacted by two friendly governments in the region to share information and they were seeking advisers to help deploy their counter terror measures.'

Just then the talk turned to the young man who accompanied the beautiful Fantegla to the party. He incidentally was now seated with Mr. Somersett.

Williams: "Lord Stanhope, what do you make of the gentleman sitting with Mr. Somersett?"

FREDERICK MONDERSON

Stanhope: "Ah, Mr. Mentuhotep. He is certainly an interesting chap."

Williams: "Admiral Reynolds, I know happens to be a good judge of men. Yet he is intrigued by him. However, he admits there is a missing element we can't put our hands on and thought you might be of assistance."

Stanhope: "There is certainly something strange about him in a nice sort of way, you know what I mean?"

Williams: "I certainly do. The Admiral mentioned the way the young woman was pulling him around as she made her introductions. What is it you told me, Admiral?"

Reynolds: "I don't know how right I am, but I thought of the 'cart before the horse' metaphor. Even Colonel Sanderson noticed it. What did you think Sanderson?"

Stanhope: "Let me add, he's Egyptian."

Sanderson: "He is certainly military from the way he walks. He may be under deep cover. He is of the nobility and quite a ladies' man' I might add.

Reynolds: "Correct, but there's still a missing element which I can't put my hands on, you know what I mean."

Sanderson: "Yes, Sir."

Stanhope: "Perhaps I can add another dimension to this discussion. While it's of a confidential nature we three share a bond and were brought here by the Admiral. The Colonel is included. He is in possession of antique jewelry dated by me to the early 18th Egyptian Dynasty, around the time of Thutmose or Hatshepsut. I examined it and found it authentic and placed a monetary value on it. Naturally he's tight-lipped about how he came into its possession."

Reynolds: "Well, as Sanderson said, he is from the Egyptian nobility and may have had it handed down as a family heirloom."

Williams: "Waiter! I believe these gentlemen can use a refill."

Waiter: "Yes, Sir, coming up."

Stanhope: "Another thing I may add, he's in possession of a necklace I have seen in the Cairo Museum."

Williams: "Stanhope, are you suggesting someone in the Museum may be funneling him antique jewelry?"

Sanderson: "Well, Admiral, if that's the case there goes your family heirloom theory. But I would venture to say such a possibility is very remote. The Museum's collections are national treasures and naturally under heavy guard. Even more important, there has not been any alarm about missing treasures."

INTRIGUE THROUGH TIME

Reynolds: "If he is nobility and involved in such a scheme, then we're dealing with a corrupt and bankrupt noble and he does not fit the type."

Williams: "Sanderson has suggested he may be undercover. If that is the case heaven help the Somersetts, because according to your 'cart before the horse' perspective, he already has control of the daughter's millions."

Reynolds: "For all we know he might be spinning Somersett a yarn right now as they sit over there."

Stanhope: "Gentlemen, let me say this, do not sell Mr. Somersett cheaply; but I will investigate the necklace further and keep you apprised."

Somersett: "Mr. Mentuhotep, may I call you Michael?"

Mentuhotep: "Yes, Sir, please do!"

Somersett: "So how do you find New York?"

Mentuhotep: "New York is a wonderfully exciting place. The people, hospitality, sites, structures, all can make a real lasting impression on someone like me, coming from a different culture."

Somersett: "Where are you staying?"

Mentuhotep: "At the Plaza."

Somersett: "OK! That is where Fantegla has her residence."

Mentuhotep: "Yes, I was surprised, yet delighted to find that out."

Somersett: "I will get straight to the point."

He was a bit nervous and thought, 'Is he going to ask me about his daughter?'

Instead Somersett said: "I have decided to purchase your jewelry collection. I think it has great historical significance and as a collector I do not wish to see it scattered among several owners."

Mentuhotep: "That is a wise decision, Sir."

Somersett: "I'm not interested in being wise. I'm an investor, a collector. It's an economic decision on my part."

Mentuhotep: "I see. You're a practical man."

Somersett: "Yes. That is why I'm prepared to pay $2,000,000.00 for the collection. It's much more than it's worth. Are you willing to sell it to me?"

Mentuhotep: "Like I said, you're wise and practical. I would have it no other way. That is a bench mark and personally I would not accept a higher bid, even if it was offered. So, consider the deal settled. I see you as a principled man and I admire you for that. I will instruct Mr. Ghafoor to hand over the jewels to you forthwith."

Somersett: "Good. What is the manner of payment that is acceptable to you?"

Mentuhotep: "Cash."

Somersett: "In that case, I'll be at Ghafoor's at noon Monday with the cash to pick up my merchandise or is there another place we can meet, say your hotel room?"

Mentuhotep: "Well, Ghafoor's is where the jewels are and where you'll pick them up."

Somersett: "So, that's settled."

Mentuhotep: "Precisely."

Somersett: "I understand there are two other pieces, a necklace and a dagger."

Mentuhotep: "Yes they are, but at this time I am not considering their sale. If I do, however, I will certainly consider giving you the right of first refusal."

Somersett: "In that case, if you deal directly with me, you can bypass Ghafoor and save the finder's fee. By the way, how much has that chiseler tried to get you for?"

Mentuhotep: "Pardon?"

Somersett: "How much is he charging you to find a buyer?"

Mentuhotep: "We have not discussed percentages."

Somersett: "In that case, give him $100,000 and not a penny more. In fact, here's what I will do for you when I bring the cash. I will parcel his portion, in an envelope, so you can do the transfer easily. Remember not a penny more. Further, if there is anything, anything, I can do for you; please do not hesitate to ask."

Mentuhotep: "Yes, Sir. I will certainly keep that in mind." Just then he thought, 'perhaps as my point man he can persuade Lord Stanhope to get me a British Passport. I recognize this travel document will cost me, but that's the price of doing business. Still, it's not time to move on this front as yet.'

As if to consecrate the deal, Mr. Somersett called the waiter who came with two glasses of bubbly.

Somersett: "Shall we drink to consecrate our agreement?"

Mentuhotep: "We certainly can." Then they drank a toast to seal the bargain.

Just then Fantegla happened over. She sat in the chair between the two men who were seated across from each other. She grasped both their hands, establishing a link between the two men who meant so much to her. With that she said: "Dad, it's getting late and I must take Michael back so we'll be going."

Somersett: "Very well, my dear. It's so nice to see you in such good spirits. I think your mother is in the house."

Fantegla: "I'll see her on my way out."

Somersett: "We're finished with our business here, so I will say good night to Mr. Mentuhotep."

Fantegla thought: 'What business were they discussing? Were they discussing me? I would certainly like to know the outcome. Perhaps I can inveigle it out of Mother later on.' With that she got up, kissed her dad good night, pulled her man to his feet, and headed straight to the door. Once inside the house she began looking for her mother who was with some ladies. She approached, kissed her saying, "See you later," headed out the front door and into her waiting limousine.

On the way home she nestled close to him, somewhat pooped from the long day, the dynamics of the party and the alcoholic beverage she consumed.

"Your parents are nice," he said.

"They mean so much to me," she replied, still wondering 'What were he and Dad discussing?' In the warm comfortable embrace on the way home, she continued to think, 'Were they discussing me?' 'Does he have any idea that we are wealthy?' Perhaps! But he has not intimated in anyway, nor has he queried about it. He interrupted her thoughts by saying: "I could use a nice hot bath." She responded, "So could I."

In an occasional glance in the rear-view mirror, the chauffeur noticed how comfortable his boss had become and he smiled. He was happy to see her happy. Then they pulled into the Plaza. Exiting, she said, "Thank you, Sidney, I won't need you anymore this evening." "Very well, Madam," he responded and seeing them enter the Plaza, he took off. It was 11:30 by the lobby clock.

Standing in front of his elevator, Gibsoni had been staring at the entrance. When he noticed the couple appear, he straightened up. As they approached the elevator, he greeted them. "Good evening, Sir. Good evening, Madam." She said nothing. Mentuhotep said:

"18." Expecting she would give a floor, she did not. They got off at 18. Mr. Busybody thought, "Umm, she got off at 18."

Colossal Anubis figure stands before various scenes of individuals and offerings in the tomb of Vizier Rekhmara at Thebes.

Another scene from the Vizier Rekhmara's tomb that so intrigued Mentuhotep, reminiscent of his father, the Vizier Puyemre.

INTRIGUE THROUGH TIME

12.   First Taste of Goodness

In that malleable frame of mind, she headed straight to the showers, set the water real warm, and did her thing. While she was in the shower, sitting on the sofa, he began to write his "to-do-list" for tomorrow, Saturday.

1. Visit the Museum; 2. Secure a good Travel Guide for Egypt; 3. Perhaps visit the New York Public Library to look over the place. He thought 'I may have to do some research about my homeland. The Met will give artifacts and pictorial graphics, but I have to get more than that. I also have to tap into William again.'

Fantegla finished her shower and headed straight between the sheets. Hearing the shower stop, he knew she was finished. So, it was his turn. 'A nice warm shower can do such wonders,' he thought. After a good soaking, toweling and pajamas, he moved to the living room, to get one last night cap. A bird landed on the balcony rail. It began whistling. He approached the door, looking at the bird, the stars, in the bright, clear, blue summer night sky, and thought of his home. The sky was in so many ways similar in illumination. It was as if he was sailing the Nile River in his boat, just peering skyward. Just then he heard a distant voice: "Come to bed, honey." "Coming dear," he responded. Soon he was traveling, again, on that seemingly majestic and heavenly, Nile, journey.

Fantegla awoke Saturday morning. Reaching across the bed, unlike the last time, Michael was there. She moved even closer to him feeling his warmth, his muscular body. Snuggling and just barely peeking out above the cover, she stared at the ceiling. 'How lucky I am,' she thought. Savoring the moment, she continued, 'It's been a while, but worth it. I must work to ensure there's more of this wonderful feeling.'

Just then she thought of Sarlinda, her childhood friend and running buddy. There was something she said at the party, about not allowing the man to play the field. He did not seem that type. His mind seems preoccupied with business, 'Is that what he was discussing with my dad?' After last night, she continued, 'The best woman won. I'm confident in and out of my clothes,' she chuckled.

103

FREDERICK MONDERSON

She did not want to be too brash last night, but Sarlinda seemed to issue a challenge. 'Poor child,' she thought, 'even if she got a slice of the bacon, and deservedly so, I've got the whole hog and intend to "mate it" for dear life.'

Just then Michael stirred, he turned, raised his arm and she slipped under; covered; it was hours before they finally got out of bed.

Beetle with outstretched wings supporting "Eye of Horus" with uraei wearing disks hoisting Ra in his bark with other forms of gold and precious stone decoration.

INTRIGUE THROUGH TIME
13. Reflections on the Party

At 10:00 am, he was up, showered, dressed and down to breakfast. She remained in a nap. Getting off the elevator he spotted William. "Good morning, Sir," William belted. "Morning, William," he responded. "Today is such a wonderful day for outdoors." "Yes," he added. "Tell me," said Mentuhotep, "Where can I buy a good Travel Guide?" "On which topic, Sir?" "Ancient Egypt," he replied.

William: "Barnes and Noble. They have an outlet somewhere in this vicinity around Forty-Fifth and Forty-Sixth Streets, but you have a wider selection at the main store on Fifth Avenue and Eighteenth Street."
Mentuhotep: "Fifth and Eighteenth? I saw the one around Forty-Fifth Street." 'Still,' he thought, 'Fifth Avenue is an important street. I'll think of it as my Nile for navigation purposes.'
William: "You can take a cab, Sir, I wouldn't walk. It's too far, nearly forty blocks away."
Mentuhotep: "Isn't the library in that direction?"
William: "Yes, Sir. It's at Forty-Second and Fifth. They're open from 11:00 am to 5:00 pm."

Looking at the lobby clock it read 10:30. He said: "OK. Thank you," and entered the restaurant for breakfast.

The waiter brought the *Times* and took his breakfast order.

The *Times* headlines for Saturday June 15, 1985 read:

Lead: "Gunmen Seize Jet in Mideast Flight. Passenger Killed"
International: "U.S. Recalls South Africa Envoy in Response to Raid on Botswana"
National: "Executives Convicted for Unsafe Workplace Conditions"
Local: "Police Say Others Saw Student Attack Officer."

At 10:50 Mentuhotep finished breakfast and the *Times*, and then walked out of the Plaza, waving to his friend William. It was a

FREDERICK MONDERSON

bright, sunny day; a day for walking. By that time 5ᵗʰ Avenue had come alive. He set out, passing stores along the avenue. There's Rockefeller Center. Soon he was passing Ghafoor's who opened at 11:00 am. Following a steady pace, he got to Forty-Second Street. He stopped at the northwestern corner of Forty-Second Street. The New York Public Library was across the street, beside Bryant Park. He looked ahead, left and right. He used the path of the sun to orient himself. The direction he came from was the north and Barnes and Noble lay to the south. To his left lay east and to his right, he remembers the West Side Highway on which he had traveled. He also seemed to remember coming from the right with Fantegla on that first night they walked. He then decided to walk two or three blocks to the left or east, to see what lay in that direction.

New York Public Library from the 5ᵗʰ Avenue and 42ⁿᵈ Street corner.

Grand Central Station's elevated colonnaded entrance, Old Glory and the Great American eagle beside Vanderbilt Avenue and 42ⁿᵈ Street.

INTRIGUE THROUGH TIME

Crossing the avenue, he headed to the left and towards Madison Avenue. Further on, he came to stand at the southwest corner of Park Avenue at 42nd Street. There he saw Grand Central Station. Gazing at the entrance façade of the building, he was impressed with its beautiful sculptured architectural features on the cornice as well as the tremendous amount of traffic that passed through the doors. Then he thought, 'I must stay on my schedule.' As he retraced his steps, his mind racing, 'There will be time for a revisit. Perhaps with Fantegla in tow, she can help me navigate some of the sites William pointed out. However, that will have to be sometime when she is not volunteering at the Veterans Hospital or the Nursing Home.'

Just then his mind returned to the lovely creature. She may be stirring by now. 'What a beautiful, fiery and exciting experience she is,' he continued. 'She seems to fit hand-in-glove like Nekajai;' and the second necklace came to mind just then. He also remembered when his father gave them both the necklaces, seeming to cement the ties. Unfortunately, he was not around or able to appreciate or even enjoy Nekajai or wear his necklace. However, 'now resurrected and with Nekajai carbon copy he was going to eat that beautiful cake and enjoy the wonderful ice-cream, as he lives and make a life for himself in this new land and time.'

Ghafoor opened his store at 11:00 am, and, as usual he soon had browsers. Still, he kept a close eye on the door to see if Mr. Mentuhotep would come in today. He was a bit nervous! None of his contacts, Lord Stanhope, Mr. Somersett, Mr. Gray, even Senator Williams, amateur collector that he is, no one had contacted him in almost 24 hours. Nevertheless, he thought, 'I'm holding the jewelry. I'm holding the cards; the prized possession is in my vault.' Still, he reasoned further about the $10,000.00 Mr. Somersett had promised. 'Now if I could sell the necklace, that's even more money, a bigger finder's fee. All is mine!' He began humming!

Mrs. Edwards woke Saturday morning. At breakfast she said to Mr. Edwards: "Morning, my sweet. What do you think of last night?"
Mr. Edwards: "I think it was fabulous," he responded. "Some of our old friends were able to attend. Lord Stanhope said he had come across about some business and he's on his way to the Middle East.

FREDERICK MONDERSON

I think Egypt. Also, Senator Williams said he had to leave early, but did not want to disappoint you."

Mrs. Edwards: "That's nice of him," she said.

Mr. Edwards: "The Senator is debating some aspects of President Reagan's budget before they break for the Fourth of July," and then summer recess. He was more in party mood. Admiral Reynolds said he got your wire aboard ship. His crew thought he was trying to make shore for "Fleet Week," but he had you in mind. His companion, Colonel Sanderson, is just back from some sort of diplomatic mission, and he was glad to bring him along, even though not invited. He knew he'd enjoy easiness with us and took the liberty to bring him along."

Mrs. Edwards: "The Admiral has always been one of our dearest friends. Since standing godfather for Michele Cheryl-Ann he has made our home a stop every time he made port. He has indeed been a true friend. It's interesting when an individual is away at the other end of the world on a military expedition and can think of you so far away, there must be some significant bond, that of friendship, that is priceless."

Mr. Edwards: "That sense of deep thinking is what I admire about you my dear; it fans the flame of our love. You have treated me so well over the years."

Mrs. Edwards: "You know when I first met you and said I'm in love, since then, my passion has not diminished one iota."

Mr. Edwards: "That sense of encouragement is what makes me go out and daily challenge the world. I have so much to be thankful for."

Ring. Ring. Ring.

"Hello, this is Ghafoor's Antiques, Ghafoor speaking."

"Ghafoor, this is Lord Stanhope. I'll be out of town for a while. I understand, however, Mr. Somersett will be in your office with Mr. Mentuhotep to conclude that business around noon on Monday. I won't be there, but you should hold my fee until further notice."

Ghafoor: "As usual, Sir. It will be here awaiting your return."

Stanhope: "OK! Bye."

INTRIGUE THROUGH TIME

Architecture against the sky has always fascinated Michael, himself an architect.

14.　　　First Thoughts

Ring. Ring. Ring.

"Hello, Egypt Air. Can we be of assistance?"

"Yes, this is Lord Samuel Milford Stanhope."

Egypt Air: "Oh, yes, Lord Stanhope, the Englishman. How delighted to hear from you? How can I help you, Sir?"

Stanhope: "I'd like a seat on your Sunday evening to Cairo. I must be there by Monday morning."

Egypt Air: "Such a celebrity as you, My Lord, only has to make the request, and we will be happy to comply."

Stanhope: "I'm happy to know I'm held in such high esteem in Egypt which I consider to be my second home."

Egypt Air: "OK. Give me a moment, let me check my listings." After a pause, "Sir"

Stanhope: "I'm still here."

Egypt Air: "Yes, I have the listing for tomorrow's flight and we have a seat available for you. How long will you be in Egypt?"

Stanhope: "I wish to be back here by next Friday."

Egypt Air: "OK. Lord Stanhope, we have a flight out of Cairo Thursday morning at 5:30 am. I can put you on that."

Stanhope: "Great."

Egypt Air: "OK. Here's your itinerary. Egypt Air 812, Seat 4C, Sunday, June 16, 1985, check in from 6:30. Flight leaves at 8:45.

FREDERICK MONDERSON

Be at the airport, JFK, two hours prior to check in. Arrival 8:20, Monday morning, June 17. Return Flight. Egypt Air 811, Thursday, June 20, 1985. Check in 5:30 am. Flight leaves 7:30 am. Arrival JFK 3:30 pm. Be at Cairo International at least two hours prior to check in. Seat number, 3C. Do you have all that?"
Stanhope: "Yes, I do."
Egypt Air: "Now, how would you like to pay for that?"
Stanhope: "By Credit Card, American Express.
Egypt Air: "One moment, Sir, while I complete this processing." After a pause, "Everything's complete, Sir. You can pick up your ticket at the Check-in desk. I'll make a special note about your circumstances. Thank you for flying Egypt Air."
Stanhope: "Thanks."

Attendant: "Admiral, are you going ashore?"
Reynolds: "As soon as lunch is over. Can you contact Colonel Sanderson?"
Attendant: "Yes, Sir, the Colonel says he will be at the Pier at 1:00 pm.
Reynolds: "What's on the menu today?"
Purser: "Shrimp scampi, steamed salmon, baked chicken. Mashed potatoes. Peas and carrots. Salad. Apple Pie.
Reynolds: Picking up the phone: "OD (Officer of the Day), let me speak to the Executive Officer."
"Executive Officer, Captain Powell speaking."
Reynolds: "Powell, this is the Admiral."
Executive Officer: "Yes, Sir."
Reynolds: "What percentage of the crew is already ashore?"
Executive Officer: "More than 75 percent of the crew, Sir. Everyone's on a week's liberty. Most are not coming aboard at nights. Is there a reason for this inquiry, Sir?"
Reynolds: "We're having a wonderful lunch and I just want to make sure the Mess Hall does not prepare unnecessarily."
Executive Officer: "Well, Sir, I will forward the stats to the Mess Hall, so they will be fully apprised, Sir. Is there anything else, Sir?
Reynolds: "No. On second thought, Captain Powell, are you going ashore?"
Executive Officer: "Well, Sir, I wanted to take in a concert at Lincoln Center with a friend of mine."

INTRIGUE THROUGH TIME

Reynolds: "Very Good. I hear Radio City Music Hall also has an excellent show. I always keep a mental picture of the legs of those Rockettes in the air."

Executive Officer: "I concur, Sir. That's the wonderful thing about our culture, we have such moving and significant symbolisms, it motivates us to serve and protect this great American nation."

Fantegla awoke feeling exotically lazy. She had not slept so wonderfully well in a long time. Getting out of bed there was a little sprite in her step, as she headed to the bathroom. Realizing she had to go and not wanting to be seen in an evening gown, she thought, 'If I'm going to spend the night here, I will have to begin leaving a change of clothes. However, I don't know how Michael will take it and I don't want to frighten him.' Nevertheless, she dismissed such thoughts and began to admire herself in the full-length bathroom mirror. 'Has one night improved upon my make-up?' she questioned. Whatever! Still, feeling fit as a fiddle, she paused to admire 'God's gift' in her endowment. Feeling pleased, she stepped into the shower and had a good soaking.

Emerging from her bath Fantegla fell into a nostalgia that led her back to the bed to await her man's second coming. First, she switched TV channels, 2, 4, 5, 7 for Oprah Winfrey, then 9, 11, 13, Cable, Travel, Disney, Cartoon Network, AMC, and so on. She was feeling restless. She listened to lite music, then jazz and none of these filled the void. Pouring a drink, she moved to the balcony to sun herself in the skimpiest attire. Actually, she began with "Tee and Tong," and then shed it for the latter. Still, there was a yearning she could not control nor satisfy. Unconsciously, she focused on the keyhole in anticipation of it opening. When this did not happen, she returned restlessly to her bed. In the deafening silence, she could hear herself saying quietly, 'Where is this man?'

Fantegla seemed to remember once being in the Caribbean, Trinidad and Tobago, for the Carnival. She was told of a young woman who had this terrible feeling. She had moved from the mildest form of this love the locals called Tobanca, to the more intense form called Pou-Pou-re. The analogy is like moving from a mild fever to a more intense fire, a burning fever that consumed her entire being. Fantegla thought her condition mirrored the latter stage. Thus, she needed a good drenching to quench the fire of her chest, her thighs,

111

her entire being. She seemed to remember the old adage: 'be very careful of what you ask for, you may get it.' She thought, further, 'I don't mind getting it, but I want it now. Where is this man?'

It was only 11:30 am, and Fantegla had to live out the remainder of the day for Michael Mentuhotep had a full itinerary slated in the day's events. Perhaps, she thought, 'the after-dinner talk and night-cap may be such that it's well worth the wait.'

New York Public Library entrance on 5th Avenue at 43rd Street.

Michael Mentuhotep now started back towards 42nd Street and 5th Avenue, to enter the New York Public Library. Standing at the 5th Avenue entrance, he began to admire the façade, its lions and columns. Then he entered this historic building. Seeking assistance, he was directed to room 215 where Egypt is represented in the Oriental Division. How strange, he thought, 'In my day the Orient was much further east, but these moderns now have created a new form of geographical classification.' Notwithstanding, he paid particular attention to the hours of operation, Tuesday to Thursday, 11:00 am to 7:00 pm and Friday and Saturday 11:00 am to 5:00 pm.

INTRIGUE THROUGH TIME

Fifth Avenue first floor entrance foyer at the New York Public Library.

Entering, his quick eye picked out the extensive, black leather bound, catalogue in the outer room. He thumbed through a few volumes noting entries on Egypt, ancient and modern. He noticed Egyptian history, architecture, art, archaeology, and then other sub-headings. Entering the small reading room, ahead on the right, he checked the shelves and noticed books, about not simply Egypt, but also China, India, Persia (Iran), Iraq, Syria. Wow! He thought, 'these were some of the ancient nations we dealt with.' Even further, 'much of the history of my time and country is here.'

From the shelves he picked up a few volumes and took a seat. These volumes included: *Ancient Egypt*: *Sources of Information in the New York Public Library* Compiled by Ida A. Pratt, The New York Public Library, 1925, Kraus Reprint Co., New York, 1969; *Topographical Bibliography of Ancient Egyptian Hieroglyphic Texts, Reliefs, Paintings,* By Bertha Porter and Rosalind L.B. Moss. Volume I: *Theban Necropolis,* Part 2. *Royal Tombs and Smaller Cemeteries,* Griffith Institute, Ashmolean Museum, Oxford, 1927; Vol. II. *Theban Temples.* Oxford at the Clarendon Press, 1929; Volume III. *Memphis*: *Abu Rawash to Dashur,* 1931; Volume IV:

113

FREDERICK MONDERSON

Upper and Middle Egypt: Delta and Cairo to Asyut. 1954; Volume
V. *Upper Egypt Sites: Deir Rifa to Aswan, excluding Thebes and the
Temples of Dendera' Esna, Edfu, Kom Ombo and Philae,* 1937.

There were people in the small room and he chose to observe how
they were serviced. He noticed you pick up a slip, fill it in with your
information, and hand it in at the desk. Then they bring you the
book from beyond the doors. He watched this process repeatedly.
Once he heard someone ask: "Do you have a driver's license?" and
they produced some card from a pouch. He thought, 'I don't have
one of these, maybe William can be of assistance.'

Someone discarded a call slip on the table and he noticed it
requested information about the author, title, volume, and date of
publication; and about the borrower, including name, address and
representative organization. Still observing the activities in the
reading room, he noticed you can even put books on reserve. After
a while he chose to leave, again noting the hours of opening and
reminded himself, he must frequent this place to get the information
he needs.

As he left the reading room and the outer room, he headed for the
exit when he noticed a guide conducting a Tour of the Library. This
group walked past him and took the stairs to the third floor. He
thought he would follow them. They stopped in front of Room 315.
They did not enter, he did. Here he noticed, the catalogs, more
people filling out call slips, handing them to a clerk at the desk and
being directed through a facing door. Passing into it, he was amazed
by its size, the number of people there and realized there were two
reading room sections. There was a big brown counter with columns
where you pick up the ordered books.

Not having ordered any books, he sat to observe. There were
reference books against the walls throughout on both sides of the
two large rooms. Then there's a big board with lighted numbers
below where people retrieved their books, before moving to the
desks with lamps, for reading and research purposes. After
observing for a while, it was time for him to leave, and this time
Mentuhotep left the building through the Fifth Avenue doorway.

114

INTRIGUE THROUGH TIME

Once outside, he turned to admire the place once more. This was a fabulous institution with a rich repository of information about all types of subjects. His mind returned to the Egyptian subject in the Oriental Collection. It reminded him of the libraries of the great temples, the "Houses of Life," at *Waset, On, Abtu,* and *Men-Nefer.* In addition to these national centers of worship and learning, smaller or satellite temples had their own libraries of accumulated knowledge, containing the ritual of the holy places.

Heading further downtown, lots of pieces in the emerging puzzle began to be put in place. He was always sharp, quick-witted with a desire to acquire knowledge, accept a challenge and best the competition. He had been taught well by his father Vizier Puyemre that he should always seek to excel in activities in which he was engaged.

Even though his father had political and other referenced power which he exercised fairly; he, Mentuhotep achieved his status by hard, diligent and resolute work, determination, an active mind and a keen sense of observation. And so, it was, as he walked down Fifth Avenue towards Barnes and Noble to acquire a Guide Book on Egypt.

His mind again shifted to the wonderful morsel he left sleeping in his bed. A big grin came to his face. 'What a woman,' he thought. He wondered if it was wise to take her to Egypt with him, but soon dismissed the idea. He returned to those intimate moments when it was just the two of them with the kissing and carrying on. It was such a long time since he felt this way, since he savored such joy. Then he realized the woman had begun to affect him, in a nice way.

Sarlinda had been up for quite a while. She was having a disturbing Saturday morning. 'I need to tell that woman a thing of two,' she thought. Sarlinda decided to make her play by confronting her friend. She felt a kind of betrayal. So, she left to set the record straight. Her chauffeur dropped her off at the Plaza, and she took the elevator to the 20th floor. She moved to room 2005, where they had spent so much time together, and rang the bell. She got no answer and thought Fantegla must be out, since it was a beautiful, sunny day.

FREDERICK MONDERSON

'Well,' she thought 'since the vixen was out, perhaps I should hit on Mr. Mentuhotep, Michael. After all, she dared me to go for it. I will give my eye-teeth for a roll in the hay with Michael.' So, she got off at 18 and rang the bell at 1825. Fantegla had struggled with Michael's absence and longed for the key in the door, as her adrenalin had begun to flow. Excited she raced to answer the door, thinking he may have forgotten his key. As she opened the door, fireworks! A proxy war! Joyful expectation turned to sudden astonishment, anger, embarrassment, shame, disappointment, betrayal!

In that fleeting moment time stood still. A thousand and one things passed through the two minds at work without a single word being said. Suddenly, they both burst out laughing, reached arms out, hugged and remained embraced in the open door. Now, if nosy Gibsoni had passed and seen them in embrace, he would, again and wrongfully think, 'some-things' going on!'

True friendship is such a powerful force it can overcome perceived transgressions. The bond was forged over mutual experiences and over time. Such a path traveled and relationship cultivated is generally hard to dismiss.

When the two women had composed themselves, Sarlinda said, "Congratulations my friend, I'm so happy for you."

Recognizing the sentiments were genuine, Fantegla simply said: "I'm happy, you're happy."
Sarlinda: "Well, I want a full report. I want details and don't spare the mustard."
Fantegla: "The first rains seemed to come after a long dry season, but after that the showers were more frequent." And so, they sat giggling, sharing a drink, two spoiled rich girls, dissecting their new toy, one playing, the other as if unspoken, seeming to say "I'm next." However, in that seductively devilish smile a question lingered on her lips: "When?"

116

INTRIGUE THROUGH TIME

Another of the buildings of the Public Library near 5th Avenue at 40th Street.

15.   The Revisit

Even though it was Saturday, Senator Williams was troubled by a dream his wife had and told him about. There had been some big explosion and loss of life, people running injured, but she was not sure if it involved Americans. It was not at home but some distant place and this troubled him. He called colleagues in various Committees as Appropriations, Armed Forces, and the Department of Defense, as well as a few individual generals. He also called Admiral Reynolds to hear if any new news had a disturbing effect. As an important supporter of defense, he was able to reach into these areas and receive credible feedback. In this respect, all roads seemed to point to all being quiet on the western and eastern fronts. Despite their reassurances he seemed concerned and reached back to those same individuals suggesting a heightened sense of security alertness. He reminded his contacts, much of the fleet was home, Congress was on the verge of ending the summer session, and also preparing to celebrate Independence on the Fourth of July. He cautioned: "This is the optimum time when our enemies may think us off-guard and strike."

FREDERICK MONDERSON

The Chairman of the Armed Services Committee was pleased with his assessment and thankful of the reminder. He promised to speak with the Chairman of the Joint Chiefs who would raise it with the Secretary of Defense, Caspar Weinberger. 'President Reagan and his advisers probably have foreseen this, but it won't hurt to remind them,' he thought.

Senator Williams requested a meeting with Admiral Reynolds at 2:00 pm, but was told 3:00 pm would be more appropriate. Still, he left his New York Office early, drove through Queens and came up on Roosevelt Island, parked and began to admire the fleet in the harbor. 'How beautiful they look,' he thought, 'the maritime might of America's defense. Still, these were beautiful yet destructive men-of-war adorning both rivers, piered with their crews ashore. They were also sitting ducks.' He seemed to remember the Japanese sneak attack at Pearl Harbor during World War II, because 'we were momentarily lax in defense vigilance.' The watch word, he remembered, was "Never Again!"

It was approaching 3:00 pm and he moved on to meet Admiral Reynolds where his carrier group was anchored around the Forty-Fifth Street pier area. Crossing the Fifty-Ninth Street Bridge, he hurried across town to the west side. He took Seventh Avenue down and, in the Times, Square area was pleased to see so many white uniforms. Each Navy man seemed accompanied by a companion, busily enjoying the hospitality of the city. Just then, he thought 'That's our boys out there. How honorably they serve. How much they deserve the liberty they have served to maintain.' He also wondered 'Where would be their next theater of service?'

Down past Thirty-Fourth Street, Twenty-Third Street, Mentuhotep was approaching Barnes and Noble Bookstore at Eighteenth Street and Fifth Avenue. Naturally his inquisitive nature was taking in every street name, store, building architectural features, mode of transportation, everything. He thought, 'America like every great civilization was not only a paragon of literary expression, but also a virtual industry of technological innovation, engineering feats and cultural synchronization that blended peoples and languages into a new personality.' The word or concept that evaded him was the

INTRIGUE THROUGH TIME

"melting pot," a term he was totally unfamiliar with. Equally, the further conceptualization of 'who is the cook stirring the pot?' is at a level he had yet to attain, being unfamiliar with many nuances of the new experience.

Empire State Building, bottom to top at 5th Avenue entrance.

He arrived at Barnes and Noble. Across the street lay the Barnes and Noble Annex. He wondered what was that all about. Nevertheless, he entered the main store. Quickly, he was directed to secure and purchase six 'Travel Books on Egypt.' Looking around further in the store, he noticed various other types of subjects and books, offered for sale. Reflecting on his time, books were made of papyrus parchment but here the books are made of bound paper. Nonetheless, with the second item of his "to-do-list" completed, he left the store.

World famous Barnes and Noble Bookstore on 5th Avenue at 18th Street.

Trying to make hay while the sun was still shining, since it was only 1:00 pm, Mentuhotep decided to take a cab uptown to revisit the Metropolitan Museum of Art. He was fascinated with his first visit. Now returned, he wants to go slow so he could really fill in gaps in understanding his country's history.

Like a computer, a hungry one at that, his mind began to absorb the various periods of Egyptian history in the display. He began with the pottery of the Prehistoric Period.

At 3:00 pm, a motor launch approached the pier at Forty-Fifth Street and shortly two line-backer type sailors approached the Senator's automobile. "Senator," they said in unison, "Admiral Reynolds requests the pleasure of your company." Leaving the car, he followed them to their motor launch, and was ferried out to the Admiral's Aircraft Carrier, the USS Enterprise. Upon arrival and with the customary 'Permission to come aboard' formalities, he was led to the Admiral in the briefing room.

Reynolds: "Hello, Senator, good to see you," the Admiral said.
Williams: "The pleasure is mutual," the Senator responded.
Reynolds: "That was some party the Edwards family threw the other night."
Williams: "It certainly was. If I could let the cat out of the bag, I was tracking your return through the Admiralty and informed Mrs. Edwards when you would be here. While she was planning the party for some time it was no co-incidence it occurred just about the time you made port."
Reynolds: "That was so kind of you. After all, that's what friends are for."
Williams: "Cigar?"
Reynolds: "Why, thank you."
Williams: "These are Cuban. Lord Stanhope presented them to me. The top brass will have a fit knowing we're smoking Cuban cigars on a US Carrier."
Reynolds: "Well, if you don't tell them, I won't."
Williams: "It's a deal."

Looking at a picture with two quotes beside President Reagan's photograph, Williams said: "Hey, I see you have these quotes of President Reagan?"
Reynolds: "He's our man. The first, 'We have been blessed with the opportunity to stand for something – for liberty and freedom and fairness. And these things are worth fighting for, worth devoting our lives to' was made March 1, of this year at the Conservative Political Action Conference."
"The Second: 'The challenge of statesmanship is to have the vision to dream of a better, safer world and the courage, persistence and patience to turn that dream into a reality,' was said in Washington, March 8, to the US negotiating team for the Nuclear and Space Arms Negotiations with the Soviet Union."

Reynolds: "Light?"
Williams: "Thank you. Actually, my reason for coming is to discuss one of my growing concerns. I fear there may be a plot against our

country and don't want for us to be caught unprepared, with our pants down, so to speak."

Reynolds: "Well, as you know, we're of like minds. Tell me more."

Williams: "Essentially, I have a gut feeling about a pending plot against our country."

Knock. Knock. Knock.

Reynolds: "Come in."

Executive Officer: "Admiral, Colonel Sanderson has come aboard."

Reynolds: "Great. Have him join us."

Executive Officer: "Yes, Sir."

Reynolds: "Let's wait for Sanderson. These Cuban cigars are excellent."

Williams: "I agree."

Knock. Knock. Knock.

Reynolds: "Come in."

Executive Officer: "Sir, Colonel Sanderson is here."

Reynolds: "Have him join us."

Sanderson: "Senator, Admiral."

Williams: "Colonel."

Reynolds: "Colonel, the Senator was telling me he fears there may be a plot against our country by foreign forces."

Sanderson: "That is standard practice, Admiral. We do have in place countermeasures."

Reynolds: "Nevertheless, let's hear him out."

Williams: "As I was telling you, I have an uncanny feeling about a possible attack in which there may be an enormous explosion with casualties, many dead and many wounded. It may not be at home, possibly on foreign soil. I contacted people at Department of Defense, Chairs of Foreign Relations, Appropriations and Armed Services. I even spoke with Generals Bradley, Davis and Newman. Naturally, I called you and set up this meeting. Armed Services promised to bring it up with the Chair of Joint Chiefs. My friends, I just don't want us to be caught flat-footed."

Reynolds: "What do you think Sanderson? Hold on." Picking up his desk telephone a voice answered on the other line: "Yes Admiral?"

Reynolds: "Have the Executive Officer join me in the Briefing Room."

Voice: "Yes, Sir."

INTRIGUE THROUGH TIME

Sanderson: "I don't expect the Russians will try anything. They are on the verge of crumbling. If anything, it has to be the Middle East."

Knock. Knock. Knock.

Reynolds: "Come in." An officer enters. "Gentlemen this is William Cockburn, my Executive Officer."
Reynolds: "Cockburn, has there been any unusual chatter, particularly from overseas?"
Cockburn: "No, Admiral."
Reynolds: "How many men are aboard ship?"
Cockburn: "Of the 5500-man crew, 1500 are still on-board ship, Sir."
Reynolds: "As we ride out "Fleet Week" I want you to maintain on board strength between 1500 and 2000. From now on, regulate all Passes so we can have those active numbers. Summon all Captains of the Fleet for a briefing at 1900 hours."
Cockburn: "Yes, Sir. Will that be all, Sir?"
Reynolds: "That's all."
Reynolds: "Colonel, what have our allies come up with?"
Sanderson: "There is nothing specific or substantial from our allies at this time."
Reynolds: "OK. Keep me posted."
Reynolds: "Would you like some coffee, Senator?"
Williams: "I would prefer a good shot of scotch."
Reynolds: "Like the Boy Scouts, I'm always prepared and so keep a nip for emergencies such as this." Then he reached into his cupboard and brought out a bottle of Johnnie Walker Black and three glasses.
Glasses all around! "Cheers." "Bottoms up!"

After a rather engaging and learning exercise at the Met, Mentuhotep chose to walk home to the Plaza. He was beaming from ear to ear. He was very happy with how his day had gone. He was particularly pleased with the history and art lesson learned at the Met. He first picked six volumes from the Museum Shop. These were W. Stephenson Smith's *Art and Architecture of Ancient Egypt* and M.A. Murray's *The Splendor that was Ancient Egypt*, Gardner's *Egypt of the Pharaohs* and Frankford's *Intellectual Adventure of Ancient Man*. The clerk seemed to sense his interest and

FREDERICK MONDERSON

recommended also, Steindorff and Seele's *When Egypt Ruled the East* and Hayes' *The Scepter of Ancient Egypt* in two volumes. Another volume, C.A. Diop's *The African Origins of Civilization: Myth or Reality* caught his eye and he picked that up too. Now armed with these important volumes he intended to fill all gaps. 'Tomorrow will be a day of reading,' while he basks in the sunshine on his balcony. Even more important, he will have the lovely Fantegla to keep him company. These and so many more things raced through his mind as he strolled home from the Met to the Plaza.

Flags of nations in Rockefeller Center Rink, viewed from the Fifth Avenue side.

The Kiosk of Seti II dedicated to the Theban Triad of Amon, King of the Gods; Mut his wife the Earth Goddess; and their son, Khonsu, the Moon God; in the Great Court at Karnak Temple.

INTRIGUE THROUGH TIME
16.   Reflections

All this notwithstanding, there was an excited anticipation as he headed to his heartthrob. It was almost 6:00 pm when he arrived at the Plaza and headed to his room. Opening the door, he found the pretty lady still there, quite comfortable, watching the evening news on CBS. She flashed him a big smile with a deep sense of expectation in her eyes. As he entered through the door, she flew into his arms. She was wearing one of those see-through jobs. Revealing, it left very little to the imagination. Below that she wore something she called "Thong" which itself said very little. As he slumped into his favorite seat on the sofa, she handed him a shot of brandy, and snuggled up close to him. "How was your day?" she asked.

Mentuhotep: "It was wonderfully exciting, my dear," he said, "particularly, as I kept you in my thoughts all day long." That one threw her for a loop.

Fantegla: "Excuse me!"

Mentuhotep: "I walked down to the Library then to Barnes and Noble and then took a cab back to the Met.

Fantegla: "The Met, again?"

Mentuhotep: "Yes, I wanted to fill some gaps in my memory about the collection and the history of Egypt.

Fantegla: "Are you sure? Or, is there a young woman who attracts you there?"

Mentuhotep: "Don't be silly. At this point in time, you're the only one for me!"

She rose from her snuggle, reaching over, grabbed him and planted a sweet juicy kiss on his lips.

Mentuhotep: "That's what I'm talking about. As I kept thinking about the young, ravishingly hot and sexy maiden in my bed last night, and the one I left, I kept wondering if she awoke. Whether she was still there and more importantly can I continue where I left off last night? These are the thoughts that kept driving me all day long, as I went from place to place with a smile on my face."

She had an idea: "Let's take a shower before dinner."

"Good idea," he thought and noticing that she lingered, he went ahead and let the hot steamy shower take care of the dirty work. As

125

he basked in its powerful and refreshing spray, he closed his eyes and attempted to really relax, releasing his negative forces. He did not notice when she slipped in the shower behind him. He was startled when she grabbed him around the waist and the hot shower seemed to fuse their bodies. Turning to face her, they began acting like young adolescents just becoming aware of their physical self. After a while, they exited the shower, got dressed and decided to have an early dinner.

Leaving the room, they headed to the elevator. Just then she said, "Let's stop at my place for a moment, I need to change."

Busybody Gibsoni was at the controls, and he said: "Good evening, Sir, Madam. Down?" She said, "Up." He wanted to know what was going on! They got off at 20 and headed to 2005.

As they entered, surveying the room, 'nicely furnished,' he thought as she slipped out of view. 'Posh!' he thought again. Just then she thought, 'I should try it here,' but said 'perhaps later.'

Several photographs were conspicuously posted and he chose to examine them. They were all with the other woman. 'What was her name? Ah, yes, Sarlinda. These two seem very close. Well, after all, in their first two encounters, at the Met and at that first dinner, they were together. Fantegla said they both Volunteer. Friendship was such a wonderful experience,' he thought, thinking back to his youth and early adulthood.

As the Vizier's son, his youth was very exciting, it was constant schooling; learning his job as an architect; military exploits; youngest Commander of the Imperial Guard; promoted Deputy in charge of the construction of the Temple of Mut in Asher; and a few visits to observe and overseer at *Djeser* (Deir el Bahari). It was always forging ahead and taking the high ground, so to speak. He never had time for anyone save Nekajai. This is why he was so fascinated by and attracted to her. He seemed to understand forging of a bond with another. Just then she emerged as beautiful as ever, clean as a whistle. "Let's go," she said, hooked arms with him and headed to the elevator.

Gibsoni was happy to see them period! He noticed she had changed. His active eye seemed to pick up things quickly, though his mind seemed to confuse them. "Here we are folks," he said and they exited the elevator and headed to the restaurant. Scanning the lobby area, Mentuhotep could not see his man William. 'Perhaps he is not at work this evening,' he thought.

When they are together, especially when linked arm-in-arm, there seems a little pep, a little spring in her step, and like this, they entered the crowded restaurant. It was Saturday night, there was a live band and there seemed much activity in the place. Waiters were busy taking orders, delivering dinners, drinks and keeping a watchful eye out for certain residents. Word must have gotten out Mr. Mentuhotep was a good tipper. As soon as they entered a waiter came to seat them at their now customary table.

On the way over, eyes turned. Some seemed full of jealousy and envy and others seemed to approve. Fantegla picked out the approving ones. They were sizing up her man! She did not like it but could do nothing. The jealous and envious ones she scorned. 'That's because you're not getting it,' she thought and, 'you're certainly not getting what I'm getting.' Anyway, soon they had navigated the questionable terrain, seated and had drinks delivered without ordering. She thought further, 'I must have Sidney deliver a case of Hennessy to Michael's room.' Then she looked at him as if to offer a toast.

Noticing that studious yet distant look on his face, she still admired it because his active mind was at work. Raising her glass, she said, "To a wonderful person, a super lover and a dynamic character." Like a ping pong backhand, he threw it back at her. "You're toasting yourself," he said, "but I'll drink to that."

One thing she noticed he was quick. His mind was sharp. It picks up things rapidly, it flips ideas. He seemed to process with the speed of a computer. Their dinner came. They sat silently. Watching each other, they were smiling approvingly. They seemed the quintessential couple. It was the cocktail hour. Tonight, was soul night, and the vocalist seemed right on target as she belted out: "When a man loves a woman;" "Me and Mrs. Jones Got a Thing Going On;" "My Girl;" Marvin Gaye's "Let's Get it on;" Barry White, Al Green, Roberta Flack, etc., etc., etc. It seemed as if she was singing for them, to them. Looking down, Fantegla could see

127

FREDERICK MONDERSON

Michael tapping his feet. She knew he was enjoying the music and the company. She reached her hand over and quietly grasped his. Squeezing it lovingly, nothing needed to be said. The promise of later, charged the air and seemed to make sparks fly.

At about 7:30, as Michael and Fantegla sat finishing their dinner and desert, just before coffee and drinks, who but Sarlinda, the gate crasher, walked in. 'The other woman,' he thought.

"Hello, darlings," she said. "I called both your rooms and got no answer. Rightly I thought you might be at dinner; that calm before their storm."
'What a wonderful use of metaphor,' he thought. Then he got a closer look at her. She was another beautiful woman without question. She was perhaps a year or so older than Fantegla. Maybe twenty-nine years old. How old is Fantegla? He wondered as he looked at her. 'Maybe if I got to see her driver's license I would know and also see what information it contained.'

"So, what are you two doing tonight?" she asked. "We have not gotten that far as yet," Fantegla responded.
Sarlinda: "The Ali-Frazier fight is on at Madison Square Garden this evening. I could sponsor the tickets."
Fantegla: "What do you think, honey?"
Mentuhotep: "I saw the billing but didn't know if you were a fight fan, so didn't bring it up."
Fantegla: "What time is the fight, anyway?"
Sarlinda: "Well, there's a boxing double-header and the preliminaries begin at nine or so."
Fantegla: "So I guess we have time to get there. Then let's finish up and catch a cab downtown."

Into the lobby and towards the door Mentuhotep stepped into the night. Who but nosy Gibsoni caught sight of him from the rear? 'Oh, my gosh,' he thought. 'Now he's got two women. What manner of man is this?'

Out the door, Gibson's idle thought counting for naught, they caught a cab and were heading downtown. Out of the cab they assumed the same formation as when they walked out of the Plaza doors. In this manner he blended well with the many pimps, players, playboys, entertainers, ladies' men, who also enter these sporting events in

INTRIGUE THROUGH TIME

like manner. This way he passed for a good local. Nevertheless, while Fantegla took things in stride, Sarlinda considered being on his arm, this up-close and personal, her rightful place. Within her sinister mind, she never forgot Fantegla's dare. Silently and stealthily, she was warming up to self-sacrifice on Mount Venus.

They got ringside seats and watched the two great fighters slug it out toe-to-toe. The fight over, the results known, they left the Garden heading uptown. An old college mate, her husband, and another friend approached and invited them to the "after-fight" party in the Penn Plaza, across the street, on Seventh Avenue. This was a Who's Who get-together and before you know it, Sarlinda's pending intentions took a back seat. All were having a wonderful time, Sarlinda was letting her hair down, so Fantegla and Michael slipped away around midnight. She would not be denied her ascent of Mount Venus. So, they caught a cab and arrived at the Plaza. This time the party after party was held in 2005. This time the sacrifices would be on familiar terrain, an altar closer to home. Tomorrow is Sunday; it's a day for reading, a day for staying in.

Ra as Khepra adorning an amulet of blue faience pendant

129

FREDERICK MONDERSON

17. At Home with the Missus

Mentuhotep awoke Sunday morning before Fantegla did. He slipped out of bed, got dressed and headed to his room and changed before going down to breakfast. The elevator man on duty was an unfamiliar chap. At the restaurant he was served *The Times* with his meal. How interesting, the news appeared on this important Sunday June 16, 1985. The Headlines read:

Lead: "Hijackers release over 60 from Jet in Algiers Airport; US to send Commando Squad"
International: "US Frustrated in Efforts to Counter Soviet Spying"
National: "Countdown on for Shuttle's Space Arms Race"
Local: "Buchanan Labels Cuomo a 'Reactionary Liberal.'"

After finishing breakfast, he headed back to his room. This day he resolved to stay in and catch up on his reading of the Egypt travel guides.

One of the first things he noticed about such books is that they began in Lower Egypt, and worked their way up river. He remembers the military campaign that went as far as *Meso Potamos* – the land between the rivers, and the description of "Going up river while going down river," and this also reminded him of the Hudson and East Rivers in Manhattan, in his new land, that flowed from north to south. Somehow, he associated this reverse orientation of the rivers with the manner in which the guide books were oriented. That aside, he also recognized that the Old Kingdom Pyramids are in the north where they rightly belong but he could not understand the Museum described in the earliest pages of the book. After all, it is a repository, after the fact, to house recovered artifacts. He also quickly noticed that the main guide books are generally written by European and American and not Egyptian authors.

Nevertheless, and quite surprisingly, he read more of the history of his nation, *Kemet*, now called Egypt and divided into "Periods," the Old, Middle and New Kingdoms, and Late and Graeco-Roman. After these came the Arabs, Muslims, Caliphs, Ottoman regimes,

130

INTRIGUE THROUGH TIME

(Mamelukes, and then indigenous Egyptians), followed by French and English rulers. This was also a part of the timeline he saw at the Metropolitan Museum of Art.

Of particular note were the first three periods he knew as the First, Second and Third Risings. The first period he remembered well for he had visited the Step Pyramid at Sakkara and the True Pyramid, "Khufu Gleams," on the "Horizon of Khufu," now called Ghizeh Plateau. As a young man, he had come with his father when he made rounds of inspection. While by the time of his Queen, there were two Viziers, one in the North and one in the South; his father, Vizier of the Southern or Upper Kingdom, nevertheless was the senior of the two officials. This was due principally because administrative and sacerdotal power and responsibility were centered in the Upper Kingdom capital and home of the God Amon-Ra at *Waset*.

As a youngster he also remembers playing within the enclosures of these structures. As a Commander of the Imperial Guard, he had followed Her Majesty there. He does remember the Proclamation that 'Citizens visit these monuments of our forefathers, our ancestors, extolling the glory of our great accomplishments!' The visitors of this age, however, were not granted access into the inner reaches of these pyramids and tombs and their contents were not exposed to public view. After all, these sacred places were designed to remain secret into eternity!

Strange he also remembers the temple of the Sphinx but not a Stela of the Sphinx. According to the book, this last was put there by Thutmose IV, who ruled after his time. He only knew of the first in this line, the Queen's father. He does remember she had a brother, now designated Thutmose III. There is extensive commentary on the art and architecture of the first and important period. The architectural innovations, and emerging decorative themes fueled by the competitive schools of art caused scholars to label this period one of experimentation and creativity. The accomplishments were so revered later generations looked back boldly to imitate the creative and inventive spirit of that age.

He remembers being beaten at school to get his work completed, for its accuracy, and once for fighting with Djhuti-Sa, because he spilled the ink in his writing palette. His father was annoyed and scolded him threateningly. Even though the culture believed 'a boy's ears are on his back and so must be beaten,' his father never liked to hit him. He was given chores to work with stable hands cleaning up after the horses. This was not a pleasant task, he remembers. As a result of the beatings by his Priest teachers, and, with instruction from his father, he learned how to control his thinking and assess situations, silently think things through before deciding on a course of action.

Perhaps the greatest gift from his father, not counting the necklace of course, is development of a keen sense of observation, the ability to quietly assess and process situations and to move with that panther-like noble posture. These traits have served him well. From his mother he learned the art of appreciation of beauty in himself, in his work and surroundings, and in a woman. He learned to appreciate beauty first in her as his mother, her gentle loving yet strong demeanor, her keen and intelligent penetration of people, things and situations and her patient, kind, yet firm, disposition. Perhaps this appreciation of beauty is what made Nekajai so attractive to him. Now he could see that beauty deep within Fantegla, and that is why they are so attracted to each other.

Continuing his reading and learning on Sakkara, Ghizeh, *Men-Nefer* (now Memphis), and he mentally stops at *Abtu* (Abydos) and Dendera. *Abtu*, now Abydos, retains a beautiful temple to Osiris, first among the westerners; that was built by Seti I of the 19th Dynasty. 'This was a good 250 years after my time,' thought Mentuhotep. While the existing temple at Dendera was built in Graeco-Roman times, he remembers being taught in school as a lad, that there was a temple at Dendera, home of the Goddess Hathor, as early as the Old Kingdom. King Pepi of the Sixth Dynasty had done repairs to it. Previously a copy of the *Book of Going Forth by Day* had been found within, during the time of King Septi. Further, as a lad, he had visited *Abtu*, home of Osiris, with his father, the Vizier Puyemre, when he executed a Royal Prescript for the temple there at that time. Even more, priests at an early temple there informed that King Narmer or Menes of the First Dynasty had worshipped there after he unified the two kingdoms. Now the guide book mentions an archaeologist named Petrie, telling how there were 10 successive temples at *Abtu* dating back to the time of Narmer.

INTRIGUE THROUGH TIME

Moving further south, Beni-Hasan was an active sports center where he attended wrestling matches, chariot races and water sports. A picture in his guide book depicts an early form of column that has survived from the Middle Kingdom at Beni Hasan. His beloved city of *Waset*, the 'Scepter,' now called Thebes and Luxor, was the busiest city of his great nation. Everything was here - temples, mansions on sprawling estates, schools of art and schools of learning, palaces, sacred lakes, civic projects, many of which he had helped erect. There were also boulevards lined with planted trees acting as shade for passersby; avenues of sphinxes to many temples, and his regiment as Commander of the Imperial Guard was housed at *Waset*; Nile Boats were numerous. His family estate was located at *Waset*. Everywhere gardens beautified the city and provided flowers for the temple ritual and the tables of nobles.

On and on and on Michael was engrossed in his reading and savoring their contents as his historic memory and experiences came back to him. He seemed to act as a starving computer that absorbed the contents of the books. He gave great meaning to the concept 'Reading is Fundamental.' He kept trying to better understand his nation's history and apply that knowledge in this new culture. Taken back and mentally journeying in the ancient culture and even enjoying the company of beautiful Nekajai, his trip was interrupted by a buzzing sound. It was the door bell ringing and there she was, the beautiful Fantegla who was beginning to look so much like Nekajai.

"Hello, you gorgeous hunk of man," she said, kissing him and passing through the door. Grasping her arm and pulling her to him he said, "Come here, you're not getting away from me," as he kissed her. There was no better place for her and there they stood, embraced and kissing in the open doorway. Just then an elderly woman passed in the hallway, noticed them; she smiled and whispered: "Young love, how sweet it is." Hearing her, they moved inside and closed the door while remaining embraced. Then they moved to the inner room and flopped down on the bed. Here they remained for hours enjoying each other on a lazy, hot, but otherwise exciting, and enjoyable Sunday.

When love is the food, no other morsel will do and so they passed the day until dinner time. There was no happier couple in the hotel as they headed to dinner to replenish their energies for the later combat in the erogenous zones. And so, they passed from Sunday into Monday morning when Mentuhotep rose from beside his beautiful plaything in the bed. Surveying the gorgeous, contented, happy face of a smiling beauty, he wanted to just lay there but duty and business called. He needed to plan his day.

Ceramic Egyptian Art intricately showcase the Ankh and twisted flax.

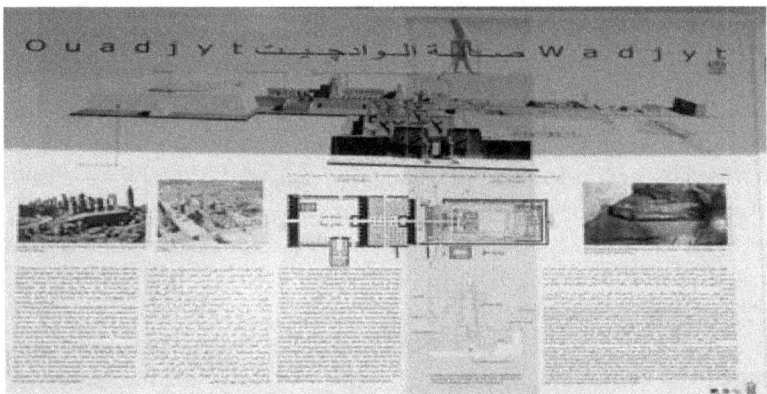

The *Ouadjyt*, between the Hypostyle Hall and Sanctuary at Karnak Temple.

"The most select of places," Karnak Temple, offers the view, literally yards from the Sanctuary or, "Holy of Holies."

18.   The Eagle Flies Today

Showered and dressed, he left for breakfast. Stopping at the desk, he enquired if the hotel had a safety deposit vault. "Yes, we do," replied the clerk. "Good," he chimed. 'I need to have a way to secure my money,' he thought. Turning, the smiling face of William greeted him. "How are you on this wonderful day, Sir?" he asked. "Very well, William" he replied. "I have a favor to ask of you later," said Mentuhotep as he headed to the restaurant. "I'll be here when you're through, Sir" he responded. Slipping William a $20.00 note, Michael moved to the restaurant. Standing at the entrance of the elevator and noting the two men in discussion and passing of the money, Gibsoni thought enviously, 'Why couldn't I have been his Man-Friday.'

Sitting at his favorite table in the restaurant the waiter brought *The New York Times*, a pot of coffee and took his breakfast order. He too received a $20.00 tip. "Thank you, Sir, breakfast coming up." He exclaimed happily in thought, 'The big dipper is a big tipper.'

FREDERICK MONDERSON

Karnak Temple's "Chief of Security" Handaka points to the two Obelisks of Thutmose I and his daughter Hatshepsut.

Glancing at the headlines of *The Times* Monday June 17, 1985, he began working on his "to-do-list."

1. Meet with Mr. Somersett, 12:00 noon.
2. Purchase a watch
3. Consult with William about a driver's license and other forms of identification
4. Purchase a set of suitcases for traveling

INTRIGUE THROUGH TIME

5. Propose an extension of the "Partnership" with Ghafoor
6. Approach Lord Stanhope about the passport
7. Plan a trip to Egypt
8. Purchase two good cameras and film, lots of film

The Headlines of the *New York Times* for Monday June 17, 1985, read:

Lead: "Gunmen Negotiate as Hostages Urge Caution from U.S."
International: "New Soweto Clash Mars Observance of 1976 uprising"
National: "Doubts Increase over Future of U.S. Based Land Missiles"
Local: "After Fire, Brooklyn Church Starts to Rebuild."

That day Monday June 17, 1985, aboard Air Egypt:

"Ladies and Gentlemen, this is Captain Mubarak. We have begun our descent into Cairo International Airport. We should be on the ground in thirty minutes. The temperature is 84 degrees, local time is 8:05 and all is well. Once we have landed, I will be back on the air with further instructions."

Lord Stanhope remained single-mindedly focused on the necklace. From the time of departure, he plotted the course of the flight throughout and hours later he retained the thought of the necklace. He had seen it in the Cairo Museum and wondered how Mentuhotep got hold of that precious national treasure of antiquity. His single-minded thought was interrupted by the Captain who announced: "Ladies and Gentlemen, this is the Captain again. Welcome to Cairo International Airport. The local time is 8:40 and the temperature is 85 degrees Fahrenheit. Please have your documents ready for Immigration. If you have a video camera in your possession, be sure to register it with the proper authorities. Once again, let me thank you for flying with Egypt Air. Have a great stay."

FREDERICK MONDERSON

Having visited Egypt numerous times on official and non-official business, Lord Stanhope quickly cleared Immigration, and knew how to go through Customs. Soon he was on his way by cab to Mena House Hotel, a place he stayed on several occasions. Checked-in, he chose to relax for most of the day, fighting jet lag. Late in the afternoon he made a sentimental journey to the Pyramids of Ghizeh to feast on the mathematical and timeless phenomenon so characteristic of the ancient Egyptian mind. Later dinner, a cocktail or two and hello to a few friends, visiting and residents, Lord Stanhope retired for the night at his favorite hotel in Cairo.

Up early Tuesday morning June 18, 1985, Lord Stanhope headed to breakfast of eggs, bacon, croissant, fruit and coffee. Milling around, he checked out the local papers, *The Egyptian Times* and *The International Tribune* simply to stay abreast of events on three continents. This finished, he hired a taxi to take him across town to the Cairo Museum of Egyptian Antiquities.

Upon arrival at the Museum there was a long line of people waiting to get in. In the line, the customary vendors approached visitors selling decorated canvas bags, toy camels, Arabic headwear and papyrus decorated with art. Lord Stanhope observed a piece of papyrus with Rameses in his chariot. When the vendor approached him, he enquired of the man: "Is this banana?" he asked. "No, this is papyrus, see the seal of authenticity," was the reply. Naturally the vendor vehemently denied he was selling banana, but the Englishman simply smiled and said: "Good art on bad paper." Just then the line started to move.

At the ticket booth a sign read: 'Admission 10 Egyptian Pounds, 10 pounds for a camera and 25 pounds for a video camera.' Lord Stanhope paid the 10 pounds for admission and 10 pounds for his camera.

INTRIGUE THROUGH TIME

Varied descriptive Cartouches or Shennus of pure gold.

In the walk across the grounds to the door his heart was racing. He thought, 'What if I am wrong?' Then he entered the building and took off to the left on the First Floor. The ubiquitous dust was there. He headed to the New Kingdom section for the location he had known beforehand. Entering the New Kingdom hall, he immediately spotted his piece. He drew closer and stood there gazing at the necklace he knew he had seen before in the Cairo Museum. Taking out his camera he chose to take two good pictures of the necklace. By that time so many people had entered the hall, tour groups with their guides; individuals like him, all closing in to see the same thing he came to see: the beautiful necklace of Princess Nekajai who lived during the 18th Dynasty.

After a while he got his pictures. Then he headed back to the front and off to the right where the library was located. He saw a few familiar faces who greeted him instantly.

"Hello, Lord Stanhope, nice to see you back."

However, they were not sure in which capacity he was visiting. Was he here on official visit for Her Majesty's Government? Is he here as part of some new archaeological 'dig?' Or, has there been some new discovery, which the Museum was not yet privy to, which he was asked to authenticate? Curiously and simply, he asked: "Has there been any breach of security lately?"

"Oh, no," he was told. "Security in the Museum has been good. In fact, we've just added two dozen more guards as part of the Tourist Police assignment. The pieces in the Museum are safe."

Satisfied with that explanation, he was convinced the clever Mr. Mentuhotep had in his possession a fake antique. Sure, it was gold and the inlaid precious stones were real. It was, however, a very good copy that Mr. Mentuhotep was holding. However, he was confident the other pieces of the jewelry now in Mr. Somersett's possession were real. He examined them twice. However, he had only seen the necklace and dagger, not paying much attention to them, and was not able to examine and give them the double take.

Nevertheless, having completed this part of his trip, he thought of once more seeing the Tutankhamon exhibit. It always fascinated him how a young king could be buried with such great wealth. 'If so,' he thought, 'imagine the wealth buried with some of the great conquerors particularly those of the New Kingdom.' Once he did Tutankhamon, his interest turned to Akhenaton, whose incomparable exhibit lay nearby. With this completed he chose to

INTRIGUE THROUGH TIME

leave the Museum. He stopped at the bookstore on the way out to see what books were new. Leaving, he caught a cab back to his hotel.

The dilemma puzzled him but not once did he entertain the thought of a second necklace! Meanwhile, the previous day, back in the United States, Mentuhotep arose Monday morning from a Sunday filled with guide book reading and beautiful female companionship.

That Monday morning after his breakfast and focusing on his "to-do-list," Mentuhotep knew meeting with Mr. Somersett was the most important development so far. He also wondered if there were going to be any problems. However, none developed after he arrived at Ghafoor's at Noon.

Mr. Somersett arrived as early as 11:30 all excited to be in possession of such rare jewelry. He was not sure about Ghafoor. What if the scoundrel had made an offer to a rival so as to get a bigger finder's fee? Fortunately, none of this happened and the exchange went off like clockwork. Mr. Somersett had brought a briefcase filled with $2,000,000 dollars in hundred-dollar bills. He shelled out the dough, giving Mentuhotep the money and collecting his jewels and left.

Next, Mentuhotep handed Ghafoor the envelope Mr. Somersett had set aside with the $100,000.00 for his fee. Then he counted out the one hundred thousand as the advance, and also handed this to Ghafoor. Expecting a larger fee, he nevertheless accepted his reward. "Now, Sir," he said, "can I sell the necklace and dagger?" "I'll give some thought to it," Mentuhotep responded. "Thank you, Mr. Ghafoor," he said and then left, heading back to his hotel with the briefcase in hand. At the Plaza, he immediately deposited his briefcase in the Safety-Deposit Box.

The next day, Tuesday, he rose early and got dressed. As usual, Fantegla was a late riser. He headed to breakfast and read *The Times* for Tuesday June 18, 1985, as he ate.

The Headlines read:

141

FREDERICK MONDERSON

Lead: "Passengers Taken from Hijacked Jet, Lebanese Reports."
International: "United Airlines Set to Buy Hertz from RCA in $587M Deal"
National: "Shuttle Lifts Off; Satellite Orbited"
Local: "4 Newark Banks Face Fines by U.S. in Cash Violations."

He then returned to his apartment to do some more reading of his Guide Books and lounge around the place. He was very happy Fantegla was spending more time around the place. She seemed to add life to the place, and so they spent more time embraced and working out.

Next morning, he entered the lobby on his way to breakfast and approached William.

"Good morning, Sir," he said. "How can I help you?" Slipping him a C-note, Mentuhotep said: "Naturally, the things I say to you are confidential!"
"Without a doubt, Sir," he responded, "without a doubt!"

Mentuhotep: "I need to get a driver's license. Do I have to stand in line or is there a quicker way?"
William: "Let me make a call. I know someone in the Brooklyn Office. I'm on the early shift next Monday. So, I can take you there and have the process done expeditiously. I'll collect the forms from the New York Office on my lunch break today. You can fill them out and we'll arrive in Brooklyn with that done. You must take a photo there."
Mentuhotep: "Go to it. I'll be back at four. I have to do a little shopping. By the way, where can I get a sturdy suitcase?"
William: "The Hotel Shop has them. Let me see," thinking, he said, "there's a leather goods store, two doors down from Ghafoor's on Fifth between Forty-Eighth and Forty-Ninth Streets."
Mentuhotep: "Ghafoor's?"
William: "Yes. They carry American Touristed. It's one of the best traveling suitcases on the market."
Mentuhotep: "Thank you," he said, and left for the restaurant. Over coffee he read *The Times* for Wednesday June 19, 1985.

The Headlines read:

INTRIGUE THROUGH TIME

Lead: "President Bars Concessions; Orders Anti-Hijacking Steps. 3 more Hostages Freed"
International: "U.S.A. Has a Plan for Red Cross to Arrange the Release of Shiites"
National: "House Vote Bans Buying MX [Missile] over Next Year"
Local: "New York Raising its Drinking Age to 21 next December."

Heading down Fifth Avenue, his thoughts next turned to Egypt. He remembered reading the selection on *Djeser*, now called Deir el Bahari. He saw a photograph of the temple but could not determine if there was development in the neighborhood that may pose a problem to recovery of his treasure. The more he thinks about it, however, the more he believes it will take two trips. The first will be to reconnoiter then perhaps he may better understand the terrain. Nevertheless, he needs a passport and a British one is desired. 'Lord Stanhope has to help with this,' he thought.

Queen Hatshepsut dances before the Ark at rest, a scene from her "Red Chapel."

FREDERICK MONDERSON

19. Return to Karnak and Luxor

With his business at the Museum in Cairo completed, Lord Stanhope still had a day to spare. He decided to take an early Wednesday morning Egypt Air flight to Luxor to visit friends. An hour after takeoff the Captain was again on the horn saying, "Ladies and Gentlemen welcome to Luxor. The local time is 9:30 am. For those of you flying on to Abu Simbel and Aswan, we'll be on the ground 35 minutes. Thank you for flying Egypt Air."

Traveling light as he generally does, and not having to wait for luggage, Stanhope was out the Airport, in a cab and heading for the city. His return flight is 5:30, so he has plenty of time to sightsee, he thought.

"Where are you heading, Sir?" asked the taxi driver.
Familiar with rough and tumble, and the tricks of the city, he said: "Take me to Karnak!"
Realizing the visitor was just off the plane, he had no luggage, so the driver said: "Is that Karnak Hotel, Sir?"
"I am not interested in a hotel named Karnak in Luxor," he responded.
"Then you mean Karnak Temple!"
Stanhope remained silent, but he noticed the driver eyeing him in the rear-view mirror. Trying to make small talk, he said: "First time in Luxor, Sir?"
"No!"
"I could show you some interesting sites," he continued. Responding in Arabic, Stanhope said to the driver: "I'm English. I read and write ancient Egyptian hieroglyphics and am very friendly with the Chief of the Tourist Police in Luxor. Now take me to the temple!"

The driver shut up instantly, accelerated the automobile and reached the temple without any detour. As Stanhope exited the cab and tried to pay him, he said: "No, Sir, pay me later. I'll wait right here for you."

Stanhope looked at him and smiled. He thought, 'Sure, you've got an all-day passenger.' Without looking back, he headed to the ticket

INTRIGUE THROUGH TIME

booth and joined the waiting line. 'This temple always draws big crowds, particularly this early in the day,' he thought. Paying his 10 Egyptian pounds for the ticket, he headed for the Pylon entrance. Karnak Temple always attracted him. He was fascinated by its history and he always felt a highly spiritual charge when within its enclosure wall.

His Oxford Dissertation was on the Wars of Seti I and as such he had to examine the Hypostyle Hall. For his doctorate at Cambridge, he contrasted early and later New Kingdom temples. He chose Thutmose III's Festival Temple the *Akh Menu* and Rameses III's worship temple in the Great Court.

It seemed odd to Lord Stanhope that this native Egyptian would stand "Between the Pillars of Truth" as if in a salutary manner.

Both had been built by a single pharaoh and were thus complete temples. Thutmose's temple was built in the 18th Dynasty, while Rameses' temple was built in the 20th Dynasty. They stood perpendicular to each other, at the rear and front of Karnak. They both stood perpendicular to the principal east/west axis at Karnak. The *Akh Menu* straddled the main axis and Rameses' temple on the north/south axis faced the central line. Rameses' temple stood before the Holy of Holies and Thutmose's Temple stood beyond the Holy of Holies. Their builders won significant military victories. Thutmose won a significant battle at Megiddo against a confederated force because of the uniqueness of his military strategy. Rameses III won a significant battle against the Confederated Sea Peoples. His strategy was to fight when he was ready and on his own terms. Both encounters are among the few military engagements preserved in the annals of Egypt. The two temples are contrasting styles of architecture.

A massive golden necklace in the Cairo Museum of Antiquities.

The *Akh Menu* has a broad open face with pillars going around the outside. There are two rows of columns on the inside. The columns have thin bases and reverse or "Tent Pole" capitals. The *Akh Menu* has clerestory windows to let light into the temple. The *Akh Menu* stood before another temple where Pharaoh Thutmose III was worshipped as a divinity. This was thought to be the rear or eastern end of Karnak in his time. The temple of Rameses III, coming later

INTRIGUE THROUGH TIME

as it did, stood at the front or western end of the temple. From within his temple Rameses could see all in ascent towards the Holy of Holies. From his principal vantage point on a pedestal, Thutmose could see beyond the Middle Kingdom Court, through the Holy of Holies, an open-ended structure into which the rays of the sun passed when it traversed overhead, and along the Central Axis right through to what became the Processional Colonnade, the Great Court and towards what also became the First or Ethiopian Pylon.

Whereas the *Akh Menu* had pillars and columns within, the Temple of Rameses had two rows of Osiride statues in the small temple Court. The *Akh Menu* had no Enclosure Wall. The Temple of Rameses had an Enclosure Wall. The *Akh Menu* was designed as a Temple of Festival to the ancestors of the King. The Temple of Rameses was dedicated to the Theban Triad of Amon-Ra, Mut and Khonsu. The *Akh Menu* had few illustrations; Rameses' temple was well illustrated. While later foreign enemies attacked and desecrated Rameses' temple as the first visible casualty of their animosity, later Christian adherents desecrated the *Akh Menu* and re-consecrated it as a Christian Church. And so on, and on, Lord Stanhope reflected.

Making his way through the temple he headed towards the "Coca-Cola Temple," beside the Sacred Lake. There his friend, "Brother" Abdul, High Priest at Karnak, ran a concession stand; but also, was overseer of all operations, digs, repairs and removal and placement of stone in the temple. Even more interesting, he was Karnak's principal ambassador, having been in the temple for more than 50 years. In that time, he has learned to greet and speak every major language of visitors who come there to see him, particularly on a return visit.

When Lord Stanhope appeared in the rear of the temple and they both set eyes on each other, the vibrancy of their embrace was thunderous. These two old friends embraced and reflected. They admired and respected each other greatly. Brother Abdul was in the temple when young Lord Stanhope did both of his dissertations at Karnak. That was a long time ago. In fact, during these studies, Brother Abdul pointed out many features to Lord Stanhope which enriched his presentations. Hence, their long-standing association

147

and friendship was a powerful motivator for the Englishman to fly to Luxor to visit Karnak. Soon his visit was over and retracing his steps he headed to the entrance.

Scarabs of gold and other precious stones.

Once beyond the walls of Karnak, he noticed his taxi-driver out chatting with other taxis and buggy or carriage drivers. One of them recognized him and said: "You're driving Lord Stanhope? Do you know he is famous here in Egypt? He is a good friend of Captain Farouk, Commander of the Luxor Tourist Police. They actually

INTRIGUE THROUGH TIME

went to school together." All Stanhope's driver could respond was, "I know this." As he rushed to him, he asked, "Where to, Sir?"

Stanhope: "Take me to Aboudy."

"Across the river on the West Bank, Sir?" he responded.
Stanhope: "Have you forgotten what I told you about the Tourist Police Chief Farouk? I need to pick up a book."
Driver: "Oh, you mean Aboudy, the bookseller."
Stanhope simply gave him the eye. Within five minutes they were in front of the most famous bookstore in all Luxor, perhaps in all of Egypt.

Looking out from his small but compact premises Aboudy saw the taxi pull up and a visitor emerge. Then he noticed who it was. His face lit up. It was the Englishman who gained fame as a great Egyptological scholar. He had known him before he was married and had children. He himself was a boy in his father's shop when the young Englishman first came to Luxor to do studies. He would come by and spend hours upon hours in the shop. They spoke Arabic. His father liked him. He read practically every book in the store, for free!

As soon as the visitor entered the store, they embraced and began to converse like long lost brothers. A couple of stuffed-shirt visitors in the store turned and wondered what was going on, but could not get it. Aboudy called his sons from in front of the store and ordered cold Coca Cola drinks and hot tea. They knew the man. They had seen him before. They heard their father tell unending tales about the young Englishman. Though he was no longer young, their friendship grew stronger over the ages.

"How are you, my old friend?" Aboudy asked.
Stanhope: "I'm well, old friend and buddy. I was checking something in the Cairo Museum. I'm just here for three days. I leave very early tomorrow, but I thought you cannot come to Egypt and not try to get to Luxor to see old friends. I stopped at Karnak to see Brother Abdul first."
Aboudy: "Brother Abdul! Oh, how's he doing? I know he's busy with the beautification of Karnak. My sons want me to get out more, but old age is catching up on me. Not as quick as I used to be."

149

FREDERICK MONDERSON

Stanhope: "Who is these days? More than 40 years I have known you and feel our bond has gotten stronger over the years. It's always nice to see and chat with an old friend."

After what looked like hours but actually no more than 30 minutes Stanhope prepared to leave.
Stanhope: "My return flight is at 5:30 and I want to get a quick walk-through Luxor Temple, before I leave. You take care, old friend."
They embraced and he departed.

Not being able to see the greeting he received at Karnak Temple, the driver observed what happened here, even though he could not hear what happened at Aboudy. Now he was a believer.
"Mr. Aboudy greeted you like a long lost relative, Sir" he said.
Stanhope: "In more ways than one. I've been coming to this shop for nearly 40 years. I knew his father. We two boys practically grew up together."
Driver: "Where to now, Sir?"
Stanhope: "Luxor Temple."

Without uttering a word, in 2 minutes he parked in front of Luxor Temple. With ticket in hand Stanhope approached the entrance. He headed north along the Avenue of Sphinxes, stopped and turned to look at the broad face of the propylon. Looking past the standing red granite obelisk and seated and standing statues, his eye focused on the inscriptions on the pylon. He was always fascinated by the depiction of the events surrounding the Battle of Kadesh illustrated there. After a lengthy pause, he turned south and approached the remaining obelisk and seated statues then passed through the Pylon entrance and into the Court of Rameses II. He remembers it was he who gave it the name "Ramessean Front."

INTRIGUE THROUGH TIME

From the West, Colonnades of the "Ramessean Front" of Rameses II (left), the Processional Colonnade (center) and Court of Amenhotep III with its colonnades (further right), and pitifully small Roman columns in forefront of the majestic Temple of Luxor.

The Triple Bark Shrine of Hatshepsut at Luxor to which Rameses II did repairs, the statues striding between the short, squat columns as if stepping into this Peristyle Court, always interested him. Another feature of note in this Court is the procession of sons of Rameses II ahead of fat cows led by priests to the illustrated Temple of Luxor on the eastern back wall. There, on the fourth cow in the Procession, a Nubian lady seems to be coming out of the cow's head. Obliquely opposite in the north-eastern front wall area is the Mosque of Abu Haggag, the patron saint of Luxor. Passing through 23-foot-high seated statues of Rameses II and the Pylon of the Temple of Amenhotep III, this gave access to the more than 50-feet high Processional Colonnade. Supposedly unfinished by Amenhotep, it bears the names of Seti I, Tutankhamon and Horemheb who all did repairs to it. The walls enclosing the Processional Colonnade were done by Tutankhamon. He decorated it with events of the procession from Karnak to Luxor and back, to celebrate the "Opet Festival." This festival was the reason for building the Temple of Luxor.

FREDERICK MONDERSON

To celebrate the "Opet Festival" the God Amon-Ra left Karnak by procession, along the river. Others, such as musicians, priests, drummers, charioteers, came by land. Upon arrival at Luxor the God Amon stayed there for 24 days in which he remained in chambers with his wife, the Goddess Mut. The celebration of joy, gaiety and sex was very intense and there was much merriment. The return to Karnak was by land along a canal. These events are depicted on the walls enclosing the Processional Colonnade. The best view is given by examining first the south end of the western wall, moving north and then moving to the eastern wall which is badly damaged. In fact, both walls of illustrations are damaged but the western wall is more easily read.

Ascending the stairs, Stanhope entered the platform and into the Court of Amenhotep with its beautiful calyx-capital peristyle colonnade. As a young man, he spent endless hours here, took many pictures and was always intrigued by the play of light and shade as the sun rose, passed overhead, crossed the river and cast back its shadows on the Court and its columns. Oftentimes he would sit in the Hypostyle Hall with its four rows of columns, just to the Court's rear, and gaze across the Court, through the Processional Colonnade and across the "Ramessean Front," past Hatshepsut Kiosk and towards the entrance Pylon. Those days of youthful admiration laid the foundation for his academic specialization in becoming a foremost authority on ancient Egyptian history and art and architecture, as well as being able to decipher Hieroglyphics.

Even more important, his easy disposition and loveable mannerism gained him easy acceptance, love and respect among the Egyptians. That camaraderie had grown tremendously over the years as a result of trust and respect.

Moving beyond the transept and circling but never entering the Holy of Holies out of respect, Stanhope soon completed his visit to Luxor Temple and retraced his steps, exited and headed for his parked ride. The driver quickly whisked him to the airport to catch his 5:30 flight to Cairo. Upon exiting he paid the driver 100 Egyptian pounds. The driver was very happy with that, and with not having to drive all day, but sit around waiting on the Englishman, whom he began to respect more as the day wore on.

INTRIGUE THROUGH TIME

Within two hours Lord Stanhope was back in Cairo, preparing to depart early the next (Thursday) morning. Reflecting on the success of his trip, he had determined the necklace was still in the Museum. He wondered, however, how Mr. Mentuhotep not simply possessed the necklace, but also how he was able to duplicate it. While he did not have a chance to inspect it, he took it for granted that it was part of the "ancient cache" which Mr. Somersett purchased. Just then it dawned on him, there was a possibility he may have to return to Cairo after he examines Mentuhotep's necklace as well as his dagger. Finally, he reasoned, must remember to get a photograph of both the necklace and dagger.

One of the last surviving Sphinxes lining the "Avenue of Sphinxes" beginning at Luxor Temple.

Ceramic Egyptian Art depicts a falcon, emblematic of the God Horus of Edfu.

153

FREDERICK MONDERSON

20.   A Gift for You, Madam

Mentuhotep found his store on Fifth Avenue, between Forty-Seventh and Forty-Eighth Streets. The name, *Luggage Express* said it all. With some help he found a 5-piece set of American Tourister luggage. He then chose two other rugged collapsible backpacks that fit one inside the other. Perhaps this will suffice since it is one inside the other. It should also muffle any sounds. Maybe that way, having secured his treasure he will be able to whisk it through customs. Nevertheless, he thought he must devise the most foolproof method of successfully carrying out his scheme.

"Please have this delivered to Room 1825 at the Plaza in an hour," he told the clerk, slipping him a $50.00 tip. "Will do, Sir. I'll handle it personally," was the response.

Passing Cartier, he was attracted by jewels in the window. To enquire further, he entered the store. 'What a fabulous place,' he thought. 'It seems, looking at the quality items, only wealthy people shop here,' he continued. At the watch counter he chose a beautiful, yet modest piece for $9600.00. "This has the most up-to-date features," the salesman told him and began explaining how they work. "We even have it in his and her set," the salesman continued. His heart thumped. He was so busily engaged, he had forgotten Fantegla. He reflected on the beautiful, soft, sensuous, and oh so sexy, piece of woman-flesh he was thankful to Amun for providing him. This was the first time he thought she made him feel this fabulous, other than being with Nekajai. But how dare he think that way?

"Sir! Sir! Sir," the Salesman murmured softly, surprised the customer seemed in a trance after he told him about the 'companion piece.' "It's only $9000.00," he said.

"I'll take them both," cried Mentuhotep, who was beginning to develop an itch for the woman. He could not help the way she made him feel. "How would you like to pay for that, Sir? Cash, check, or credit card?" the Salesman asked. "You need two pieces of identification if paying by check or credit card."

INTRIGUE THROUGH TIME

"Oh, not to bother," Mentuhotep replied, "that will be cash." Having paid, he slipped the Salesman a $50.00 note and had Fantegla's piece gift wrapped. Then he headed back to the Plaza.

Besides the thought of retrieving his treasure, another nagging idea plagued his active mind. He knew he was in the city and realized there were many different things here compared to his city. Nevertheless, he saw no slaves. In his warlike times many defeated peoples were made slaves and then given to temples of the Gods. Some were even owned by wealthy nobles who employed them as field hands on their estates in the countryside. He also realized he had not been outside the city limits.

'Maybe Fantegla can help in this respect. Maybe she knows more about this,' he thought as he entered the Plaza. Seeing William, he nodded to him and he responded.
William said: "Sir, your package was delivered to your room a few minutes ago. Ms. Somersett signed for them." "Thanks," slipping him $10.00. Climbing into the elevator, thinking deeply about his woman, he forgot to request a floor. However, his man Gibsoni was on the case and simply said, "Here we are, Sir, 18th floor." Our Hero turned with a smile and handed him $20.00.

Mentuhotep rang his doorbell. Fantegla thought, 'Another package?' Opening the door and seeing him, she broke into a big grin and hugging him looked and felt very much in the mood. Fixing him a drink, she asked: "How is your day going so far, honey?"
Mentuhotep: "Very well, gorgeous. In fact, I've been thinking of you all day long. I could use a good massage and some pampering."
'You mean my specialty,' she thought. "Ok, let me get at your shoulder," and she began disrobing him.
"Lie on the sofa, dear," she said as if preparing him for the sacrifice on her altar. Just then she noticed his new watch. "Nice trinket," she said. "Oh," he responded, turning over on his back and pulling a little gift-wrapped box out of his pocket. He handed it to her. Fantegla's eyes lit up. Opening the box, she was exceedingly pleased and examining it further she realized: "It's his and hers," she exclaimed. Just then she straddled him, reaching down began kissing his lips, neck, bare chest and away they went. It was hours later before they came up for air. For them, lovemaking was getting

155

FREDERICK MONDERSON

more frequent, exciting and long lasting. Fireworks seem to explode time and time again, when they combat in the erogenous zones.

When things quieted down in room 1825 and Mentuhotep and Fantegla lay relaxed, he remembered William had pointed out Circle Line from the west side highway. He asked: "Honey, have you been on Circle Line?"
"Oh, yes," she responded. "There are two- and four-hour tours. The two hours trip just sails to nowhere but the four hours one circles Manhattan Island. They're sailing every hour. Perhaps we can take a trip tomorrow."
"Great Idea," he said laughingly, "I thought you'd never ask." And then they laughed with, and at each other, before the next hook-up.

It was Wednesday evening and the Ladies Bridge Club was conducting their June Meeting. More than sixty members were in attendance and a few husbands had followed their wives. The President and other Executive Members presided over the meeting. The Secretary read the Minutes of the last meeting which was circulated. Only one correction was reported. Mrs. Jefferson pointed out her first name as a typo which should read Clarissa instead of Charisma. "All in favor of adopting the minutes with the corrections please say Aye."
"Aye! Aye! Aye!"

"The Treasurer has presented the group's financial report for the year ending June 30, 1985. All expenses are paid. A substantial sum is in the bank and two annual payments made on the mortgage. Twelve new members are added according to the Membership Chairman. Four enrolled with Life Membership status and the others opted for annual membership. Of the latter, two are leaning towards life membership at the end of their first year. There are now eighty-five active members. Since the last quarter two elder members deceased and were sent flowers while a delegation attended their funerals. Saturday July 15th is the club's annual extravaganza and the Social Committee reported four hundred tickets already sold, of which two hundred were corporate buys. Bridge, Pinochle, Rummy, Spades and Dominoes will host competition in the day-long event. Darts and Ping Pong are also being considered but these will be worked out later by the Social Committee. Prizes will be awarded to winners in each field."

INTRIGUE THROUGH TIME

Window at the New York Public Library on 42nd Street, New York City, where knowledge is dispensed so students can enrichen their minds for the future and Michael was pleased to be in such a place.

21.　　The Bad News

Ring. Ring. Ring.

"Hello. Ghafoor's Antiques. Ghafoor speaking."

Hospital: "Mr. Ghafoor, this is San Bernadine Medical Center in Los Angeles, California. Mr. Ghafoor your daughter Angeline was admitted with a rare blood disorder that is creating spinal and liver disorders. We are conducting tests and warn you, as the designated next of kin, this is a very serious condition that may require extensive rehabilitation."

Ghafoor: "Please keep me informed. I will be at the hospital early next week, perhaps Monday."

Hospital: "Her current medical coverage will cover all the tests and the first 10 days of hospitalization. However, upon completion of the tests, we may have to have her see a specialist or two."

Ghafoor: "Spare no expense. I will make a preliminary payment on all costs when I get out to Los Angeles next week. Please take care of my only daughter, the apple of my eye."

FREDERICK MONDERSON

Hospital: "We certainly will, Sir. We provide some of the best medical care in the state and take pride in our service."

Lord Stanhope flew in from Cairo on Thursday, arriving at JFK at 3:00 pm, and headed to his room at the Plaza. He was a bit under the weather, fighting a bout of diarrhea as well as jet lag. Nevertheless, he called and set up an urgent meeting at Ghafoor's between himself, Mr. Somersett, Mr. Wisenthal and Mr. Gray. He scheduled it for 11:00 am, Friday morning.

Golden Ankh inlaid with precious stones serving as an amulet.

INTRIGUE THROUGH TIME

22. Tours and Historic Places

Mentuhotep was up early, had breakfast and realized Sarlinda was joining them.

The *Times* of Thursday June 20, 1985 read:

Lead: "U.S. Warns Shiites about Becoming Global 'Outcast'"
International: "Four U.S. Marines Slain in Salvador"
National: "House votes to renew Output of Nerve…"
Local: "Billing Error Cost Transit Authority Millions."

Thursday morning at Noon Sarlinda, Fantegla and Mentuhotep arrived at the Brooklyn Museum on Eastern Parkway in Brooklyn. A new exhibit opened in the new wing donated by a wealthy but anonymous donor. Entering, at the desk, they were asked to join as members of the Museum and all happily complied.

Intricate decoration of Ionic Columns on the Cornice supporting a Pediment enclosing a wonderfully carved winged figure with companions at the Brooklyn Museum of Art.

Passing the Museum Shop, which they promised to visit on the way back, the group headed to the rear for the elevator to the Third Floor. Ushered to the rear of the Third Floor, they entered the Egyptian Gallery. Very compact, yet extensive, Brooklyn boasts one of the most renowned collections in the world. While not as extensive or

159

expansive as the Metropolitan Museum of Art, it rivals it in select pieces. In addition, the Brooklyn Museum houses the famous Wilbour Egyptological Collection of books, the Wilbour Library. Upon enquiries they were told by a guard that the library, naturally a research center and equally very extensive, is housed in limited space. As a result, one has to call ahead for an appointment to visit and use the facilities.

As the group walked along Eastern Parkway, this afforded another view of the   entrance to Brooklyn Museum and the NO. 2 and 3 trains.

From his readings, Mentuhotep realized Rameses was an Egyptian pharaoh of a later dynasty and he was pleased to see "his name written in the Colonnade" here.

Two hours later, after a very enlightening visit they chose to visit the Museum cafeteria for brunch, and there the talk got to tomorrow's one-day visit to Washington, DC. Sarlinda complained

INTRIGUE THROUGH TIME

of not being informed beforehand, so she could plan her Friday, and be available for the trip.

Fantegla, sensing her disappointment said, "Don't feel sad honey, on Saturday we will do Circle Line so you can come along." "Is that OK, my sweet," she asked, turning to Michael. "But of course," he responded, realizing Sarlinda had eyes on him. He also entertained the thought quietly, 'What would Fantegla think if I sex that!' He, however, chose not to go there.

Now relaxed and refreshed, they exited the Museum after visiting the Museum Shop, where he purchased a Travel Book on Egypt, and headed for the Subway ride uptown. Just then, Sarlinda said: "Let's look at some flowers in the Brooklyn Botanic Garden."

Fantegla, wanting to return to the fiery zone with Michael, chose to be a good sport and said: "OK."

Newly renovated Brooklyn Botanic Garden Eastern Parkway entrance.

They entered the Brooklyn Botanic Garden from the Eastern Parkway entrance. The flowers were just coming into bloom, the first few weeks into summer. Gardens were always a favorite of

161

FREDERICK MONDERSON

Michael's. He had trees to provide shade on his estate and a garden not only beautified the place but also provided flowers daily for his table. In addition, in his work at the Temple of Mut in Asher, he supervised the clearance of areas beside the Sacred Lake, where flowers were planted to not simply beautify the temple, but also provide flowers for the daily ritual of the Goddess' worship. After a while they exited the Garden on Washington Avenue and started walking back to Eastern Parkway; he in the center, with both women clinging to him.

Clara Barton and Prospect Heights High Schools were just letting out around 3:00 pm, and our Hero was really surprised to see so many young people exiting, excited, bags on their backs, in colorful fashionable attires.

One of the 'fresh kids,' said: "Oh, yes, Mister, two wives, way to go!" Then everyone smiled.

Clara Barton High School for Health Care Professions on Washington Avenue opposite the Brooklyn Botanic Garden.

He turned to Fantegla and asked: "Honey, did you attend such a school?"

"Yes, I did, but not here. My school is located in Queens, New York. But I did go to Hunter College of the City University of New York. It is a short distance uptown from the Plaza." As they walked, he began to get a better external view of the Museum's architecture.

INTRIGUE THROUGH TIME

The names written on the cornice and front of the building impressed him. He knew right away this was a special honor, similar to having ones "name written in the colonnade."

Prospect Heights High School is the other educational institution Mentuhotep and the ladies observed as kids exited after a day of instruction.

Walking past the Museum's entrance he kept reading the names written on the building's face, but instead of entering the subway for the No. 2 Train, Fantegla kept walking along the Parkway. They kept going west and she said: "Honey, this is Mount Prospect Park right next to the Garden."   At the end, they encountered the Brooklyn Public Library, main branch in the Grand Army Plaza square. Standing him in front of the Library she also pointed out the entrance to Prospect Park. Turning he noticed the Arch of the Soldiers and Sailors War Memorial Monument and he knew right away it had historical significance. He stared at the chariots and the winged angels blowing their trumpets. He remembered his chariot and thought these people must have idealized the horse. He also paid attention to the colonnades on the monument.   For the average visitor or resident, it became a part of the landscape, but he seemed to know its meaning as he gazed upon it. They kept walking, and then he noticed the fountain behind.

FREDERICK MONDERSON

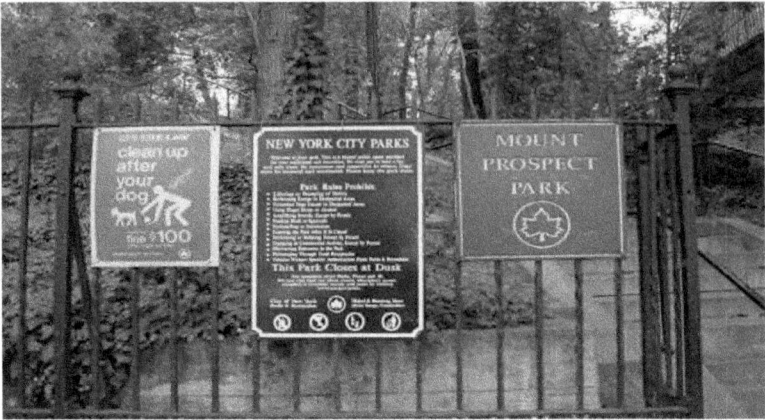

Mount Prospect Park between the Brooklyn Botanic Garden and Brooklyn Public Library on Eastern Parkway in the Grand Army Plaza vicinity.

Bust of President John F. Kennedy with the Fountain in the rear at Grand Army Plaza Memorial site.

Sarlinda wanted to enter and kick up some water, but they decided to board the No. 2 Train at the Grand Army Plaza stop heading back to New York. All this notwithstanding, these visits to cultural institutions, libraries, wherever, are expanding and extending the current memory of a man transplanted to a new time. Each incident and nuance, thought pattern of reflection into his ancient past further enhances his brain capacity. The end result is a greater human being

INTRIGUE THROUGH TIME

with a true sense of conscious and historical continuity, strong physical frame and a remarkable ability to adapt in a new environment. His handsome face, charming personality, and noble demeanor reinforce the view we have a superman in the mix.

Another view of the fountain with its mythological figures in the Grand Army Plaza Memorial site.

Not even he realized his financial largess from the sale of his jewelry, the net unrealized riches of his lady and the potential wealth from his hidden treasure will make him a rival of some of the super-rich families in America. As long as he continues the escalation of acquired knowledge, for this gentleman, truly the sky is the limit.

Fantegla, having dismissed her chauffeur upon their arrival at the Museum, had decided to ride back via the subway, Number 2 Train. Once inside he was fascinated by an underground train thinking for sure slave labor may have dug this deep into the bowels of the earth. He remembered how in his time prisoners of wars were made slaves. Marched back to the capital they would be distributed and given to temples of various gods. These in turn would be used as labor for building projects, farming and even applying their skills to craft making. He noticed the name of every stop on the line. He observed ads in the train while still keeping an eye on both of his companions. At Times Square, 42nd Street, they moved across the platform to the Number 1 Train. Getting off at Rockefeller Center they walked back to the Plaza and headed straight to the Restaurant.

Grand Army Plaza Station on the Number 2 and 3 lines.

While Mentuhotep did stop for breakfast on his way out to the Museum, on his return this time his favorite waiter, Basil approached with the *Times* and menu. Having read *The Times* earlier he still perused some pages he may have glossed over. For lunch the ladies chose mutton curry, rice, peas and carrots, spinach and corn. He chose baked salmon, baked potato, squash, eggplant and spinach. For dessert, they chose apple pie, and he custard with a sprinkling of spice. They all had coffee and he a double shot of Hennessy. The ladies chose sweet Gallo white wine. However, while eating he kept noticing the lead article in *The Times*. Nevertheless, he also kept a close eye on the two ladies paying particular attention to their beauty, their happy almost joyful expression when they're all together. It's as if they're enjoying a threesome without the actual intercourse. Still, a wicked thought crossed his mind, what happened if he broached the question, but thinking further, left it there. Then they retired to his apartment, and spent two hours on the balcony sipping brandy and watching the lights of the stars flicker on the green of the park on a clear summer night. Soon Sarlinda's chauffeur arrived to take her home. The others spent the night chit-chatting and preparing for Friday's Washington, D.C., adventure.

View of Grand Army Plaza Sailors and Soldiers Memorial from Prospect Park entrance across the street.

Close-up of "Defenders of the Union 1861-1865" at Grand Army Plaza Soldiers and Sailors Memorial, with its chariot that fascinated Mentuhotep and brought back memories of his distant past.

FREDERICK MONDERSON

Friday morning, they rose early, indulged in the zone for a while, showered, dressed, and were down to breakfast by 9:00 am. They enjoyed Continental Breakfast with coffee. He took *The Times* to read on the way and by 10:00 am Fantegla's chauffeur, Sidney, had them on their way. Speeding south down Fifty-Ninth Street, he headed east on the West Side Highway. Mentuhotep began noticing the beautiful buildings lining the west side. Then Fantegla told him, "Tomorrow, when we do the Circle Line, I promise to explain a bit more about the names as the view is better from the river." Just then, Canal Street sign came up. They turned into Canal Street and then into the Hudson Tunnel and towards New Jersey. Coming out of the tunnel they saw the signs, for Highway 1, 9, NJTP and before long they were heading south on I-95. As she nestled in close to him, he began reading *The Times*, for Friday June 21, 1985.

Lead: "U.S. Aides Say Hostages Release Would Free 766 Held in Israel; Formal Link of steps Barred."
International: "Hostages at Beirut Hold News Conference: Beseech U.S. Not to try a Rescue."
National: "$2.5 Billion Voted in House on Missile Shield"
Local: "Met Will Eliminate its National Tour after 1986."

Main Branch of Brooklyn Public Library, Grand Army Plaza.

Promptly at 11:00 am, Lord Stanhope arrived at Ghafoor's and soon realized Mr. Somersett, Mr. Gray, Mr. Wisenthal and Ghafoor were all there, and pacing nervously and excitedly wondering, why he had them assemble there.

INTRIGUE THROUGH TIME

"Gentlemen, we have a situation," he said.

"Oh, my God," exclaimed Ghafoor, instantly feeling guilty about the jewels he brokered. Trying to stay calm, Mr. Somersett was also nervous because he had purchased the jewels for a hefty sum.

Wisenthal, who had not been part of any consideration thought 'Well, it's a good thing I did not get involved.' Mr. Gray simply looked at Somersett sympathetically.

"Oh, no, it's not what you think," exclaimed Stanhope. "The jewelry you bought is as authentic as possible. It's truly 18th Dynasty, belonging to the Theban School, sometime between the reigns of Thutmose I and Hatshepsut." You could feel the sighs of relief as the tension lessened. Continuing, Stanhope said: "The issue here is not those jewels, but the necklace Mr. Mentuhotep has in his possession, on his neck."

Ghafoor: "Honestly, I was a bit nervous about that piece. While he flaunted the others and allowed me to take photographs, he only flashed the necklace and dagger. Still, I gave him the benefit of being an honorable man, a gentleman."

As former Commander of the Imperial Guard, Mentuhotep was impressed with this statue of a fighting soldier.

FREDERICK MONDERSON

Somersett: "I must thank you for putting my mind at ease, Lord Stanhope, but if I'm to bid on the other pieces I want watertight authenticity, otherwise I'm not interested."

Gray: "I'm sitting this one out."

Wisenthal: "Since I was not able to secure anything in the first lot, I'm naturally curious and excited, but I await Lord Stanhope's judgment, for, after all, he is the expert par excellence."

Stanhope: "Gentlemen, I think we're climbing up the wrong tree. Here's my take on this. When I saw that necklace, I instantly recognized it. I had seen that piece of jewelry before in the Cairo Museum. So naturally the thought came to me, was it stolen? Is the one Mr. Mentuhotep holding a fake? Is the one in the Museum a fake? Thus, I took a short trip to Egypt and visited the Museum in Cairo. Much to my surprise the necklace is where I saw it. I also enquired of one of the Museum officials if there had been any theft there lately and she informed me there was no such thing. In fact, security had been tightened. The Tourist Police added 20 new guards to the Museum so that seems out of the question."

Dr. Martin Luther King stands as a "Stone of Hope" from the "Mountain of Despair" in his Washington Memorial.

Somersett: "OK. Then what's the next logical step?"

Stanhope: "There are a couple of scenarios we could pursue. First and foremost, I must examine Mr. Mentuhotep's necklace. I must

170

give it a thorough going over, the full treatment. Once I'm certain it's truly authentic then there's the next step I must take."

Wisenthal: "And what is that?"

Gray: "The questions are, firstly, does he suspect we may be on to him? And secondly, if he is, will he allow you to examine the jewelry? After all, we have the domino theory here."

Somersett: "Hold on, gentlemen, I'm convinced Mr. Mentuhotep is an honorable man. My daughter Fantegla has spent a lot of time with him and she's convinced he's the genuine article. In fact, she called me early this morning to say they're on a day-trip to Washington, D.C. right now. They're driving up. Would you believe he never enquired about her wealth? He seems unconcerned and knows nothing about her or her family's fortune. This is not the actions of a man of questionable integrity. All he knows about her family is that the father forked-out two million dollars for the jewelry and may be rich. He is not sure if I'm a collector or intend to re-sell the jewelry."

Wisenthal: "What is the second option you have considered, Stanhope?"

Stanhope: "After I have verified the authenticity of his piece, then I will return to Cairo and request an examination of the museum piece. That should not be a problem because they are familiar with my work. Even more, the Curator is a schoolmate of Mrs. Stanhope, and I can easily claim she sends greetings before I turn on the charm."

Gray: "You were always good at that, you silver-tongued devil."

Wisenthal: "Let's fast forward beyond option two. What happens next?"

Stanhope: "Quite frankly, gentlemen. I don't have a clue. Option two has two parts. If the museum piece is a fake then Mr. Mentuhotep has to answer why he is holding the real McCoy and the Museum isn't. If the Museum piece is genuine, I don't know what to do. I haven't got that far as yet. I have not thought that out. That is as far as I can think of right now."

Somersett: "OK. Let's get Mr. Mentuhotep and his necklace here Monday 11:00 am, when Ghafoor opens."

Ghafoor: "I'm booked on a 1:30 pm flight out of JFK for Los Angeles. My daughter has developed a serious medical condition and I must fly out there. They're conducting tests. The store will be open, however, and you gentlemen have the run of the place."

FREDERICK MONDERSON

The Lincoln Memorial with its majestic 36 "Proto-Doric" columns representing the 36 states of the Union at the time President Lincoln was assassinated.

Wisenthal: "Sorry to hear about your daughter, old friend."
Gray: "Yes, do keep us informed."
Somersett: "Remember Ghafoor, we've been friends for a long time and through this difficult time, that's what friends are for."
Stanhope: "Yes, old buddy; God go with you. Blessings on your daughter, and I'm sure we all wish she pulls through."
Ghafoor: "Thank you, gentlemen."

Rear of the Capitol Building entrancing the Grand Marble Terrace affording the panoramic view of the Great Lawn with the Navy and Marine Memorial. This is probably one of the buildings with the most columns anywhere in the United States and perhaps the structure most frequently photographed, particularly by tourists.

INTRIGUE THROUGH TIME

Senator Williams arrived in Washington, D.C., and headed to his office in the Senate Building. He intended to deal straight from the shoulder and immediately called the Chairs of Armed Services and Foreign Relations Committees. He also reached the Majority Leader. In fact, he called a dozen members of key committees who in turn called other senators from both parties. After all, he is a master of logrolling, so he got things going. The significance of Senator Williams' action is he set in motion a chain reaction of events and concerns that the capital was buzzing about, particularly amidst the current crisis of the hijacking. The buzz about security, readiness, even spilled over to social issues of concern as the nation prepared to celebrate July Fourth, 1985. Still, it was never more secure! That weekend the talking heads making the rounds on Sunday morning television, for the first time in a long time, seemed meaningfully concerned about the issues facing the nation.

Defense Secretary Caspar Weinberger; Secretary of State George Schultz; David Stockman, Budget Director; Treasury Secretary Donald T. Reagan; as well as William Casey of CIA; and Volker at the Federal Reserve; all were on television promoting President Reagan's military spending, Star Wars, SDI, what the full response should be to the Lebanon mess and whether tax reform is truly good for the nation. Ed Meese seemed to be keeping his powder dry.

By 2:00 pm, Friday afternoon, Fantegla and Michael arrived on Independence Avenue, beside the Capitol Building and both the Madison and Jefferson buildings of the Library of Congress. They decided on a walking tour and asked Sidney her driver to drive down Independence Avenue and cross over to meet them at the other end of Constitution Avenue. Leaving the Madison Building they walked toward the spouting fountain of Greek Gods fronting the Jefferson Building of the Library of Congress and towards the Supreme Court Building. There they saw a concession stand and decided to buy a Guide Book of Washington, D.C., to make their trip even more informative and exciting.

173

FREDERICK MONDERSON

Another view of the Capital Building with its wonderful esplanade lawn.

Still, another panoramic view of the front of the Capital Building from the Jefferson Library of Congress building.

The National Library of Congress is the world's largest library with more than 120,000,000 items on its 500 miles of bookshelves.

Michael was instantly fascinated with "Colonnade City." It took him back almost immediately to the colonnades of his time from the

INTRIGUE THROUGH TIME

earliest at Sakkara to that of Karnak, during the time of Thutmose I and even the wonderful use of this feature at *Djeser*, today's Deir el Bahari. At Deir el Bahari, his superior Senmut, the Queen's architect, used Beni Hasan, later called "Proto Doric" columns, as well as regular columns in the Hathor Shrine and square pillars along with Osiride figures at this his favorite temple. Oh, how he remembers the slopes on the side of the mountain where he hid his treasure. Still deep in thought, he could feel Fantegla tugging at his arm.

At the Thomas Jefferson Building of the Library of Congress' Bransfield "Wheel of Knowledge," Michael was shocked to see his nation stood at the "12 O' Clock," head or foundation of this "fountain of wisdom," instrumental in furthering the pageantry of human intellectual growth.

Nevertheless, as they moved towards the Supreme Court, he kept gazing at the colonnades surrounding the Capitol Building. Even the Dome had columns. Next was the Supreme Court, home of the nine justices. Our man kept being surprised with this particular architectural feature. Standing in the hundred-foot oval plaza,

FREDERICK MONDERSON

flanked by two seated marble figures flanking the main entrance, often described as "Contemplation of Justice," they looked at the sixteen marble columns at the entrance and above the caption read: "Equal Justice under Law." They circled the building and on the east side the inscription read: "Justice the Guardian of Liberty."

He also remembered and again equated this caption with the honor of having one's "name written in the colonnade." Crossing over and coming around the side of the Capitol Building they arrived just below the Grand Marble Terrace. Here they were treated to the spectacular panoramic view of looking down the Great Lawn towards and past the Washington Monument, to the Lincoln Memorial beyond. The Reflecting Pool could not be seen as yet. The United States Botanic Gardens lay to their left just away from the Capitol Building. His keen eye seemed to notice the Washington Monument lies almost midway between the Capitol Building and the Lincoln Memorial Building. With that they took off heading in that direction.

The Temple of Karnak's Hypostyle Hall "roots" of the "knowledge Wheel" and the Washington Monument, Seti I before Amon-Ra, Ptah, and Sekhmet and Ptah.

INTRIGUE THROUGH TIME

The Washington Monument amazed Mentuhotep as he remembered the "Tekhens" or Obelisks of his day especially of those erected by his Queen and her father at Karnak Temple.

Walking on the Great Lawn or National Mall, described as "An ideal stage for national expressions of remembrance, observance and protest," and with the Smithsonian Castle on the left with Mr.

FREDERICK MONDERSON

Henry's statue before it; the Guide Book noted there were sixteen museums in the Smithsonian Institution with nine on the National Mall. The Museum of the American Indian is one of the nine and it lies just before the Castle on the Independence Avenue side. Elsewhere on Independence Avenue they could make out government building after government building with their white marble colonnades at their sides and front. On the Constitution Avenue side of the Mall stood the National Gallery of Art, and the New National Museum, but also government buildings in red granite with the same features as on Independence Avenue.

The Jefferson Building of the Library of Congress.

Once past the Smithsonian on the left they moved quickly and on and on they kept going, until they reached Monument Grounds, and the Washington Monument. His heart almost stopped beating. Silently he asked 'Where did they get this *Tekhen*, today called an obelisk.' Upon closer observation he noticed it's not like those of his time. Whereas the *Tekhen* of his time consisted of a single piece of stone cut from quarries, this Washington Monument was made of put together stone. It stood nearly five hundred and fifty-six feet, made of marble, granite and interior ironwork, and boasted an "unadorned Egyptian Obelisk" at its apex. It should be added, an obelisk is a pyramid upon a high base. As they walked around the Washington Monument, he was, however, fascinated by the great spread of "Old Glory," the numerous flags of white, red and blue surrounding the Monument. These sort of reminded him of the temples and their flagstaves which flew national, Nome and temple flags. They also seemed to remind him of the White Crown sitting on the Red Crown, encompassing the Blue waters of the Nile.

After circling the Washington Monument, they paused to the left on the Independence Avenue side. From there they could see both the Jefferson Monument off to the left across the Tidal Basin, and the White House far off to the right on Pennsylvania Avenue. It was as if the standing nineteen-foot figure of Jefferson in his rotunda was keeping an eye on both the Washington Monument and the White House. Incidentally, the Jefferson Memorial Rotunda was modeled after the Parthenon of Rome. Annually this Memorial plays host to a memorial service, Easter Sunrise Services and the Cherry Blossom Festival. From this spot at the Washington Monument the Reflecting Pool came into proper view and they could see the Washington Obelisk reflecting in the pool as they looked toward the Lincoln Memorial.

Mr. Thomas Jefferson stands majestically in his Memorial looking across the Pond pass the Washington Monument and towards the White House.

179

FREDERICK MONDERSON

Moving back across and then further down the Great Lawn on the Constitution Avenue side, they passed the Nurses' Memorial, Wall of the Vietnam Veterans' Memorial, and the statues of three soldiers, two white and one black, coming out of the rice paddy in Vietnam. To their left they could get a better view of the Reflecting Pool and further on the Tidal Basin.

From there they could also see the F.D. Roosevelt Memorial near the Mall along the Tidal Basin and Cherry Tree Walk on the Independence Avenue side. Further on they saw the soldiers of the Korean Memorial, a whole company coming through a rice paddy field.

Then they came to the west end of the National Mall at the West Potomac Park and end of the Reflecting Pool. They approached the steps of the Lincoln Memorial to the sixteenth President of the United States. It boasts a Hypostyle colonnade of thirty-six fluted columns, one for each of the 36 states in the Union at the time of Lincoln's death. There are also two others in the rear. Ascending the steps of the Lincoln Memorial they turned and looked back over the distance they came. Across the Reflecting Pool, to the Washington Monument, they could better see the obelisk reflecting under the glare of the bright sunshine. To Mentuhotep this reminded him of the Greater Court at Karnak. The Capitol Building with its columns further on in the distance, completed 'one of the most spectacular sites on the face of the earth,' Fantegla told him. He agreed wholeheartedly. They took the time to read the left wall Gettysburg Address made by Lincoln, and the other inscriptions on the right wall. Pausing to reflect on this solemn place, he seemed to sense this was a great man and the events of his time were equally great.

Retracing their steps back to Constitution Avenue, they arrived at the waiting limousine. Then they drove around looking at a few important buildings.

First, the Mormon Temple at Sixteenth and Harvard Square in the North West; Constitution Hall on D Street, also in the North West; and several other buildings including the Bureau of Engraving that prints money and stamps, with its more than twenty Proto-Doric columns. Then they swung around to the Executive Office Building

INTRIGUE THROUGH TIME

with its nine-hundred Doric columns at Pennsylvania Avenue and Seventeenth Street. Leone Battista Albertini in his *Ten Books on Architecture* at Leoni in 1755, said regarding a building like the White House, such a "Palace…should stand in the Heart of a City, it should be easy of access, beautifully adorned, and rather delicate and polite." That is why this "American Treasure," the "People's House," seems so centrally located at 1600 Pennsylvania Avenue. On the way out, they viewed buildings of the Treasury, the Ministry of Agriculture, the National Gallery, Canadian Embassy and the Naval Memorial. After a brief pause, they headed back to the Highway to connect with I-95 North for New York.

The National Archive, another colonnaded building that attracted Mentuhotep's attention.

Pretty soon Fantegla was in her favorite and comfortable nestling position. Snuggled next to him she asked: "What do you think?" All along Michael had been mostly quiet taking in the sites as she pointed them out. Walking briskly and silently, that keen sense of observation and quick-witted mentality; that had endeared him with the Queen, earning him the position of Commander of the Imperial Guard; metaphorically speaking, enabled him to fill his mental tank.

As if digesting everything before he answered, he then said: "It's the most exciting modern experience I have ever had." Looking at him seductively, she thought, 'except,' as if reading her mind, he

181

FREDERICK MONDERSON

grasped her hand gently, and said: "except, when I'm with you, sweetheart."

As if rewarding his confession, she reached up and kissed him passionately. In that embrace she felt lost but secure, then slouched back to enjoy the ride. Hours later, they were back in New York, arriving at the Plaza. "Thank you, Sidney, for a wonderful ride. I will not need you anymore until tomorrow."
Sidney: "Always willing to be of assistance, Madam."

Refreshed, they came down to dinner. Over cocktails they ordered steamed lobster, baked potato, broccoli, cheese, garlic sauce, and lemon. He also ordered mustard, vinegar and pepper in a sauce.
"Do you know lobster is an aphrodisiac?" she asked.
"I didn't know that," he responded.
"I'll show you when we get upstairs," she added.

They both laughed. When the meal was over, like two young lovers they retired to his room to hibernate.

Circle Line's emblem where the group took the 4-hour ride.

Golden bracelets in the Cairo Museum of Egyptian Antiquities.

182

INTRIGUE THROUGH TIME
23. Circle Line Incident and After

Saturday morning Mentuhotep was up very early. As usual Fantegla still slept. He showered, dressed and headed to the Restaurant, his favorite table and waiter. Over breakfast, he kept eyeing *The Times* top stories for Saturday June 22, 1985.

Lead: "Shultz and Perez Agree to Oppose Shiites …"
International: "8 Days of Mideast Terror; the Journey of Flight 847"
National: "Man Kills Mother and Self at State Dept"
Local: "Vendors of Food Face New Limits on Street Sales."

He looked for William to complete the arrangements for securing the Driver's License on Monday, sometime in the afternoon. For some reason his man could not be found. Then he returned to his room. Fantegla was just coming out of her slumber. The phone rang. It was Sarlinda. She came to accompany them to the Circle Line cruise. Sister Girl jumped out of bed, showered and was dressed. She joined her friend, along with Michael in the Restaurant. Now fully awake, she was ready to take on Circle Line as well as Sarlinda. She had realized her friend was intent on taking her up on the dare. Then she thought, 'Not to worry, I've got this.'

Sidney was waiting with a beaming smile on his face. Just back from his Washington, D.C., triumph, he was ready for Circle Line. Soon they were off down Fifty-Ninth Street, pass Columbus Circle, and onto the West Side Highway. Just before Forty-Second Street, they came upon Circle Line. Fantegla and Sarlinda got out, while Michael remained in the car with Sidney. The ladies went to get tickets for the four-hour cruise.

With tickets secured, they lined up and waited to board. Soon they were aboard and sailing. They chose the top deck so as to get the best view of the New York Skyline. As soon as they set sail down the Hudson, Fantegla began pointing out buildings along the New York skyline with which she had some familiarity.

First, she pointed out the Chrysler Building just off Forty-Third Street. The Empire State Building at Thirty-Fourth Street and the

FREDERICK MONDERSON

Jacob Javits Convention Center was next. At Twenty-Eighth it was the Madison Belvedere. The New York Life Insurance Company is around Twenty-Sixth Street and the Chelsea Piers between Nineteenth and Eighteenth Streets, with the New York University buildings nearby. The US District Courthouse, Woolworth Building, Bank of New York Building and the Federal Reserve Bank of New York were all pointed out before the four buildings, two with towers in the World Trade Center complex.

Soon they were making the turn to go up the East River and there she stood, the "Lady of the Harbor," the Statue of Liberty. Fantegla announced she had read somewhere this statue, given by the French just before 1876, America's Centenary, was actually meant to celebrate the American slave woman freed from slavery; for the statue had chains around her feet that were broken, signifying French recognition of American slavery being abolished.

Up the East River they turned. The boat seemed to make a sudden turn and Sarlinda, standing very close to Michael, fell into his arms. From there she kissed him on the lips, right in front of Fantegla, right there on Main Street. Michael, with his hands full, returned the favor, right there in front of Fantegla, who seemed to think, 'Poor thing, she doesn't get any, so what. Even if she gets a slice of the bacon, I've got the whole hog.' Still, the shameless hussy seemed to think, 'Well, I've got my pound of flesh.'

They headed upriver on the East Side. First 1 New York Plaza, 55Water Street, Towers One and Two of the World Trade Center, and the Woolworth Building were within view. Ahead lay the Brooklyn Bridge but to the left, again, the Woolworth Building and Verizon structure just beyond the Brooklyn Bridge. Then they passed Jacob J. Javits Federal Building and Citicorp near the Manhattan Bridge, then the Baruch Building near the Williamsburg Bridge. Next Fantegla pointed out the Georgetown Plaza around East 7th Street, the Con Edison Building and Empire Blue Cross, Blue Shield around 41st and 42nd Streets. The United Nations Secretariat Building is located off 42nd Street and next the Queens Borough or 59th Street Bridge. She again pointed out the Citicorp Building around 96th before they made the turn around George Washington Bridge and headed back to the Pier. It was quite a day and Fantegla realized Sarlinda would stop at nothing to get a piece of Michael's apple.

INTRIGUE THROUGH TIME

They returned home a bit tired of all this sightseeing and both Michael and Fantegla felt the need to relax and recharge their batteries. Sarlinda left for Queens. After some resting, they came down for dinner and found the restaurant crowded with weekend city revelers. They passed the night uneventfully.

Something happened to these two people. For the next week they remained in their room. Fantegla caught the flu and Michael got it from her. They never left the room for the next eight days. It was room service and *The Times* all along. Michael read *The Times* religiously and he read the travel guides he purchased at Barnes and Noble and the books he got at the Met and the Brooklyn Museum. All week long the *Times* depicted the threatening challenges of the times.

Sunday June 23, 1985

Lead: "U.S. Warns Shiites of consequences on the Hostages"
International: "Marines' Killers will not Escape, Reagan Promises"
National: "Survey finds Security at Airports Usually Serious, Sometimes not"
Local: "Signs of Economic Revival Abound in Northeast."

Monday June 24, 1985

Lead: "329 lost on Air India Plane after Crash near Ireland. Bomb is Suspect as Cause."
International: "Blast Kills 2 as Cargo is Unloaded from Canadian Airliner in Japan"

National: "Astronauts hold News Conference from the Shuttle"
Local: "City Services Found Improved."

Tuesday June 25, 1985

Lead: "Shiite Insists U.S. Pull its Warships back from Coast"
International: "Recorders Hunted in Air India Crash"
National: "Part of Tax Plan May be rewritten by Administration"
Local: "Reporter and 2 Others Guilty of Fraud for Insider Trading."

185

FREDERICK MONDERSON

Wednesday June 26, 1985

Lead: "U.S. Gives Warning of Reprisals Aimed at Lebanon"
International: "Pressure Mounts on Shiite Leader"
National: "Pension Dispute Creates Impasse in Budget Talks"
Local: "Rise of Up to 6.5% in Stabilized Rents is set for New York."

Thursday June 27, 1985

Lead: "Lebanese Militia Frees a Hostage Who's Ailing"
International: "U.S. is Reported to be Weighing Shiite Offer on Moving Hostages"
National: "House Would Curb Anti-Satellite Test"
Local: "Tentative Pact Set in Walkout at City Schools."

Friday June 28, 1985

Lead: "U.S. Says 7 Missing Must Also Go Free with Air Hostages"
International: "U.S. Will End Curbside Check-In as Part of Drive on Airline Terror"
National: "House Broadens Spying Death Law"
Local: "Stockman Says Tax Increase may be best Budget Solution."

Saturday June 29, 1985

Lead: "Hostages Expected to Go Free after Moving to Syria, Today"
International: "32 Hostages Given Bouquet in Beirut"
National: "Index that Shows Economic Trends Advances Sharply"
Local: "Court Overrules Order by Koch on Sexual Bias."

Sunday June 30, 1985

Lead: "Release of Hostages Put off as Lebanese Call for Promise that U.S. Will Not Strike Back"
International: "Pretoria Troops Kill Namibians in Angola Raid"
National: "Pentagon Study Faults Security of Contractors"
Local: "Decade after the Cutbacks New York Is a Different City."

Another classic rear view of the Lincoln Memorial with its 36 Doric columns, one for each state of the Union in the year the President was assassinated.

Back entrance of the White House in Washington, DC with its fountain.

24.   First Necklace Challenge

Awakening Sunday morning, June 30th, they ordered Room Service breakfast that came with *The Sunday Times*. Remaining in his room all day Sunday, first Mentuhotep read the papers then followed with his Egypt Travel Guides. He remained fascinated and surprised at the things that happened in his country after his untimely demise. Significantly, however, these reading caused his mind to traverse

FREDERICK MONDERSON

time back and forth from the then familiar to the now emerging familiar. Late in the afternoon the phone rang. It was Mr. Somersett.

Somersett: "Hello, Mr. Mentuhotep. How are you today?"

Mentuhotep: "Very well, Sir."

Somersett: "I'm getting together with Lord Stanhope and a few friends at Ghafoor's tomorrow at 11:00 am. Can you do us the honor of joining us at that time?"

Mentuhotep: "No problem, Sir."

Somersett: "One more thing. Can you bring your necklace and dagger so Lord Stanhope can examine them and give us a ballpark figure in the event you decide to sell! Quite frankly, my two friends are envious of my recent purchase and those two items have been on their minds unendingly. Let me say also, I'm not about to let them win in any bid race."

Mentuhotep: "I'm so glad to hear of the heated interest. I'll be there tomorrow."

Somersett: "Thank you." 'Flawless,' he thought.

Necklaces similar to the one in Cairo and one worn by Mentuhotep.

Rising early Monday morning, before Fantegla, he got dressed and went to breakfast, and, as usual, "dressed in his dagger." The necklace he removed and placed in a pouch in his breast pocket. The restaurant staff was glad to see him. He thanked them all for room service and handed over an envelope with $300.00. He read *The Times,* Monday July 1, 1985.

Lead: "39 American Hostages Free after 17 Days; Go from Lebanon to Syria and Head Home"

INTRIGUE THROUGH TIME

International: "In Beirut Hooded Men Tell of Captives Release"
National: "Space Arms Projects Ignite Debate on U.S.-Soviet Science Exchange"
Local: "AIDS Children Struggle with Tragic Legacy."

He even saw a small piece about an African Street Festival going on at Boys and Girls High School in Brooklyn. It started Thursday evening and would last through Wednesday July Fourth. He seemed to remember his African neighbors, especially the Envoy who brought one of his chests of treasure.

Upon arrival at Ghafoor's he met the Proprietor, Mr. Somersett, Lord Stanhope, Mr. Gray and Mr. Wisenthal. After the introductions, Ghafoor asked to be excused as he had to get to Los Angeles.
Stanhope: "May I see the treasure, Sir?"
Mentuhotep: "Certainly," removing the necklace from his pouch and dragging the dagger from his waist.

Something struck Stanhope as odd. The fact that he carried a dagger in his waist and the manner in which he drew it out was reason for thought. However, this was just a passing thought, and he began to concentrate on the jewels. "Can I take a photo of them?" he asked.
Mentuhotep: "No objections."

Lord Stanhope began to meticulously examine each piece. First the necklace, then the dagger but he kept eying the necklace, the main object of his interest. He stopped for a breather; took a photograph of each piece, and then back to the necklace. After a long while he murmured 'definitely Theban School, 18th Dynasty, Late Thutmose I, early Hatshepsut.' Then he spoke, "Gentlemen, this is the genuine article, the Real McCoy. It is Theban School, 18th Dynasty, Late Thutmose I, early Hatshepsut, no doubt." Then he did the same with the dagger with the same results.

Putting away his tools he turned and looked at Mentuhotep, thinking, 'What manner of man is this?' 'How did he get hold of the necklace especially?' 'Did he have inside help at the Museum to make the switch?' 'How could the Museum officials be so wrong, insisting they had the original piece?' All these questions were turning around in his head. Naturally he was quietly elated, ecstatic

189

FREDERICK MONDERSON

to have such wonderful ancient Egyptian jewelry in his grasp, allowed the privilege of authenticating them, and most importantly being able to determine their monetary value.

Mentuhotep, on the other hand, began to study Lord Stanhope. He thought, 'Here's an English Lord, a nobleman like myself, extremely versed in the cultural history of my experience more than I can ever be in his, at home in Europe, America, Egypt.' 'How can he be helpful to my agenda?' 'What role can he play in recovery of my treasure?' 'I can certainly use him to authenticate my jewels when they're recovered.' Even further, he thought, 'I must come up with an angle to have him help me secure a British Passport for my travels. This, however, is not the right time. A move as delicate as this must be timed propitiously and executed with graceful finesse. I imagine it will be a costly venture, but well worth the investment.'

With the business at hand completed, Mentuhotep gathered up his property and said: "Gentlemen, I bid you farewell," and he was gone.

Once he left, Somersett broke the ice. "Well Stanhope," he said, "What's your next move?"
Stanhope: "I must return to Cairo to complete some business there."
Wisenthal: "What sort of business? Is it in connection with these jewels? I want to be given a chance to secure at least one piece."
Gray: "I will not be left out of the bidding."
Somersett: "My friends, if as Lord Stanhope claims, these jewels may all be related. Who knows how Mr. Mentuhotep secured them? He has always acted as if they are his personal possessions. In that case they all belong together. As such, I must secure these additional pieces to make the collection complete. I must keep them in the family, you know what I mean."
Wisenthal: "Lord Stanhope, what do you think these two pieces are worth?"
Stanhope: "I would have to make one final examination but based on its rarity and Theban style, I'll say the necklace is worth three million and the dagger valued at about five million. As I said, I must look at them again."
Gray: "Well, Sirs, there is the challenge. Who will bell the cat?"
Wisenthal: "Lord, you never answered my original question, 'What sort of business?'"

INTRIGUE THROUGH TIME

Stanhope: "Well gentlemen, as I should let you know, we have a stalemate here. There are two necklaces I have seen. I examined Mr. Mentuhotep's and found it to be genuine. I must assume the one in the Museum is a fake. What I can't understand is how Mr. Mentuhotep has been able to pull it off."

Wisenthal: "I will not bid on any product that is tainted by fraud."

Stanhope: "I am certain there has not been any outcry of theft of jewelry, whether public or private. That is why I reassured Mr. Somersett that his purchase was genuine. What I must do is return to the Museum and seek to examine the necklace they have. That will put to rest a lot of concerns and answer many questions."

Gray: "When do you intend to leave?"

Stanhope: "Egypt Air has a flight out on Tuesday evening and one in Thursday morning. I will make the arrangement soon."

Somersett: "To save time, you could probably make the arrangements from this phone."

Stanhope: "Good idea." And, he left to make the necessary arrangements.

Ring. Ring. Ring.

"Hello, Egypt Air."

Stanhope: "Yes, this is Lord Stanhope. I'd like to reserve a seat on your flight to Cairo tomorrow evening."

Egypt Air: "Very good, Sir. Have you traveled with Egypt Air before?"

Stanhope: "I have."

Egypt Air: "OK, Sir. Let me bring up your name and profile! The Computer Screen read: Lord Samuel Milford Stanhope. Egypt expert! Frequent Flyer! Status – Excellent! Extend the warmest cordiality to this gentleman."

"Hello."

Stanhope: "Yes."

Egypt Air: "Lord Stanhope. I have your information. I'm exceedingly pleased to serve you."

Our flight tomorrow July 2, 1985, Number 811 leaves JFK at 9:00 pm. Check in is between 6:00 and 7:00 pm. Your seat number is 5B. Time of Arrival in Cairo, is Wednesday morning, July 3, 1985 at 8:30."

Stanhope: "Very good."

Egypt Air: "When are you returning, Sir?"

191

FREDERICK MONDERSON

Stanhope: "Thursday morning."
Egypt Air: "That's flight 812, Thursday, July 4, 1985. Departs Cairo International, at 6:30 am! Check in is at 4:00 am. Time of arrival at JFK is 3:30 pm. Your seat number is the same, first class, 5B. Is that satisfactory, Sir?"
Stanhope: "It is."
Egypt Air: "I see we have your American Express Card number on file. Will this be the method of payment, Sir?"
Stanhope: "Yes."
Egypt Air: "Very good. That's all done, Sir. Thank you for flying Egypt Air. Have a good flight. Enjoy."
Stanhope: "Thank you."

Returning to the group he said, "Well, that's taken care of."
Somersett: "The marvels of modern technology!"
Gray: "Stanhope, this is a kind of curve ball but tell me, since you're such an expert on the ancient Egyptians, 'Did they think like us?'"
Stanhope: "Of course they did. Well, in a way they did not. You must understand in their time thought happened on a kind of *Tabula Rasa*, a clean slate. Much of what they did and created was original. Their writing, religion, building, art, technology, science, medicine, were all original creations that would have a tremendous impact on later peoples and time."
Wisenthal: "So if a man from that time came to live among us, he could fit in easily."
Stanhope: "Well, as you know that is not possible! However, even though he may fit in some respects than others, he may appear a fish out of water."
Somersett: "I imagine our method of transportation would certainly baffle him."
Stanhope: "The seasons and temperature of our time would certainly cause him to wonder. Our culture and buildings would be strange and our political systems and prejudices may alarm him. But, all in all, he could fit comfortably well in our culture if he has the ability to adapt."

192

INTRIGUE THROUGH TIME

Dr. Susan Smith-McKinney Nursing and Rehabilitation Center in Brooklyn which does such excellent work and where Ghafoor's daughter Angeline was transferred for treatment from San Bernadine Medical Center in Los Angeles, California.

25.   Ghafoor in Los Angeles

Ghafoor arrived at Los Angeles International Airport and took a cab to San Bernadine Memorial Hospital. He identified himself as the parent of Angeline Ghafoor. Doctor Joseph Vincenti was paged and met Mr. Ghafoor in the Visitor's Waiting Room.

"Pleased to meet you, Sir, my name is Dr. Joseph Vincenti, and I'm the physician assigned to treat your daughter. Her condition is serious and difficult. We have conducted some tests and determine she is suffering from a neurological disorder that has paralyzed her spinal column. This condition will require extensive and long-term rehabilitative care. While she is not in a coma there are many similarities. She is conscious of people and her surroundings but unable to do anything about it for herself."
Ghafoor: "What are the chances of recovery, Doctor?"

193

FREDERICK MONDERSON

Vincenti: "Her vital signs are good but we cannot explain her inability to respond to stimuli. I want to get your permission to bring in two specialists from Europe to examine her. They are top of the line experts in the field of Neurology. However, this line of specialization and treatment may be costly."

Ghafoor: "Spare no expense. This is my only daughter. My beloved and I will spend my last dime to see her well again."

Vincenti: "In that case I will go ahead and bring these two specialists to examine and treat her. In addition, I wish you to be prepared for long-term rehabilitative care."

Ghafoor: "Like I said spare no expense!"

Vincenti: "There is an excellent long-term rehabilitative hospital in New York, in Brooklyn. The name is Dr. Susan Smith-McKinney. They have state of the art equipment and medical therapy. Even though with some patients their procedures seem slow and tedious, they have gotten excellent results in rehabilitation. Even more important, it's in New York and will be less intensive a commute for you."

Ghafoor: "I would like to thank you for your kind and sensitive concern. Rest assured I will do everything within my power to provide the funds, to treat my daughter. May I see her now?"

Vincenti: "Yes, Sir. At this time, she is in Intensive Care. After our discussion I will arrange for her to be housed and treated in a private room with all the amenities to treat her condition."

Ghafoor: "Again, I want to thank you, Dr. Vincenti."

Vincenti: "Well, here we are. Please put on this lab coat and a mask before we enter her station."

Before entering the Intensive Care cubicle where his daughter lay, Ghafoor looked like a very troubled man, shaken and troubled. When he walked in, he noticed the many contraptions to which she was hooked up. As he drew nearer, his daughter recognized him and her eyes lit up. There were counteractions on all the machines as their numbers fluctuated tremendously. Clearly, his coming had made an impression on her. He grasped her arm and they held and supported each other. It was as if his coming had given her a new lease on life. Tears came to her eyes and to his.

He bent over and whispered in her ears, "I'm here for you. I've arranged for you to get the best care and I'll have you transferred to a hospital in Brooklyn, for rehabilitative treatment. Rest assured I will spend my last dime to try and see you well." Somehow, she

INTRIGUE THROUGH TIME

managed a smile and so did he. Then he bent over and said to her: "Do not be afraid, my sweet. I've always raised you to be a fighter. I'm here to remind you I'll always be in your corner. Do not worry about the expenses. If I have to, I will sell my shop. What I want you to know is I'm firing your will to be well. It's up to you. I must leave you now. Goodbye. I will keep in touch with the hospital." Then he leaned over and kissed her. She managed a smile. In his imagination he thought he heard her say: "Thank you, Dad." Then he was off.

On the way home Ghafoor began thinking how he would handle this unexpected development. He even toyed with the idea of offering Mr. Mentuhotep a partnership if he would advance some of the cash.

Majestic view of the Capitol Building with its esplanade garden, lawn and statue.

Miniature souvenirs of the Washington Monument and the White House.

FREDERICK MONDERSON

26.   Champion of US Security

Senator Williams was making waves across the board in Congress. On Sunday June 30, 1985, morning Talk Shows, *Face the Nation*, *Meet the Press*, *This Week with David Brinkley*, the talking heads from both sides of the aisle were echoing Williams' idea of security for the nation. He had carried the ball well. Hawks were beating war drums; doves were beating peace drums; all were concerned, a hole in the "safety net" meant Medicare, the Voting Rights Act, unemployment, Social Security reforms, Health Care, were all Achilles heels of the nation.

Despite the furor from both sides in 1985, President Reagan submitted a budget with the greatest spending for the military in peace time; while cutting social issues with his proposals for welfare reforms, trimming entitlements, giving tax breaks disguised as tax reforms and issuing threats to labor, behave or else. He also proposed greater block grants to states allowing them greater autonomy in the area of states' rights. The conservative "far right" and business community began trumpeting Reagan as the greatest president ever! Those poor souls feeling the bite of his teeth, the slice of his knife, and the burden of his boot, begged to differ.

Through it all, Senator Williams of New York's favorite party, emerged as the great champion in defense of the nation. He was a master of logrolling. Even more important, he relished in the perception created, that even if others had recessed, he remained on guard in defense of the nation. Political cartoons depicted him as a poster boy for the military.

Meanwhile, during the early days of July, things moved rapidly. Fantegla had her friends over to her apartment on Monday. That day William helped Michael complete the driver's license registration process. This time, Fantegla, Sarlinda and Kasheisha left to visit the Bronx Zoo and Botanical Gardens. They stopped to see Grant's Tomb and the Cloisters on the way back. In a way, he was thankful for Sidney and Fantegla's Limousine.

196

INTRIGUE THROUGH TIME

Tuesday July 2, 1985, Sarlinda met them at breakfast. He checked *The Times*. Fantegla was pleased he was such an avid reader who wanted to keep abreast of what was going on.

Tuesday July 2, 1985, they got ready to visit the Intrepid Naval Museum on the West Side Highway. At breakfast he checked *The Times*.

Lead: "Israelis Set to Release 300. U.S. Opens Diplomatic Drive to 'Isolate' Beirut Airport"
International: "Ex-Captives Say Gunmen Planned to Kill Military Men One by One"
National: "High Court Bars Public Teachers in Church Schools"
Local: "New York City Weighs Tapping Hudson Water"

Golden Scarab studded with precious stones attached to a chain.

197

FREDERICK MONDERSON

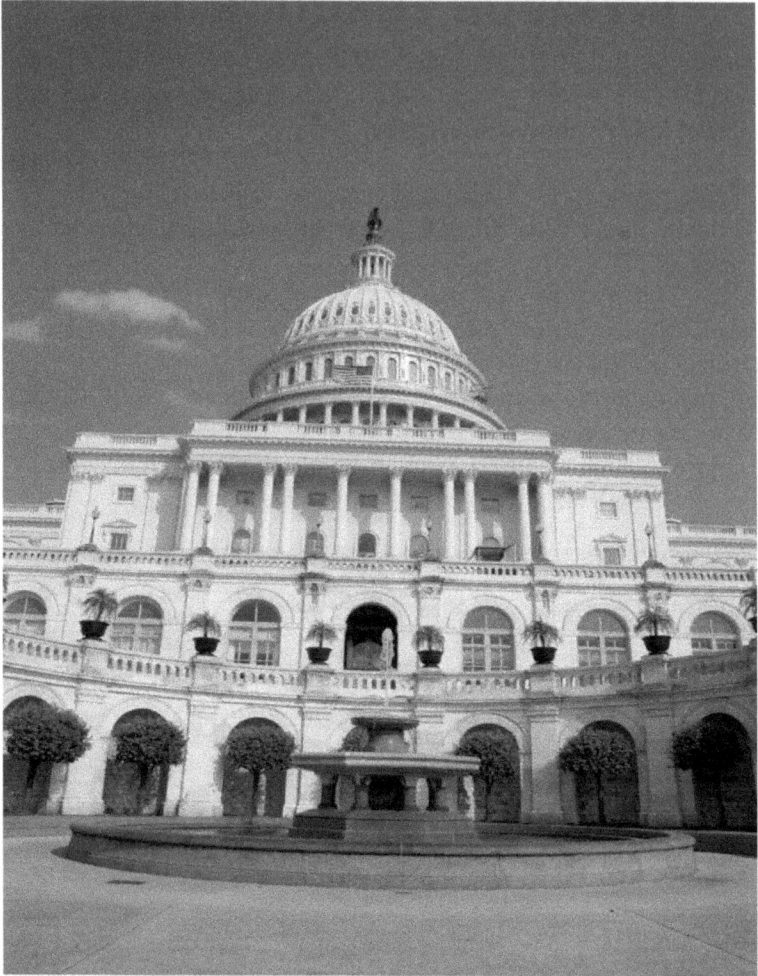

Close-up of the fountain before the Grand Marble Terrace at the rear of the Capital Building.

Miniature souvenir version of the US Capital Building (Right) where the laws are made and the Jefferson Memorial (left), honoring a great President.

INTRIGUE THROUGH TIME

Khepra the "Sun God" at the Entrance to the Cairo Museum of Egyptian Antiquities.

27.   Return to Cairo Museum

Lord Stanhope touched down at Cairo International Airport at 8:33 am. After Immigration and Customs, he decided to head directly to the Museum even before he checked into a hotel. Standing in line at the entrance waiting for the 10:00 O'clock opening, his mind kept racing back and forth between Mr. Mentuhotep and the necklace. As the doors opened, he entered and was spotted by an official.

FREDERICK MONDERSON

Champollion and Samuel Birch

Official: "Hello, Lord Stanhope, what brings you back so soon?"
Stanhope: "I'm concerned one of your important pieces may be a fake!"
Official: "Impossible! We have the tightest security here. Which piece do you think is compromised?"
Stanhope: "I would like to examine Lady Nekajai's necklace."
Official: "Sir, we have the highest respect for your knowledge and concern for our cultural history, but I don't see the need for this request. Besides, Lady Nekajai's necklace is one of the most valuable and highly guarded and regarded pieces in our collection. Nevertheless, I will allow you to examine the necklace."

Along with two guards, the official and Lord Stanhope removed the piece from its case. Within no time he began to inspect this most cherished piece. He looked at it over and over and concluded: 'Pure gold, authentically 18th Dynasty, Theban School, Thutmose I, Hatshepsut reign.' Looking at the official he said: "Your piece is genuine. It's the real McCoy!" Then he repeated himself, "18th Dynasty, Theban School, Thutmose I or Hatshepsut's reign."
Official: "That is what we concluded. Will that be all, Sir?"
Stanhope: "Yes. Certainly! Sorry about wasting your time."
Official: "I know your expertise is legendary, so I have to assume there's more to this than you're telling me."
Stanhope simply nodded his head, thinking, 'How true you are! How true you are!'
As he exited the Museum, he turned to admire names illustrated on the Cornice who have imprinted on the history and culture of ancient Egypt. These were, sort of, his predecessors.

INTRIGUE THROUGH TIME

Erik Monderson stands before the Sphinx in the Garden, before the entrance, to the Cairo Museum of Egyptian Antiquities.

FREDERICK MONDERSON

Mythical and actual names of personalities in Egyptian History - Osiris, Typhon, Horus, Menes, Athotis, Ousaphais, Miebais, Kaiechus, Binothris and some of the great minds who helped lay the foundation for the discipline of Egyptology and the correct telling of the *Story of Egypt* included – Zoega, Akerblad, A. Peyron, E. De Rouce, Th. Deveria, Chabas, Leemans, Nestor Lhote, and Prisse D'Avennes.

Kings of the Old and Middle Empires – Including Cheops, Chephren, Mycerinos, Anou, Ounas, Teti, Papi, Amenemhait, Ousirtasen and Kings of the New Kingdom and Later - Ahmosis, Amennothes, Thoutmosis, Hatshopsuit, Harmais, Sethosis, Ramesses, Menephthes and Shishak.

Psammetichus, Nechao, Apries, Amasis, Cambyses, Darius, Artaxerxes, Amyrtaeus, Nectanebo and Herodotus, Eratosthenes of Cyrenaicus, Manetho of Sebennyta and Horapollon Nilous.

INTRIGUE THROUGH TIME

Rulers of the Alexandrian and Graeco-Roman Age - Alexander, Ptolemaeus, Cleopatra, Caesar Augustus, Fl. Vespasianus, Ael. Hadrianus, Diocletianus, Theodosius, Justinianus; and, modern scholars who laid the foundation for the new discipline - Birch, Wilkinson, Hincks, Lepsius, Duemichen, Ebers, Goodwin, LePage-Renouf and Vassalli.

28.   Independence Day
State of Mind

Mentuhotep woke early Wednesday July 3, 1985. He thought of going for a walk across town. He had always traveled west across 59th Street. He had not gone east, so he thought he would explore that area since his Lady was not up as yet. His preparation routine completed, he headed down to the restaurant. Over coffee he checked The *Times*. Its headline read:

Wednesday July 3, 1985

Lead: "Pres. to Meet Gorbachev 2 Days in Fall in Geneva"
International: "Grymyko Made Soviet President by Gorbachev"
National: "Tennessee Prison Erupts"
Local: "New York's Top Court Rejects Conservator Rules."

Breakfast finished, he left the restaurant and encountered William in the lobby.

"Good morning, Sir. How are you today?"

"Fine, William" he said, "I am going for a walk in the opposite direction. What can I expect to find?"

William: "Well, Sir, nothing much really. You have Madison Avenue, Park Avenue, Lexington Avenue, 3rd Avenue, 2nd Avenue, 1st Avenue and then the Franklin Delano Roosevelt Highway, the FDR, which we rode coming back from Brooklyn. Nearby you will find the 59th Street Bridge and also the tram car to Roosevelt Island where there is a hospital for some kind of care. There are also a few hospitals on that side, including Sloane Kettering Hospital for Cancer Care. That is closer to 65th, or so, Street."

Mentuhotep: "Ok, William. Thanks. I just wanted to stretch my feet a little, that's all."

William: "Good Luck."

For the rest of the day, upon his return he lounged around with Fantegla, huddling, snuggling, a little hanky-panky, sipping Hennessy and reading his guide books. This is how they passed the day on the eve of the big national holiday. Later they went to dinner and returned for some cozying up.

The morning of July 4, 1985, Mentuhotep arose early and began reading one of his Egypt Guides. He looked at a photograph of *Deshret* or Deir el Bahari Temple. He wanted to be very familiar with the place near where his treasure lay. As he read further, he began to think 'how has the area changed?' He thought further, 'I must make a trip to do a survey of the area and to determine a plan of attack.' Just then Fantegla woke and they ordered room service for breakfast. The hotel delivered *The Times* and he quickly checked the lead stories.

INTRIGUE THROUGH TIME

United States Supreme Court with its magnificent colonnade and its composite capitals very much impressed Mentuhotep on his trip to Washington, DC.

Lead: "Shultz Suggests More Soviet Talks are a Possibility"
International: "China Releases a Catholic Priest who was Jailed Nearly 30 Years"
National: "CBS Trying to Block Turner Bid to Buy $1Billion of Their Own Stock"
Local: "Brother of Slain Student Indicted; Policeman Cleared in the Killing."

After their meal they laid back in bed and she told him Sarlinda and Kasheisha were coming, at about 1:00 pm, to take them to the African Street Festival at Boys and Girls High School on Fulton Street in Brooklyn.

Sidney the chauffeur stood outside the Plaza when Sarlinda and Kasheisha arrived. He phoned his mistress they had arrived and soon both she and Michael came down. One group of happy campers set out for Boys and Girls.

FREDERICK MONDERSON

Across 59th Street, round about Columbus Circle and again across 59th Street, then down 9th Avenue to 42nd Street and across to the West Side Highway. Passing the Intrepid Naval Museum and the Circle Line Pier, Fantegla said jokingly, "You remember?" and he responded "I do," looking at Sarlinda who blushed because she accidentally fell into his arms while they were on the middle deck, and on top of that she had passionately kissed him on the lips. Surprisingly, while alarmed, he had responded. After all, she was a beautiful woman in his embrace and Fantegla, somehow, seemed not to disapprove.

Soon they were past the World Trade Center, through the Tunnel and out passing the South Street Seaport, exiting the FDR North for the Brooklyn Bridge. Across the bridge they sped, exiting the ramp and left on Tillary Street past New York City Technical College, across Flatbush Avenue and on to Park Avenue then down Utica Avenue. Just before Fulton Street they got out and walked over to the Festival. The fee of $7.00 was paid by Sarlinda who bought the 4 tickets and then they had their hands stamped and entered the grounds.

For three hours they walked around examining sculpture, art, linen bags, books, and sampling food offered by merchants. Kasheisha had her face painted. They passed a tent that read: "Get your fortune told." No one seemed to want to look into the future. Next, they moved over to the music and listened intently. Michael could be observed tapping his feet to the beat of a popular song. After a while they grabbed their purchases, headed out the gate and rendezvous with Sidney, at this time out of his car, sipping a Coca Cola classic and chatting with a local. Soon they were on their way back to the Plaza.

Senator Williams had left to rendezvous with the Fleet Commander, Admiral Reynolds, on the afternoon of July 4th, 1985. When he arrived at the pier at the appointed hour, an escort was waiting. By launch to the carrier, request to come aboard, approved, the senator was ushered into the briefing room. Admiral Reynolds, his Executive Officer, Colonel Sanderson, as well as a frigate and two destroyer Commanders were joined by two Submarine Commanders. Naturally, because of Senator Williams' position as a member of the Defense and Foreign Relations Committees, as well as his hawkish position on American readiness and defense, he was allowed to be in on this high-level naval meeting. As a former naval commander himself, he understood the nature of the meeting and his role as a civilian.

Nevertheless, the meeting centered on the previous discussion held with the smaller group, the Senator's concerns and America's military readiness. Admiral Reynolds welcomed him, "Senator, we have reviewed your proposition. I'm sure you're familiar with everyone here."

Williams: "Gentlemen."

Reynolds: "Now that "Fleet Week" is over, we're all being sent on different assignments in different theaters of operations. My carrier group is heading back to the Eastern Mediterranean. The two submarines are heading to Western Europe. The destroyers are heading through the Panama Canal, across the Pacific and into the Persian Gulf. The significant understanding among us is that we make every commitment to keep our forces and people vigilant and in a state of readiness. We're all agreed we cannot be caught with our pants down in this age of uncertainty."

Williams: "Gentlemen, let me assure you, though Congress is in recess for the 4th of July, and soon for summer vacation, I want to assure you I will not fall asleep at the wheel. I'm going to Washington tomorrow, Thursday, to confer with the Secretary of Defense, Caspar Weinberger, the chairs of Foreign Relations, Armed Services and Appropriations. I spoke with two members of the Joint Chiefs and they agreed to ask their Chairman who will forward to the President, the need for a comprehensive review of our state of readiness."

Reynolds: "Very good, Senator. Gentlemen as I told you we can rely on the Senator to keep our torch burning. Therefore, we're all-in agreement, though we have our official and unofficial marching orders, we must stay in contact. I will be the liaison with the Senator and relay any new information that does not come through the official channels. We must rest assured that our group is monitoring developments that have a bearing on the defense of our nation and our people. Therefore, let me wish you all a successful tour, and God willing, we'll meet again."

All: "Hear. Hear. Hear."

FREDERICK MONDERSON

All: "God Bless America."

Senator Williams was on an early Thursday morning flight to Dulles Airport by 10:00 am. He headed straight to his office on Capitol Hill. He immediately began making phone calls and shaking up Washington by insisting our state of readiness is questionable. This position was very consistent with President Reagan's call for a greater military buildup. Challenges from the Soviet Union, China over Taiwan and the unsettling situation with the Arab-Israeli conflict require a different approach to our defense security concerns at home and abroad. Equally, "constructive engagement" with apartheid South Africa was also undermining our credibility as a moral force within the world community. These then became some of the issues the Senator and some of his supporters began to raise on the Hill.

Nonetheless, as budget negotiations began to take center stage, the President's call for a military buildup, domestic agendas began to suffer and coalitions emerged between democrats, liberals and grass roots organizations. They insisted welfare reforms, unemployment amidst prosperity, less government as opposed to it being a gadfly of social conscience, forming a safety net, union busting, and states' rights are antithetical to America's long-term viability. Our man, Senator Williams, nevertheless, was caught in the midst of all these new developments.

The International Trade Building named in President Reagan's honor.

INTRIGUE THROUGH TIME
29. Necklace Debacle and Eyes on Egypt

On the flight back to New York that Thursday, Lord Stanhope was now in a quandary. He had examined both necklaces and found them both to be genuine. The next day the old gang met. Ghafoor had returned from Los Angeles. He was seen as sad. His only daughter was in a terrible condition. This was not the same man who left for the hospital.

Mentuhotep woke that morning Friday, July 5th, 1985. He was asked to meet at Ghafoor's at 11:00 am. He showered, dressed and headed down to breakfast. His favorite waiter appeared with the menu and *The Times*. He slipped him a $20.00 tip.
"Thank you, Sir," he gratefully responded, then delivered the scrambled eggs, beef sausages, croissant and coffee.

The Times headlines read:

Lead: "OPEC Oil Ministers Meet amid Discord on Pricing Policy"
International: "Spain's leader Drops Top Aides in Big Shuffle"
National: "Private Hospitals are now Offering Health Insurance"
Local: "Puzzle in Brooklyn. The bizarre sinking of a 20-Block area."

Mentuhotep finished his meal, was still sipping his coffee and also reading *The Times*. His mind turned to the morning's meeting. He hoped it would be brief. He also thought it was time he had approached Lord Stanhope about the British passport. However, he was not sure how to bring it up. After all, this was a very respectable British Lord and you don't just go up to him and say: "Sir, can I have a British passport?"

His mind shifted back to his warm lovely companion still asleep. How she affects him! Her parents approve of their relationship since she has been very happy lately. In fact, at the party they treated him kindly. Mr. Somersett was very pleased with his purchase and equally pleased the way she stuck to him. Or was it the other way around? Nevertheless, Fantegla has in so many ways, replaced Nekajai in his thoughts and in his life. 'She is such a superb lover. One thing I can say for sure, her style of lovemaking is nowhere near times of old. This modern stuff is too much,' as he smiled.

As he finished his breakfast and left the restaurant, he saw William standing near the elevator chatting with Operator Gibsoni. He walked over and William approached.

"Good morning, Sir" he said.

"Good morning, William," Mentuhotep responded.

William: "Everything's set for Monday afternoon, Sir. I will meet you at 2:00 pm, Monday. We will go downtown to the New York Motor Vehicles office. There is a friend there who promises to expedite the process. You do have to take a photo there. However, while you won't get the license then, you will get a receipt saying the process is in motion.

Mentuhotep: "Very good, William. I'll meet you outside at 2:00 pm." Slipping him a $100.00 note he said: "Here, you take care of things. Give him what you think is fair. See you later." Then he exited the Plaza.

As he turned for Ghafoor it hit him. 'Why not ask Mr. Somersett to run interference with Lord Stanhope. He said ask him if I needed any type of help. That's it! Ask Mr. Somersett to speak to Lord Stanhope about the British passport!'

Within minutes Mentuhotep walked into Ghafoor's. The proprietor, Mr. Gray, Mr. Somersett, Mr. Wisenthal and Lord Stanhope were all there, talking.

Somersett: "Good Morning, Mr. Mentuhotep. I know you know everyone. We were just talking about Ghafoor's poor daughter stricken with a difficult neurological disease and it will take some time for her to recover."

Mentuhotep: "I'm very sorry to hear of your plight, Mr. Ghafoor. Naturally, one is always willing to help a friend at such challenging times. That's what friends are for. How can I help?"

Gray: "I suppose all that we can do is pray for the young lady."

Wisenthal: "So true."

INTRIGUE THROUGH TIME

Somersett: "Lord Stanhope, now that we have Mr. Mentuhotep here, can you bring us up to speed. Tell us what you found. I think the last question was, 'What's your next move?'"

Stanhope, looking directly at Mentuhotep said: "Quite frankly, gentlemen, I went to Cairo and examined the necklace of Princess Nekajai. I found it to be genuine. I found it had not been moved in any way. Even the impression of its laying in place had not been disturbed. What we have here gentlemen are two necklaces that are identical, that are genuine and both are traceable back to the same time in ancient Egypt."

Mentuhotep responded as if he had gotten a body slam, but his cool demeanor disguised it. Still, it was obvious, but the group thought he reacted to his name being called and realizing that he had come under suspicion, that they were talking about him. Nevertheless, he was not there, he was lost, he was elsewhere.

Mentuhotep heard a distant voice calling to him. "Michael! Michael! Michael!" It was Mr. Somersett. He seemed so distant. They were all embarrassed. They thought he reacted in this way because as honorable men, they treated him with suspicion. The universal guilt meant they owed him an apology.

In reality, Mentuhotep reacted to the name Nekajai. Lord Stanhope said he examined her necklace in the Cairo Museum. This took him back to the night of the banquet when his father Puyemre gave them both the necklaces. He thought about their good times; the flowers he sent her; and was jolted because he was on his way to meet her when he met the fateful accident.

After a while he came back to normal.

Stanhope: "Are you okay, old chap?"
Somersett: "Are you alright, son?"
Gray: "Ghafoor, let's have some tea or coffee."
Ghafoor: "Coming up!"
Wisenthal: "Mr. Mentuhotep, please let me apologize for the group for even initiating this line of inquiry. After all, we're dealing with an important issue here and it also involves lots of money."
Mentuhotep: "I understand, gentlemen. Apologies accepted."

FREDERICK MONDERSON

Ghafoor brought the coffee and the discussion shifted to his daughter.

Golden Necklace and blue stone in the form of a Lotus flower.

Gray: "So, how's the young lady?"

Ghafoor: "She is in a semi-coma. She recognized me. We held hands. Two neurological experts are flying in from Europe to examine the tests they took and to give us a new diagnosis. The reality is she has to undergo extensive rehabilitative therapy and they recommended a long-term facility, the Dr. Susan Smith McKinney in Brooklyn. It will be easier on me not having to fly out to Los Angeles."

Wisenthal: "That's good."

This distraction aside, all eyes and thoughts remained on Mentuhotep. Perhaps now he may not want to offer the necklace or the dagger for sale.

Wisenthal: "That original question, Lord Stanhope, 'What is your next move?'"

Stanhope: "I must return to Egypt. I will have to investigate the existence of two identical necklaces. I will consult the Museum's Library to see what I can find out."

Mentuhotep: "I would like to travel to Egypt to see this other necklace that has caused all this controversy."

Somersett: "That's a good idea. It may take your mind off the unfortunate situation." With that the meeting broke up and they started to leave.

"One moment, Lord Stanhope," said Ghafoor.

"Yes, Ghafoor" he said, "How can I help you?"

Ghafoor: "I need to speak with you for a moment." Taking him aside he said: "I'm holding a check for $25,000.00 for services rendered by you."

Stanhope: "Very good, I will spend it wisely."

Mr. Somersett had his car and chauffeur outside. As he entered the vehicle, Michael approached.

Somersett: "Sorry about all this, son. How's Fantegla? Her mother and I have great confidence that you are an honorable man. Remember, if there's anything I can do for you, please do not hesitate to ask."

Mentuhotep: "In fact, there is something you can do for me, Sir."

Somersett: "What is that?"

Mentuhotep: "Well, Sir, fact is I lost my travel documents and I need a passport. A British passport will do, but I am afraid to ask Lord Stanhope."

Somersett: "I see. Let me talk to him. Here he comes now. You go. I will call you at the hotel about 5:00 pm."

As Stanhope emerged, Somersett said: "Samuel, can I have a word with you?"

Stanhope: "Why sure, my good friend."

Somersett: "Let me get right to the point. Mr. Mentuhotep wants to go to Egypt to see that necklace."

Stanhope: "OK."

Somersett: "But he needs a British passport."

Stanhope: "What?"

Somersett: "It will make things easier for him."

Stanhope: "So you want me to get him a British passport?"

Somersett: "Yes. We owe him something of this magnitude because of the embarrassment. He acted in good faith throughout."

Stanhope: "It's very difficult and expensive to get a British passport for a non-British citizen."

Somersett: "So what are we talking about?"

Stanhope: "Between $25,000.00 and $50,000.00. I have lots of palms to grease."

Somersett: "Let's set the bar a little higher. Let's say $100.000.00. If he does not pay, I will. We owe it to him! After all, if there's any more jewelry, we want the inside track. Don't you agree?"

Stanhope: "I most certainly do. Let me get back to you. Have him give me two photographs with the signed application and I will work on it. I may have an application in my valise. Let me check." After a while, he said: "Here we are. Get this back to me as soon as possible. I'm leaving for Egypt tomorrow evening. If I have it with me, I can have it issued in Cairo."

Somersett: "No. It will be best if issued from New York. That will explain his first travel using this document."

Stanhope: "Let's say we meet again on Friday. I'm on a turnaround flight and will be back Thursday."

Somersett: "Very good. Have a safe trip. Very good work you do, my friend."

Stanhope: "Thanks."

Saturday morning the young couple rose early and came down to breakfast. *The Times* stayed focused on the continuing hijack situation and other issues. He and Fantegla planned to spend the day

INTRIGUE THROUGH TIME

with the Somersetts. They were to drive up to Martha's Vineyard, Massachusetts. Sidney collected the Somersetts and away they went. They stopped at Hyannis Port and then drove back to New York. It was an exciting day filled with laughter and joy.

Lord Stanhope arrived in Egypt and headed to the Cairo Museum. Upon arrival he was ushered to the library, "To check something." Two hours after checking the records of the early 18th Dynasty, he was shocked to realize, Lord Puyemre, Vizier to Queen Hatshepsut had two necklaces made for his son Mentuhotep and the Lady Nekajai. The necklaces were given to them at the Queen's Banquet. Within a week or so, the son had an accident and died. Mummified, he was buried in the Valley of the Nobles.

'So now it makes sense,' he exclaimed quietly. 'Therefore, Mentuhotep is a nobleman who can possibly trace his background and family heritage to that Vizier. How remarkable! No wonder he claims it is a family heirloom. I guess I must help him get back to his country. Perhaps in the long run he may be of assistance to me.'

Upon his return Stanhope kept his promise and secured the British Passport for Michael Puyemre Mentuhotep. Mr. Somersett paid the sum of $100,000.00 and they felt the embarrassment was finally satisfied. Much of what Stanhope found out he kept to himself, thinking, 'you can't divulge all you know.'

An assortment of amulets in gold and precious stones.

INTRIGUE THROUGH TIME
30.   Return to My Homeland

Soon Michael had arranged a trip to Egypt with Fly by Night Tours. The itinerary of fifteen days, while in Cairo, called for visits to the Cairo Museum of Egyptian Antiquities, the Pyramids of Ghizeh, the Step Pyramid at Sakkara and the Memphis Museum. They would stay at the Mena House Garden Hotel in the capital, and the possibility existed they would have a few additional visits, that would be optional. Soon they landed in Cairo, and with Immigration and Customs cleared, they were driven through the street of Cairo to the Hotel just down the street from the Pyramids.

The first day they paid an early visit to the Pyramids of Ghizeh. Mentuhotep was surprised to see how, since his "last visit," the Pyramid "Khufu Gleams," had suffered so tremendously. The members of his group chose to enter but he chose to walk around and view the building from the outside as if paying respect for the sanctity of the king's final resting place. He noticed the Pyramid Boat Museum and suggested they visit it when the group assembled. After the Boat Museum, they moved to the panoramic view of the Pyramids in the distance. After this they headed to the Step Pyramid at Sakkara.

Sphinx of Ghizeh, thought to have the face of Pharaoh Khafre of the 4th Dynasty but others think this unquestionably Negro face may be as old as 10,000 years. Michael remembered this figure of a statue.

FREDERICK MONDERSON

Entering with their tickets at the Sakkara enclosure, and while everyone was amazed at this ancient African architectural wonder, he stood motionless. He seemed to be saying a prayer perhaps thanking the gods for bringing him back to this holy site, he had visited previously. He was thankful it was still standing and he had the extraordinary privilege of being able to stand and admire it one more time. He thought of the first time the Vizier Puyemre brought him here, as a lad, while he was on an official visit of inspection. They never got far beyond the Great Court.

Erik Monderson stands within this, the earliest constructed colonnade that entrances the Step-Pyramid at Sakkara, built by Imhotep for Pharaoh Zoser, 2600 B.C., that Mentuhotep visited with his Queen more than 3500 years ago and thrilled to see it still stands.

INTRIGUE THROUGH TIME

On the way back from Sakkara they stopped at a Carpet Factory and some people made purchases. Then they stopped at a restaurant for lunch, and finally a stop at the Memphis Museum to see remains of a once great city he knew.

Visitor in the Great Court of the Step Pyramid at Sakkara, first seen by Mentuhotep more than 3500 years ago.

The Cobra Frieze still stands in the Great Court at Sakkara.

FREDERICK MONDERSON

Cairo Museum of Egyptian Antiquities where Mentuhotep was flabbergasted at seeing a statue of his Queen, Hatshepsut, so well preserved, almost lifelike.

The third day they visited the Cairo Museum of Egyptian Antiquities. There were throngs of people coming and going. Many were intrigued by the treasures of Tutankhamon. He observed the two black statues of the boy king at the hall's entrance; the boats; ushabtis; walking sticks; chairs; jewelry; mask; shrines, etc. He saw the chariot of Thutmose IV and paused to admire it. However, the greatest thrill he experienced was on the first floor in the New Kingdom section. There, there, surrounded by scores of admiring people, lay the necklace of Princess Nekajai. Inching his way

INTRIGUE THROUGH TIME

forward, he stopped dead in his tracks and a tear came to his eyes. A nearby kid tugged his mother's hand and speechlessly pointed to the grown man crying. He saw him but thought, 'If you only knew, sonny. If you only knew!' He stood there with his hands on his chest, seeming to make philosophical and perhaps spiritual contact with Nekajai through his necklace; and, by sending a telepathic message to connect with her through the other necklace. 'Perhaps she could see and understand,' he thought. He also thought of his parents and his sister.

On the way out they visited the Museum Shop and he picked up a popular Guide Book. Leaving the Museum, they headed to the bus, for the ride across town to the hotel. Throughout, he kept thinking of Nekajai and being thankful, maybe she too had reincarnated in Fantegla! Together again, they would enjoy what they were unable to in the past existence. Now they would live life and be doing things he was never able to do in his past existence. They would be happy and perhaps provide those grandchildren his parents were never able to see.

The next morning at the domestic airport, the Egypt Air flight from Cairo to Luxor took off and landed within two hours. The group was housed at the Sonesta Hotel.

Modern day entrance to the Temple of Karnak. Still, this was different to Mentuhotep's day when the entrance was through today's Fourth and Fifth Pylons.

FREDERICK MONDERSON

Six o'clock wake up, breakfast and by 7:30 and they were off to Karnak Temple. Arriving there by 8:00 and with tickets secured, the guide began the tour. Through the Avenue of Croix-or Ram-headed Sphinxes and beyond the Ethiopian First Pylon, into the Bubastite Court, they observed to the left a Kiosk of Seti II, dedicated to Amun, Mut and Khonsu, the Theban Triad. In the middle of this Great Court stands an altar and sphinx of Tutankhamon, a Kiosk of Taharka, colonnades north and south, and Temple of Rameses III in the Court's southeast corner.

Gate-keepers to the Temple of Karnak where Mr. Mentuhotep was surprised to see the temple's expansion with a Great Pylon and Avenue of Sphinxes added "after his last visit."

Next is the Second Pylon built by Horemheb and Rameses I. Then they entranced the magnificent one hundred and thirty-four-column

INTRIGUE THROUGH TIME

Great Hypostyle Hall, built by Rameses I, Seti I and finished and decorated by Rameses II. Beyond this is the Third Pylon of Amenhotep III who also erected the Processional Colonnade of the Hypostyle Hall. A Central Court stands between the Third and Fourth Pylons where Thutmose I erected two obelisks. The Fourth and Fifth Pylons were built by Thutmose I. This Court, with one of two remaining standing Obelisks of Thutmose I, then the Osiride Statues of Thutmose III and Hatshepsut's remaining obelisk as well as Thutmose III's Sixth Pylon; all, stood before the Sanctuary or "Holy of Holies."

Mentuhotep was pleased to view the two obelisks of the Queen's father Thutmose I (left) and Hatshepsut (right) herself, as well as ruins of the Processional Colonnade and other columns of the Hypostyle Hall at Karnak Temple that were added after his time.

Beyond this most sacred place, the Middle Kingdom Court entrances Thutmose III's Festival Temple, the *Akh Menu*. Much of this area is enclosed in Rameses II's "Girdle Wall." South of the wall is the Sacred Lake and beside this Brother Abdul's "Coca Cola Temple." Between the Girdle Wall and the Sacred Lake near the "Coca Cola Temple," Taharka the Ethiopian, built his temple designed to celebrate the Decan or Ten Day Festival. Lying near the

FREDERICK MONDERSON

Sacred Lake, the Guide pointed to Queen Hatshepsut's fallen obelisk whose upper portions show the lady in close proximity to the God Amon. Reversing their path, it was on to Luxor Temple.

At the Temple's entrance Mr. Mentuhotep's Guide, Jiusi Cummerson, makes a point of exclamation to Officials who guard the portal.

Happy to see these relics of his Queen, the colonnade made Mentuhotep really nostalgic. He remembered his years as a builder, even though only the first or inner section of Karnak was finished in his time. When he visited Luxor, this was not the smaller temple in front of which Queen Hatshepsut had built her Kiosk to the Theban Triad.

INTRIGUE THROUGH TIME

Ruins of the decorated ceiling and columns of the Hypostyle Hall in the Temple of Karnak. Window gratings above are for the Clerestory that let light into the Hall.

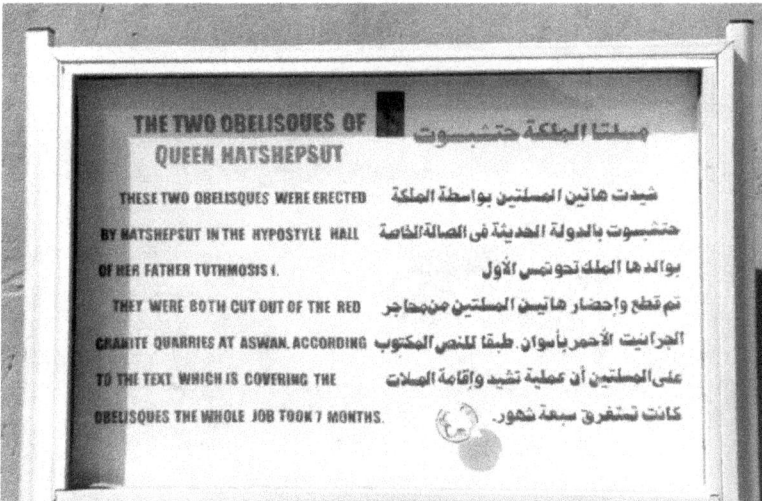

THE TWO OBELISQUES OF
QUEEN HATSHEPSUT

THESE TWO OBELISQUES WERE ERECTED
BY HATSHEPSUT IN THE HYPOSTYLE HALL
OF HER FATHER TUTHMOSIS I.

THEY WERE BOTH CUT OUT OF THE RED
GRANITE QUARRIES AT ASWAN. ACCORDING
TO THE TEXT WHICH IS COVERING THE
OBELISQUES THE WHOLE JOB TOOK 7 MONTHS.

مسلتا الملكة حتشبسوت

شيدت هاتين المسلتين بواسطة الملكة
حتشبسوت بالدولة الحديثة فى الصالة الخاصة
بوالدها الملك تحوتمس الأول

تم قطع وإحضار هاتين المسلتين من محاجر
الجرانيت الأحمر بأسوان. طبقا للنص المكتوب
على المسلتين أن عملية تشيد وإقامة المسلات
كانت تستغرق سبعة شهور.

Mentuhotep was thrilled to see this sign of his Queen's obelisks.

Our Hero was thrilled to see part of the second of his Queen's obelisks, as it lay beside the Sacred Lake, as a native Egyptian, Brother Abdul, passes nearby.

Brother Nasser, in traditional Egyptian attire, stands near Hatshepsut's fallen Obelisk beside the Sacred Lake.

INTRIGUE THROUGH TIME

Seti I Presents a "Table of Offerings" to Ptah, God of artisans in Karnak's Hypostyle Hall, northern section.

Mentuhotep was ecstatic to see the Sanctuary, called the "Red Chapel," he helped build for the Queen as part of her efforts praising Amon-Ra, "King of the Gods."

Seti I stands before Amon-Ra in feathers while holding scepter and ankh in Karnak.

Beyond the Obelisk and entrance pylon at the Temple of Luxor, Michael broke into an exasperated smile just to see his Queen's Kiosk to the "Theban Triad" still standing, though in changed surroundings.

As he approached, from the west and looking south, the succeeding colonnades brought tears of joy to his eyes and joyful feelings to his heart. This site took him back to Washington, D.C., that city of colonnades! Now he could see the connection; the origins of

INTRIGUE THROUGH TIME

American governmental, civic and domestic architectural history and the source of all of its knowledge lies here in North Africa, in Egypt, in the Northeast African Nile Valley, in its temples and civic and social structures.

Passing beyond the Pylon with scenes from Rameses' *Battle at Kadesh*, they entered into the Court of Rameses II, the "Ramessean Front." This court, with an illustration of the Temple of Luxor on the inner face of the South western wall is a popular tourist site. It depicts a procession of the sons of Rameses II and priests leading fat cows to the Temple of Luxor. This Temple of Luxor was designed for Amon to celebrate the Opet Festival. As such it was called the southern temple, *Southern Isut*, or Amon's Temple of the Opet festival.

Luis Casado before the entrance to Temple of Luxor with standing statues replaced and one obelisk and one seated statue before the Pylon. Reliefs on the Pylon tell of the events of the Battle of Kadesh fought by Rameses II a conflict fought after Mentuhotep's time.

On the left as you enter and above the north-east corner of Rameses' Peristyle Court is the Mosque of Luxor's Patron Saint, the Syrian Abu Haggag. On the right of this is the Bark Shrine of Hatshepsut dedicated to the Theban Triad. He remembered it well for he had

229

been there many times. From between the column, particularly on the left as visitors enter, statues seem to emerge from between the columns. There are altars remaining *in Situ* in the Court's center. Beyond this Court is the Processional Colonnade of Amenhotep III which also bears the names of Seti I, Horemhab and Tutankhamon who repaired it. Walls enclosing the columns on both sides depict the events of the procession from Karnak to celebrate the Opet Festival and the return journey. Stairs lead to a higher-level Court of Amenhotep III with papyrus bundle calyx capital columns. This particular feature shows a fundamental aspect of Egyptian temples; as one enters the inner sanctum, the floor rises and the roof lowers so as to arrive at the highest point in the structure, where the god rests. This magnificent court attracts untold numbers of photographers who are fascinated by the play of light and shade on the columns, as the sun passes overhead.

Striding statues seem to emerge from between the columns in the "Ramessean Front" of the Temple of Luxor. Altars also adorn this Peristyle Court.

Next is the Hypostyle Hall, redecorated by Roman troops who removed some of its columns. Then there is a chamber of the Divine King Amenhotep III; a second antechamber; and birth and coronation rooms. There is finally the Sanctuary or "Holy of Holies," rebuilt by Alexander the Great, after it was wrecked by attacking hordes. At this point, its retrace steps to board the buses for the ride back to the hotel.

INTRIGUE THROUGH TIME

Looking west towards the Nile River at the double row of clustered papyrus bud bundle columns in the Court of Amenhotep III, a bonanza for photographers.

The third day they crossed the river to visit the Valley of the Kings and later their mortuary temples. They were given three tombs in the Valley of the Kings in their option. He chose the Tombs of Seti I, Rameses III and Tutankhamon. These tombs he had read a great deal about. They were the largest except for Tutankhamon, the smallest in the valley, most colorful and so most popular. The Guide in the Valley was a female named Erica Greenhouse, on loan from Chicago House in Luxor. She was very knowledgeable and gave rather extensive descriptions of the tombs of Seti I and Rameses III.

FREDERICK MONDERSON

Mr. Mentuhotep stopped for lunch at a popular Restaurant on the West Bank and shared a joke with two Egyptian officials. Mr. Monsoor (left) and Mr. Ibrahim (right) who were ecstatic about something Michael said.

Seti's was the largest tomb in the valley, very well preserved. The Sculptures: "In the *First Passage* consist of lines of hieroglyphics relating to the King Sethi I, or Osirei, 'the beloved of Ptah,' who was the father of Rameses II, and the occupant of this tomb. In the staircase which succeeds it are on one side thirty-seven, on the other thirty-nine genii of various forms; among which a figure represented with a stream of tears issuing from his eyes is remarkable from having the (Coptic) word *rimi*, 'lamentation,' in the hieroglyphic above."

"In the *Second Passage* are the boats of Kneph; and several descending planes, on which are placed the valves of doors, probably referring to the descent of Amenti. The goddess of Truth or Justice stands at the lower extremity. In the small chamber over

INTRIGUE THROUGH TIME

the pit the king makes offerings to different gods, Osiris being the principal deity. Hathor, Horus, Isis, and Anubis, are also introduced."

"On the pillars of the *First Hall* the monarch stands in the presence of various divinities; who seem to be receiving him after his death. One of the most interesting subjects here is a procession of four different people, of red, white, black, and again white complexions, four by four, followed by Ra, 'the sun.' The four red figures are Egyptians, designated under the name *rot*, meaning 'mankind;' the next, a white race, with blue eyes, long bushy beards, and clad in a short dress, are a northern nation, with whom the Egyptians were long at war, and appear to signify the nations of the northland; as the Negroes (called *Nehsi*) the southland; and the four others, also a white people, with a pointed beard, blue eyes, feathers in their hair, and crosses or other devices about their persons, and dressed in long flowing robes, the east."

"On the end wall of this hall is a fine group, remarkable as well for the elegance of its drawing as for the richness and preservation of the coloring. The subject is the introduction of the king, by Horus, into the presence of Osiris and Hathor."

View of Luxor Temple's Colonnade in the Court of Amenhotep III, from the street on the east side near the entrance to the Mosque of Abu Haggag.

FREDERICK MONDERSON

INTRIGUE THROUGH TIME

Majestic Processional Colonnade of Amenhotep III with seven pairs of calyx capital columns at the Temple of Luxor. Inner walls at fore and aft of the colonnade (east and west) depict events of the "Opet Festival," the purpose for building the Temple of Luxor.

"The subjects in the succeeding *Passages* refer mostly to the liturgies or ceremonies performed to the deceased monarch. In the *Square Chamber* beyond them the king is seen in the presence of the deities Hathor, Horus, Anubis, Isis, Osiris, Nephthys and Ptah. The 'Liturgy of Ra,' which occurs on the passage of walls of this top, as well as in other royal tombs in this valley, has been translated, and is worthy of study."

"The *Grand Hall* contains numerous subjects, among which are a series of mummies, each in its own repository, whose folding-doors are thrown open. It is probable that all the parts of these catacombs refer to different states through which the deceased passed, and the various mansions of Hades or Amenta."

After some forty minutes they emerged from the Tomb of Seti I, amazed but very enlightened. The temperature was different in there also. The Guide explained this is what has helped preserve the decorations even though visitors have not been kind to it leaving their marks of graffiti. Then they were off to the second tomb, that of Rameses III. Their reason for this is that the lines for

Tutankhamon were too long and they reasoned by the time they did Rameses III; it would get shorter.

Erika explained the same protocol applied to this as the previous tomb. Neither touching the wall nor leaving any unwanted evidence within. Then they entered:

THE TOMB OF RAMESES III

She explained: "The Tomb of Rameses III is commonly called Bruce's Tomb. It was discovered by the Traveler Bruce. It is also called *The Harper's Tomb*. This name is derived from the famous picture in one of the chambers of the men playing the harp. The execution of the sculpture is inferior to that in No. Seventeen [Sethi] but the nature of the subjects of this tomb is more interesting."

In its plan, it's a little smaller than Seti's Tomb. Very much defaced: "The subjects in the first passage, after the recess to the right, are similar to those of Seti's and are supposed to relate to the descent to Amenta. The figure of Truth, and the other groups in connection with that part of them, is placed in a square niche. The character of the four people in the first hall differs slightly from those of the former tomb."

"Four blacks, clad in African dresses, being substituted instead of the Egyptians, though the same name, *Rot*, is introduced before them."

"*Left Side* (on entering), *First Chamber*. Here we have kitchen scenes. The principal groups, though much defaced, may yet be recognized. Some are engaged in slaughtering oxen, and cutting up the joints, which are put into cauldrons on a tripod placed over a wood fire. In the lower line a man is employed in cutting a leather strap he holds with his feet."

"The *Second chamber* merely contains emblems and deities. In the *Third chamber* are birds, and some productions of Egypt, as geese and quails, eggs, pomegranates, grapes, with other fruits and herbs, among which last is the *ghulga,* or *Periploca sycamore* of Linnaeus' classification. This plant resembles a form of ivy, which is unknown in Egypt. The figures in the lower line are of the god Nilus."

"The principal figures of the *Last chamber* are two harpers playing on instruments of not inelegant form before the god Moui, or Hercules of the Greek. From these the tomb receives its name. One (if not both) of the minstrels is blind."

"Right side (on entering), first *chamber.* Several boats are seen with squared checkered sails. Some have spacious cabins and others only a seat near the mast. They are richly painted, and loaded with ornaments. Those in the lower lines have the mast and yarn lowered over the cabin."

"The *second chamber* contains various arms and warlike implements of the Egyptians. These include knives, quilted helmets, spears, daggers, quivers, bows, arrows, falchions, coats of mail, darts, clubs, and standards. On either side of the door is a black cow with the headdress of Hathor, one accompanied by hieroglyphics signifying the North, the other those of the South. These symbols intimate that these are the legends of Upper and Lower Egypt. The blue color of some of the weapons suffices to prove them to have been of steel."

"The *third chamber* has chairs of the most elegant form, covered with rich drapery, rightly ornamented, and in admirable taste. The beauty of Egyptian furniture is demonstrated here. It shows that at the time of the XXth Dynasty the Egyptians were greatly advanced in the arts of civilization and the comforts of domestic life. Displayed here are sofas, couches, vases of porcelain and pottery, copper utensils, caldrons, rare woods, printed stuffs, leopard-skins, baskets of a very neat and graceful shape, and basins and ewers, whose designs vie with the productions of the cabinet-maker, complete the interesting series of these paintings."

"The *fourth chamber* contains agricultural scenes. It shows the inundation of the Nile passing through the canals, sowing and reaping wheat, and a grain which from its height and round head appears to be the *doora* or sorghum, as well as the flowers of the country. Still, however successful the Egyptians may have been in seizing the character of animals, they failed in the art of drawing trees and flowers, and their colored plants would perplex the most profound botanist."

"In the *fifth chamber* are different forms for the god Osiris having various attributes."

"In the *sixth chamber* are rudders and sacred emblems." Greek graffiti indicate the tomb was open during the time of the Ptolemies.

After this they moved to the Rest House and refreshed a bit. The heat of the Valley had begun to take its toll and refreshments were in order. Then they joined the much-shortened line for Tutankhamon.

When it came to Tutankhamon's small but popular tomb the Guide Erika simply said: "Since most of the treasure found in this tomb is in the Cairo Museum which you saw, I will simply allow you to peruse it on your own. So many people come here to see and try to understand how so much treasure could be found in such a small tomb." The word "treasure" hit a note with Mentuhotep and he wondered if he would get a chance to inspect his ancient hiding place. After this third tomb was finished, it was time to return to the bus and make the trip out and around the Valley to visit Deir el Bahari Temple of Queen Hatshepsut.

As an afterthought she said, "Of course, there is a short cut for the hardy among you who can cross over the mountain. This trip does give you a 'Bird's Eye View' of the temple and surrounding area." Just then our Hero saw his chance and took it. He said: "I would love to cross over the mountain and get a good photo of the temple from that height."
"Well," she responded, "I could get you a Guide but you would have to pay him. That is not part of the tour itinerary. In addition, there is a risk but you look sufficiently fit to make the trek."
"That's not a problem," he said.

At this point Erika called over to one of the Guides she knew who was sitting in the Rest House. "This is Jiusi Cummerson, an

FREDERICK MONDERSON

experienced Guide," she said to him. "Jiusi, this is Mr. Mentuhotep. He wants to crossover to get a photo from the 'Bird's Eye View.'"

Jiusi: "Pleased to meet you, Sir. There is no better Guide," he said. Continuing, he added, "I will not set a price but leave it to your discretion."

Mentuhotep: "OK. Let's see how well you perform." Then they were off, as the others headed for the bus.

Outside the Sonesta Hotel in Luxor stands Tourist Guide Jiusi Cummerson who took Mentuhotep across the mountain to view the temple from the "Bird's Eye View."

INTRIGUE THROUGH TIME

Retracing their steps and passing signs of several tombs, they began the ascent of the mountain. As they climbed higher the Valley seemed to get hotter; yet still, they climbed. Almost to the top along the route a young man stood selling cold bottled water. This was indeed a luxury at this point and naturally cost more than the bottled water one can buy elsewhere, in the streets, but particularly in the hotel. It was, however, worth it to help cool the heat.

As Mentuhotep and Jiusi sat there sipping the cool refreshing water, they looked back at the route they came.

Jiusi: "From here you get a panoramic view of the Valley, its roads leading to the various tombs and a good view of the Rest House. There is talk of moving the Rest House in the event there may be other tombs in the spot where it is."
Mentuhotep: "This is such a wonderful view."

.Then they turned and began the trek across the difficult terrain of the mountain. After a rather hard trek they arrived on the other side. The Nile in the distance came into view. The green banks juxtaposed to the desert made a striking contrast.

Soon the route of the buses came into view and as they came across the top, the outer reaches of the temple came into view.

"Wow," thought our Hero. Even though he had visited the temple in ancient times, he had never been to the mountain top. Then he began to make out the First Court, First Ramp and the 11th Dynasty temple of Mentuhotep, beside that of Hatshepsut. This made him remember his namesake. He thought, 'My father, Vizier Puyemre named me after the famous 11th Dynasty Monarch who united Upper and Lower Kemet (Egypt) and established the Middle Kingdom. This structure is also the prototype of the Queen's temple which my supervisor Senmut copied but added greatly to in terms of space, lines and beautification.' After all, this temple is where he began his apprenticeship as an architect.

FREDERICK MONDERSON

Jiusi: "You have not seen anything as yet, Sir. There is a better view still to come."
Mentuhotep: "Lead the way," as he began snapping pictures.

And so, they traversed the path heading to the 'Bird's Eye View.' Just then they saw a red building on top of the mountain.

Now defaced with graffiti, this building served as residence of archaeologists when the Temple was cleared in the 1890s.

Jiusi: "That was the residence of an official who cleared the temple nearly a hundred years ago. It is not now used. Sometimes rich Americans come here, rent it and stay, claiming they want the quiet of the mountain to contemplate. I once brought a wealthy American from Chicago named Peter Stephenson. He spent fourteen days there."
Mentuhotep's active mind now saw his opening and took it.
Mentuhotep: "Can you still rent it?" he asked.
Jiusi: "I'm sure," he said, "But they want a lot of money claiming the quiet therapy of the mountain is worth much more than the cost of a room in a busy hotel."
Mentuhotep: "Who do you see about that?"
Jiusi: "The Local Council has an office that handles such matters in conjunction with the Tourist Board. Personally, I think, as long as

you pay the asking price, they have no objection. The rental fee helps in the upkeep, repairs and so on."

Mentuhotep: "OK. It's good to know."

Jiusi: "There! The temple! Let's move a little further out."

'Wow!' Mentuhotep thought, this is wonderful.

Mentuhotep uttered aloud: "This is a fantastic view."

Jiusi: "This spot is called the 'Bird's Eye View.' You can make out the important parts of the temple. There you have the First Court, First Ramp and Lower Colonnade; the Second Court, Second Ramp and Middle Colonnade; then there's the Upper Terrace Colonnade and closer to the mountain, the Upper Court with the Sanctuary up against the mountain base. As we begin the descent the temple's view gets even better."

While Jiusi kept pointing out more features, Osiride statues of the Queen, Mentuhotep kept thinking 'this residence is ideal for me.'

The Temple of Hatshepsut at Deir el Bahari, from the "Bird's Eye View." From left, First Ramp and Lower Colonnade in the First Court; Second Ramp and Middle Colonnade in the Second Court; the Hathor Shrine just left of the south half of the Middle Colonnade with the Middle Kingdom Temple of Mentuhotep II further on; just barely peeping out at the northern end or right of the Middle Colonnade is the Anubis Shrine. The Upper Terrace with remaining Osiride Statues of the Queen gives entrance to the Upper Court with its Hypostyle Colonnade fronting the "Holy of Holies" against the mountain wall.

Mentuhotep kept snapping pictures as any tourist would. However, his keen eyes and active mind kept looking and thinking. Soon they began the descent. The group by now had arrived at the temple's entrance and kept scanning the mountain to see if they had made it across. Soon they were spotted and you could hear a cheer. They soon started snapping pictures of them coming down the mountain. The group was really happy to see them since there was some risk in the journey across. Once they had reached the level of the temple, given his ticket he moved to enter.

Turning to Jiusi, he thanked him exceedingly and paid him $100.00 American dollars. This was much more than the trip was worth but our hero was thinking ahead. Jiusi, very pleased, said: "Sir, if there is anything you ever need, please give me a call. Here is my card." And he was off. Then they entered the temple.

As Mentuhotep surveyed the mountainside, the Temple began to take shape in the distance.

First Erika took them to the Punt Colonnade and then the Hathor Shrine. She crossed the Second Ramp and visited the "Birth Colonnade" where the Queen had her "virgin birth" recorded next to the Anubis Shrine. Further north, lay the unfinished Northern Colonnade. They could get no further, the sun was getting hotter and the ascent of the second Ramp to the Upper Terrace was blocked. A Polish Archaeological Team was doing repairs to the

INTRIGUE THROUGH TIME

Upper Terrace and Upper Court where the "Holy of Holies" is located against the mountain.

Another image of the Queen that escaped the destroyer's hand with minimal damage.

Retracing their steps, they returned to the Bus and were whisked back to the river for the trip across. Boarding another bus, they were

FREDERICK MONDERSON

returned to the hotel, tired, hot, but very satisfied with the day's outing.

This was a familiar scene to Mentuhotep as he tried to remember his days as Commander of the Imperial Guard, particularly while visiting the temple with the Queen.

The next day was an off-day. Mentuhotep came to breakfast since he is an early riser and to his surprise, Jiusi showed up.
"Hello, Sir" he said.
Mentuhotep: "How are you today? What brings you here?"
Jiusi: "Well, Sir, you were so generous to me yesterday, I thought I may be able to show you around some on this your day-off."
Mentuhotep: "What do you have in mind?"
Jiusi: "In the Valley of the Nobles, the Tombs of Sennufer and of Vizier Rekhmara are open. Perhaps we can do one."
Mentuhotep: "Did you say Vizier Rekhmara?"
Jiusi: "Yes, Sir. That is what I said, but if you want to do Sennufer instead, that's OK. There will be no charge for my services, but you do have to buy a ticket and perhaps tip the keeper."
Mentuhotep: "OK. As soon as I finish my breakfast we can be on the way. Do you have a boat?"
Jiusi: "It's all arranged."

INTRIGUE THROUGH TIME

Mentuhotep, finishing his breakfast, said: "Let's go."

They took a cab to the river and boarded the felucca "Nile Lounge."

Jiusi: "This is Abdul; he will take us across the river and wait for you to be brought back. Fifty Egyptian pounds will be sufficient."
Abdul: "Pleased to meet you, Sir. I heard so much about you from my friend. It's so nice to meet nice Americans.
Mentuhotep: "Well, I'm Egyptian. My parents are Egyptian, I'm just from America."
Abdul: "America is Number One."
Mentuhotep: "Yes, that is true."

And so, they began to cross the river. However, after a while, Mentuhotep began to think. 'Imagine the tomb of Vizier Rekhmara. I wonder if there is one for my father. Nevertheless, the thought of visiting a tomb of one who held the office of my father is very special for me.' Soon they were across and took another taxi to the Valley of the Nobles.

At the ticket booth they purchased "Ten Egyptian Pounds" tickets and headed for the tomb. Mentuhotep fumbled and Jiusi slipped the keeper 10 Egyptian pounds with the compliments of the American. This was indeed a marvelous tomb, similar to that of his father Puyemre.

THE TOMB OF VIZIER REKHMARA

"The Tomb of Rekhmara - is by far the most curious of all the private tombs in Thebes, since it throws more light on the manners and customs of the Egyptians than any hitherto discovered."

"In the Outer Chambers on the left hand (entering) is a grand procession of Ethiopian and Asiatic chiefs, bearing a tribute to the Egyptian monarch, Thothmes III. (See Wilkinson's *Ancient Egyptians*, vol. I. pl. ii). They are arranged in five lines. The first of the uppermost consists of blacks, and others of a red color from

245

the country of Pount (Punt), who bring ivory, apes, leopard skins, and dried fruits."

Tomb of Vizier Rekhmara showing workers of every industry and their overseers.

"In the third line are Ethiopians, who are styled 'Gentiles of the South.' The leaders are dressed in the Egyptian costume; the others have a girdle of skin, with the hair, as usual, outwards. They bring gold rings, and bags of precious stones or rather gold-dust, hides, apes, leopards, ebony, ivory, ostrich eggs and plumes, a camel, leopard, hounds with handsome collars, and a drove of long-horned oxen."

"The fourth line is composed of men of northern nations, clad in long white garments with a blue border tied at the neck, and ornamented with a cross or other devices. On their head is either a close cap, or their natural hair, short, and of a red color, and they have a small beard. Some bring long gloves, which with their close sleeves indicate as well as their white color, that they are the inhabitants of a cold climate."

"In the fifth line Egyptians lead the van, and are followed by women of Ethiopia (Cush), 'the Gentiles of the South,' carrying theirs in a pannier suspended from their head."

The next day Jiusi returned to be his guide at the Ramesseum and Medinet Habu. Jiusi reserved the same boat and they crossed the

246

INTRIGUE THROUGH TIME

river after Mentuhotep had his breakfast. The day before he had begun to feel the early signs of diarrhea but Jiusi suggested he use lemon to curb this malady. He said: "Cut a piece of the lemon with the skin and chew it finely and that should help greatly. That is why we seem to drink so much lemonade and we are not affected."

They arrived on the Plain of Thebes and decided to visit the Medinet Habu temple first, then to do the Ramesseum. They secured tickets and drove up to the site.

Entrance façade to the Medinet Habu Temple Complex, where, further within, the Mortuary Temple of Rameses III is located.

First, they noticed a restaurant across from Medinet Habu named Hatshepsut and Mentuhotep found this amusing. They seemed to be paying tribute to his Queen. As they approached the gate of the temple, they noticed the outer wall with its image of the king smiting Egypt's enemies. Passing through the security gate they entered an outer gate with two seated statues of the lion Goddess Sekhmet nearby.

The First Pylon depicts the king on the left half, smiting an enemy before Amun-Ra, tutelary deity of *Waset* (Thebes) who hands him a curved sword or scepter. On the right half the same scene is repeated but this time the God represented is Ra-Horakhty. Passing through the Pylon, he entered the First Court and was told this front with its pillars or Osiride Figures fronted a palace of the king situated perpendicular to the temple, but adjoining it. There were decorations on the wall, but the outer face of this wall giving entrance to the next or Second Court, showed the King receiving a curved sword from Amon accompanied by his consort Mut, the earth goddess.

Columns of the First Court at Rameses III's Medinet Habu Temple.

In this profusely decorated Court, the king is shown in many attitudes, holding audience with his generals, smiting enemies, in his chariot inspecting his troops, viewing processions of sacerdotal, bureaucratic and military orders of the kingdom, counting hands of defeated enemies, being fanned by his sons, making offerings to Amon Ra, etc.

Next Mentuhotep passed through to the Hypostyle Hall whose roof has fallen. Column stumps show this Hypostyle Hall had four rows of six columns split by the axis aisle. The walls of this part of the main temple were profusely decorated with the king depicted before enthroned and standing figures of Amon-Ra and his consort Mut and son Khonsu. There are inscribed images of other gods on walls in this now roofless rear area. Two additional smaller halls sport eight columns, each again split by the axis aisle and then there are pillars in the "Holy of Holies."

Side rooms left and right were dedicated to various gods represented in this temple. The Guide pointed out many themes and features of this temple were copied and removed from Rameses II's mortuary temple the Ramesseum, which they would visit next. Backtracking and nearing the entrance, Jiusi pointed to nearby standing remains of other temples built during the earlier 18th Dynasty. He seemed to remember, and the Guide Book pointed out, Queen Hatshepsut built a small temple at Medinet Habu. Then they were out and off to the Ramesseum.

Excellent view of columns of the Vestibule, Osiride statues and Hypostyle Hall of the Ramesseum, Mortuary Temple of Rameses II.

Ramesseum, Temple of Rameses II. Four Osiride figures of the King before the Porch ascent to the Vestibule then Hypostyle Hall with its umbel capital Processional Colonnade and flanking columns.

Arriving at the Ramesseum, they entranced from a side pathway in the Second Court beyond the Second Pylon. This bypassed the destroyed First Pylon and First Court, where the King's Palace stood perpendicular, fronted by two rows of 8 columns. In this open Second Court, with two lines of two, and one of one, columns and two lines of facing Osiride Figures, the shattered and fallen seated colossal stands before the visitor. While the head was visible on the ground, the enormous toe seemed to get more attention. Then they began an ascent of stairs into the temple past Osiride figures of the king. Passing through a Vestibule they encountered more Osiride figures of the king before entering the Hypostyle Hall with its thirty-six flanking columns and twelve in the Processional Colonnade displaying open umbel capitals. Atop these columns evidence remains of clerestory windows. There are two succeeding smaller Hypostyle Halls. The second of these is the chamber with astronomical subjects on the ceiling. These stand before the "Holy of Holies."

Pausing a moment to appreciate the colonnades in this temple, Mentuhotep felt a sense of pride, admiration and sadness for the things that had happened to his glorious country. He thought of Puyemre and his unending struggles to make truth, justice and righteousness essential features of his culture. Her was a noble who embodied the principles of Ma'at. His consideration for the poor, the homeless and voiceless, as well as sponsoring the creation of art and architecture, efficient administration of the country and dispensing of justice, were all attributes he thought may have earned his father the right to have his name "written in the colonnade," somewhere. Yet still, he thought, the ravages of time and man can tear down so much that such enormous artistic and administrative effort was expended to put up. With that they returned to the taxi for the ride back to the boat and the journey across the river.

Jiusi had paid the taxi driver and the boatman. Once across, he walked Mentuhotep to his cruiser. Mentuhotep thanked him enormously and gave him another $100.00 American dollars and left.

INTRIGUE THROUGH TIME

The next day the group was booked on a day trip to Abydos and Dendera. Since Abydos is further, that's the one they visited first.

Behind a colonnade of twelve decorated pillars are seven entrances to the Temple of Seti I at Abydos. Rameses II closed all but one entrance, as he completed the temple of his father. A decorated First and Second Hypostyle Hall with two and three rows of twelve columns respectively inclines upward to a platform fronting the seven shrines of this temple. The seven divinities worshipped in this Temple of Seti I at Abydos are, from right to left, Horus, Isis, Osiris, Amon-Ra, Harakhte, Ptah and Seti. The third shrine of Osiris opens into an inner sanctuary of Osiris that also houses a Kiosk to the triad of Osiris, Isis and Horus. There is a second adjoining inner sanctuary of Osiris and additional sanctuaries for Ptah-Seker, Nefertum, and Sanctuary of the Boats, a Hall of Sacrifice, as well as a Corridor or Gallery of Kings that gives entrance to a corridor with a set of stairs leading to the Osireion in the rear.

Next it was Dendera on the way back from Abydos. Dendera is a Graeco-Roman temple built during the reigns of these periods. However, evidence links it with the earliest times of Egyptian history. Remains of the Enclosure Wall show how it looked back when the temple was in use. A dromos leads to the Great Court and the famed pronaos with a central aisle that splits four rows of six columns, the first being screened. It has a smaller Hypostyle Hall and two vestibules before the "Holy of Holies." There are numerous adjoining rooms for books, garments, and liquid and solid offerings for the ritual. This temple also has crypts underground that contain depicted images of the gods. It has a roof chapel to Isis and a small shrine with courtyard for the Goddess Nuit who gives birth to the sun every morning and swallows it up at evening time. A Mammisi on the outside allowed for the accoutrement of the goddess. This temple has three depictions of the twenty-three crowns of Egypt. After that, it was back to the bus and heading back to the Nile Cruiser. They returned at the end of the day, tired, but very enlightened by evidence of the day's outing.

FREDERICK MONDERSON

They were set to sail about 7:00 pm for Aswan so as to be able to arrive at the first temple, Edfu, at first light the next day. They had stops planned for three temples before they arrived at Aswan.

As the sun began to set, from the deck of the Nile Gleanings, they got their last views of its magnificence over the western hills. And so, they sailed south. The first stop was Edfu, temple of the falcon God Horus. Upon arrival at Edfu, from the boat they boarded horse drawn buggies for the ten-minute ride to the temple. This shocked Mentuhotep that they retained this form of transportation but more importantly it reminded him of his chariot days.

The decorated enclosure wall of the temple is intact. Both halves of the massive entrance stand majestically depicting Horus and other deities in ritual display. Entering the gate, just to the right lay the Sphinx of Edfu, from Greek times. Though Edfu is a "Greek Temple" built by Egyptian and Nubian builders, it retained New Kingdom features of the Library, Colonnade, Hypostyle Hall, Great Court, Roofed Ambulatory, Nilometer, etc. Two statues of the falcon stood in front of the pylon and two in the Court before the screened entrance to the Hypostyle Hall. This Court has a Peristyle Colonnade of thirty-two columns going round in three sides. It also has a roofed Ambulatory.

The large Hypostyle Hall has three rows of six Columns split by the central aisle. This large Hypostyle Hall entrances to a smaller Hypostyle Hall with three rows of four columns, also split by the central aisle. Then three Vestibules follow before the "Holy of Holies."

Passing through a side door gives access to an ambulatory called the "Corridor of Victory." Here the mythological tale of the trial between good and evil, Horus and his evil uncle Seth, is graphically depicted. To the rear in the corridor, there's a plan of the temple with Horus presiding. Going around there is a Nilometer on the eastern side of the "Corridor of Victory." Mentuhotep was familiar with this aspect of the prehistory, the time of the rule of the Gods. As an educated man, architect, Imperial Commander, he was affiliated with temples and knew something about their esoteric knowledge. Soon they returned to their carriages and were taken back to the boat and off they sailed.

The next stop was Esneh with its market for cotton on way to the temple in the center of town. Standing a good forty feet below street level, the guide explained the land was built up by centuries of inundations of the river depositing silt and sedimentation. Within the inner great hall stood four rows of six massive columns, thirty-seven feet high equally illustrated and each comprising a separate type of capital. The first row is engaged to the entrance wall and the other three are freestanding. There is a north and a south gate or doorway. Several features in this temple can only be seen here and nowhere else. The pregnant Isis with the baby in the amniotic sac is one such feature. However, Khnum, god of this temple, making man on his potter's wheel can also be found at Philae, temple of Isis, removed to Agilka Island. Esneh boasts one of three surviving zodiacs in Egypt today. The others are at Kom Ombo and Ed Dayr.

The next stop was Kom Ombo, double temple of Gods Sobek and the elder Horus, Haroeis. They arrived just before dusk and he was surprised to see so many cruisers moored in a line and side by side. His vessel was fourth abreast. To exit they had to pass through the doors of the other three ships before they were ashore.

They entered a lighted temple through a dilapidated enclosure wall into a double court, each with eight columns on two sides, for the respective deities in this double temple. The double entrance to the temple proper had two uraei above the cornice. The one of Haroeis or the elder Horus sits on the left and that of Sobek the crocodile is on the right. There was a large columned Hypostyle Hall, profusely illustrated with two aisles leading into a smaller Hypostyle hall. Then there are three succeeding vestibules that lead to the twin "Holy of Holies." Each was administered by a separate priesthood dedicated to each respective God. A corridor lay between the outer face of these rooms and the inner face of the outer enclosure wall. In this back corridor several colossal figures are depicted and on the opposite wall Isis is shown seated, pregnant, in the birth chair. Beside her lay illustrations of medical instruments and a basin for the attending physician to wash his hands. Soon they returned to the boat and off they sailed further south.

Many persons including Mentuhotep stood on the top deck leaning over the rails to observe the navigation of the locks. Music from the bar at this level and busy waiter contributed to the party-like atmosphere as the captain waited his turn to enter the locks. Just then Mentuhotep noticed the lighted bridge spanning the Nile. 'I see they did bridge the wider river,' he thought. He had seen the smaller bridges in the Cairo environs. He felt proud his nation had kept pace with modern times. Sometime in the wee-hours of the morning they made port at Aswan. Later that day they transferred to the Oberoi Hotel across the river on Elephantine Island.

The next day, wake-up was 6:00 am, breakfast and then onto the ferry boat to waiting buses. They passed the High Dam and the Lotus Memorial, symbol of Cooperation between the Soviet Union and Egypt. Then they boarded motorboats to visit the Temple of Isis, now relocated from Philae to the Island of Agilka. This famous landmark and monument has long been called the "Pearl of the Nile," or the "Garden of the Nile." Mentuhotep remembered this location for he had made several trips here to collect good stone for several projects in his time. The temple in his time looked different. However, Aswan is where both King Thutmose I and Queen Hatshepsut quarried the stone for their obelisks. Soon they docked at the Temple of Isis.

Golden breastplate in the Cairo Museum of Egyptian Antiquities.

254

INTRIGUE THROUGH TIME

"Kiosk of Trajan" at the Temple of Isis. Fourteen screened columns, each with a different capital. It's a wonderful tourist attraction at the Temple of Isis on Philae relocated to Agilka Island.

Ascending the stairs, they entered the Dromos to the temple. To the left and beginning of the Dromos lay the Kiosk of Nectanebo and a nearby Nilometer. The Kiosk is dedicated to Hathor, goddess of beauty and pleasure. She is shown with cow's ears. To the right lay seventeen undecorated columns of the First Eastern Colonnade, fronting the temples of Asynapsis, the Nubian Deity Mandolist, and Imhotep, who built the Step Pyramid. To the left lay the Western Colonnade with its thirty-two decorated columns, some with palm trees, papyrus plants and other flowers and deity decoration.

Through these doors one enters the Court of the Temple of Isis with its First Pylon proper. In this courtyard an altar bears inscription and the name of Taharka of the XXVth Dynasty. To the left lay the Mammisi, Birth House of the God, whose fronting columns, can be seen, from the river. Nearby steps lead down to the Nilometer, that is considered an essential feature of a river temple. To the right lay the Second East Colonnade with elaborate capitals topped by a row of uraei or cobras.

To the rear lay other structures and off to the left the famed Kiosk of Trajan, sits beside the little chapel to Hathor. Trajan's Kiosk, with entrances from both the river and the land, is a magnificent structure with screened columns and wonderfully varied capitals. Retracing their steps visitors returned to the boat and then a long walk to the Temple of God Mendulese, of Kalabsha. As time permitted, a short five-minute walk took them to Beit Wali Temple of Rameses II. Both these temples were in Nubia and threatened with being submerged in Lake Nasser, when the High Dam was constructed. These visits completed, it was back to the boat to the bus, and then the ferry to Oberoi Hotel.

The next day they set out by bus for Abu Simbel, Temple of Rameses II, with the twin structure of his wife, Queen Nefertari. While Rameses' temple was dedicated to four gods, Ra-Horakhty, Amon, Rameses himself and Ptah; Nefertari's temple was dedicated to Hathor, goddess of love and beauty.

Upon arrival they purchased tickets and with a Guide specially trained for Abu Simbel, they were ushered towards the temple. Coming round the side of the mountain where the temple is now located, after **UNESCO** relocated this wonderful structure, four colossal seated statues at the façade greeted them. Three sat complete upright, but a fourth had its head and crown broken with these pieces lying on the ground. Upon entering the first hall eight colossal standing statues of the King greeted them. This hall was decorated with the king in various attitudes, riding in his chariot, assaulting an enemy, with his queen, both making presentations to the gods, etc. A second, though smaller hall, was similarly decorated, and this led to the entrance of the "Holy of Holies," with the four divinities of the temple enthroned. There are several side rooms, profusely decorated with the king in numerous attitudes before the gods, viz., making presentations with both hands, with a single hand, with hands empty, kneeling, standing and so on. After picture taking, they exited to make room for other visitors with other groups. Looking out from the terrace of the temple they stood beside many smaller figures standing in the forefront of the seated colossal. On both sides of the seated statues and entrance to the temples are depictions of bound prisoners and other themes. Then it was off to the Queen's temple.

INTRIGUE THROUGH TIME

Erik Monderson stands before the Western Colonnade at Isis Temple.

Philae Temple of Isis. Dromos or walkway with the East Colonnade (right) and First Pylon to the temple beyond the First Pylon opening.

Essentially similarly decorated, this temple has images of Ptah, Horus, Hathor, etc., and the king and queen making presentations to Hathor, offering flowers, shaking the sistrum or rattle, the goddess' symbol and so on. Taken to higher heights by stairs, they get a behind-the-scene view of the temple as it's dug into the mountain. Surprisingly they emerged on the back of the mountain at a higher level than when they entered the structure. After this it was back to the bus and the trip back to the ferry and the hotel. After a long day, dinner was served. Then a short lounge stay for cocktails, bed and early morning flight back to Cairo.

A day later they flew out of Cairo and landed in New York. Fantegla and Sidney were there at JFK to greet him when he emerged from Immigration and Customs.

"How was your flight, honey?" she asked.
"Smooth," he replied, meaning 'as smooth as you.' They headed to the Plaza.

For days Mentuhotep reminisced with Fantegla about his trip to Egypt. She was naturally fascinated and expressed the view she had to go too. He promised this would become a reality one day. Much of his regular routine was pursued, but he kept reading *The Times*, Guide Books and books on art and architecture. W. Stephenson Smith's *Art and Architecture of Ancient Egypt* became a veritable source of reference for him. A few he had picked up at the Cairo Museum were added to his collection. He was particularly impressed with the book by Cheikh Anta Diop entitled *African Origins of Civilization: Myth or Reality*. Quite frankly, he was surprised at the need for such a book. Though he knew his people considered they are special, he did recognize they were essentially similar to their African neighbors in language, culture and religious beliefs and practice.

INTRIGUE THROUGH TIME

On the Nile River, feluccas moored beside the Oberoi Hotel Landing with Cruise Ships in the distant rear; one of which took Michael across the river and back.

31. Ghafoor Partnership and Return to Egypt

Ghafoor approached him with a proposition. He explained his financial plight because he had to pay quite a hefty sum to first cover expenses at St. Bernadine Hospital for the treatment for his daughter. The experts he imported were costly. However, they did help. There was some improvement by the treatment they recommended, but now the part of rehabilitation began to be the issue. His daughter was transferred to the Dr. Susan Smith McKinney Nursing Home and Rehabilitative Center in Brooklyn, New York. The first month after his daughter was stricken has cost him half a million dollars. As such, Ghafoor made him an offer.

Ghafoor: "Mr. Mentuhotep, I have a proposition for you. I'm sure after our first meeting I used the word "partnership" in that discussion. Well, I'm strapped for cash and so would like to offer you a real partnership in Ghafoor's Antiques."

Mentuhotep: "What precisely is your proposition?"

Ghafoor: "Sir, if you will advance me $600,000.00, I will give you fifty-one percent of my business. The only reason I am doing this is because of my daughter."

Mentuhotep: "I understand your plight and will be willing to accommodate. Draw up the papers and by next Monday I will give you the cash. Is that satisfactory with you?"

Ghafoor's: "Yes, Sir. I would ask only one thing."

Mentuhotep: "What is that?"

Ghafoor: "That you do not, at this time, seek to change the name of the business."

Mentuhotep: "By all means no! I like the name Ghafoor's Antiques. In fact, I may be interested in you doing some traveling to secure similar antiques, not necessarily from Egypt but other places to expand our vision. The future is the key, I'm sure you know this."

Ghafoor: "I agree with you one hundred percent. The papers will be here for you to sign next Monday. I wish to thank you very much for helping me at this critical time."

Mentuhotep: "That's what friends are for, but also this is a business undertaking and I'm happy to be your partner."

Two weeks after he became a partner with Ghafoor, Mentuhotep contacted Fly by Night Tours and made a reservation for his return to Egypt. He had Mr. Gray write him a letter of Introduction to the Luxor Tourist Board, requesting his rental of the premises atop the mountain at Deir el Bahari. It simply stated, "Mr. Mentuhotep represents Gray's Gallery of New York, and would like to rent the premises atop the mountain to observe and paint the Temple of Hatshepsut at Deir el Bahari from the "Bird's Eye View," as the sun wanes against the mountain backdrop, creating the wonderful color scheme. Please give all assistance and cooperation in this venture. Thank you." Signed, Mr. Gray. With great ease Fly by Night Tours was able to acquire the residence and had Mr. Mentuhotep's itinerary drawn up. His Egypt Air travels were arranged and so too his Nile and Atlantic cruises.

On his return to Egypt Mentuhotep's accommodations were again at Mena House in Cairo. His whole itinerary was planned with military precision and pretty well researched. He decided to spend a day in Cairo to do some sight-seeing trying to reconcile himself with the changes in his country nearly four thousand years later.

INTRIGUE THROUGH TIME

His taxi wound its way through the city, first to the Citadel and then to the Mosque of Mohammed Ali. There were a few other places he wanted to visit primarily to admire their architecture. Still, he thought of Cairo as a sprawling, heavily populated dusty city. Then again, it was a sort of desert city, so he thought nothing of this. Still, looking at the heavy and rapid flow of traffic, of people and vehicles, he wondered whether chariots could handle the pace. Even further, his only recollection of that type of chariot mayhem was in his military engagement against the Bedouin. In that encounter there were casualties from sword play, lances and arrows, as well as from chariots trampling the enemy. Here he saw no casualties or accidents. It was simply an orderly, yet, mad interplay of people and vehicles, in peaceful coexistence.

Both sites he found fascinating. The high walls of the Citadel in a wonderfully precipitous location overlooking the city, the eerie site of prisoner cells and the seeming impregnable nature of the fort, made it a site to behold as a popular tourist attraction. As a modern Police Museum, it displays some of the most heinous evidence of torture in that place of detainment. He was again taken with the colonnade at the Mosque of Mohammed Ali and impressed with the Mosque of Suleiman Pasha.

Back in his hotel room Mentuhotep began to review his final campaign. Everything must unfold with the military-like precision he had planned. Fly by Night Tours had arranged his rental of the house on the mountain for ten days. He would stay at the Luxor Hilton when he arrived and the next day will move to his elevated residence. He must remember to offer a special thank you to Mr. Gray, for providing the letter of reference that helped him get the residence to paint the temple from the "Bird's Eye View." He checked his paint supplies and equipment – paint, brushes, sketch pads, canvass, pins, tape, easel, umbrella, collapsible seat, paint containers, a large pot-spoon, pencils, erasers, two cameras, film, water bottles, munchies, candy, and practically anything he would need. He further examined his easel. The spike-tipped legs will double as his pick-axe. The two carry-on pieces of luggage contained his supplies. One, however, contained the collapsible but sturdy back-packs he purchased in New York, in which to hold his jewelry once secured.

He is to board the African Queen for a Nile cruise to Cairo on the afternoon of the tenth day. He is expected to board the Nile cruiser between 2:00 and 3:00 pm for 4:00 pm departure. Once back in Cairo, Fantegla will join him for a few days of sight-seeing. They will stay again at Mena House for four days, three nights, then board the Danish Cutter for a Mediterranean and Atlantic cruise home. The reward of having Fantegla at his side, upon successful completion of his expedition, is fitting payment for a flawlessly executed plan. He remembers hearing a song in New York entitled "Big Ship Sailing on the Ocean – Leaves no Commotion." But he remembers also it's not the size of the ship, but its motion in the ocean, and he intends to have a wonderful time. 'It's my time,' he thought.

Mountain View of buses in the Temple's staging area showing the contrast between desert and plain and the Nile River way in the distance.

32. Treasure Hunt at Luxor

Mentuhotep arrived at Cairo Domestic for his flight to Luxor Airport. Within two hours he was upriver and on way to the Sonesta Hotel. One of the first people he called was his Valley of the Kings Guide Jiusi Cummerson, who was to help him get situated in the residence on the mountain. On this side of the river, that first night, he was told of Sound and Light at Karnak Temple and decided to take in the show. He was really surprised with the manner in which they replicated the priestly ritual in the temple. Absent the many people in attendance, he felt as if almost home. It's a pity he could not be home alone! However, that's where he will be on the mountain.

Very early the next day Jiusi arrived at the Sonesta Hotel. After a heavy breakfast Mentuhotep made his move. Packing two bags, one with clothing and equipment and the other with foodstuffs for his stay, he headed across the river for the slopes beside Deir el Bahari. By 9:00 am, he was at the summit and was settled in his new digs. "Thank you very much," he said to Jiusi. "Come check on me every third day." He then offered him two hundred American dollars, a very substantial sum. On that day, the current exchange rate was 5.4 Egyptian pounds per US Dollar.

"Thank you very much, Sir. I will pick up whatever supplies the Sonesta has prepared for you. The phone works. Here's my number – 453-2786. Call me anytime for whatever. There are numbers for the authorities, the Tourist Police and other entities on a chart next to the phone."
"Thank you, Jiusi," said Mentuhotep and they parted.

The first thing Mentuhotep did was to set out his art supplies, and paste on the wall some trial pieces of the temple he had prepared beforehand. In so doing his cover was well established in the event he had surprise visitors. Sometime before 3:00 pm he appeared on the ledge of the mountain. He began taking Polaroid photos of the temple from the "Bird's Eye View." He also descended the mountain somewhat ostensibly taking additional photos from different elevations. In fact, he was marking out the distance from the Summit to the approximate location of his principal interest. With all photo taking completed, he returned to the Summit and to his residence. Working quickly, his photographs were also taped to the wall. By 5:00 pm he appeared on the ledge near the "Bird's Eye View." He quickly set up his umbrella, easel and collapsible chair, and then got to work. Working quickly, he had several sketches completed. However, while reduced in size, he could be observed from the temple grounds below. Thus, he made every effort to blend in with his surroundings. In fact, a few tourists who came over the mountain passed nearby and noticed his unfolding work. Comments and pleasantries were exchanged and they began their descent of the mountain.

Atop the trail from the Valley of the Kings that Mr. Mentuhotep had traveled, the "Bird's Eye View" showing the First Ramp, First Court and Lower Colonnade; Second Court, Second Ramp and Middle Colonnade; and Upper Terrace, Upper Colonnade and Upper Court housing the Sanctuary with the mountain as a backdrop.

Every tourist who made the trek across the mountain from the Valley of the Kings was accompanied by a native Egyptian Guide. Because of his timing, setting up his cover, they were able to observe and publicize his work to concerned onlookers below. True to form, approaching nightfall, his operation was well-executed. He had established his beachhead and in fact, "taken the high ground."

INTRIGUE THROUGH TIME

Second Ramp in Second Court to the Middle Colonnade, the Upper Terrace above with its columns and surviving Osiride Statues of the Queen that entrances the Upper Hypostyle Court fronting the "Holy of Holies" built against the mountain as a backdrop.

Soon the phenomenon he came to observe and paint began to materialize, and he, surprisingly, had begun to capture it on canvass. Yet, he vividly remembered the description of this remarkable scene from one of the Travel-Guides he had read and brought with him. Taking out the Guide he read and simultaneously observed as the phenomenon unfolded: "As the sun nears the horizon, the eastern cliffs of the Valley appear rich in yellow light with purple shadows deepening to crimson at sunset; there rises a bright rosy band across the eastern sky, higher and higher the sun wanes, with the dark blue of night below it, and the brightness of the day still above. This fades as it nears the zenith, and then the western sky from a golden glow darkens to a rich tawny brown, fading into purple and so to blue on either side; this brown, however, never gives place to blue, but gradually becoming spangled with the stars it deepens to blackness of night."

FREDERICK MONDERSON

Standing there with great admiration and in fascination, he remembered when he first saw this scene. It was right after his appointment as Commander of the Imperial Guard. He had followed Her Majesty Maat-Ka-Ra, Hatshepsut, from the palace to the temple for the dedication ceremony. It seemed as if it was only yesterday this had occurred. However, while he kept observing the changing dynamics, he also kept an eye on events below. After the last of the visitors leave, the temple was secured, and a while later the guards chained the fence and left. He sat there well past nightfall observing the temple in its rich black stillness. Yet, the white limestone seemed to shine beneath the starry night sky. He was alone on the mountain yet there was sufficient starlight for him to complete his work.

Having conquered his space, place and time, as his plan calls for, he decided to establish a routine for the first three nights; as precaution, in the event he was being observed. He did not want to be caught flatfooted, sort of with his pants down. He did, however, descend down the mountain and demarcate the precise location of his treasure. 'It's only a matter of time before the next phase is implemented,' he thought.

Next morning before 10:00 am, he had official visitors. Guides, Tourist Police, Regional Administrators, etc., came ostensibly to see how he was doing, but in actuality to see what he was doing.

"Good morning, Sir," said one of the visitors who walked through his open door.

As if expecting this reception, he turned from his work of establishing a palette for his art. "Good morning, gentlemen. Good to see you," he greeted them. "Are there any problems," he was asked, as the visitors fanned out in the room examining his tools, and the trial pieces, the sketches, the photographs on the walls, and his supplies. Once they were satisfied with the legitimacy of his work, he was bid "Good luck," and they were off. He then returned to his work. Everything was proceeding like clockwork.

Mr. and Mrs. Somersett had invited Fantegla to dinner one evening. She arrived in a colorful gown. Sidney her chauffeur, had first

INTRIGUE THROUGH TIME

noticed her dress, and big smiling, happy outlook. In the drive over, while she kept staring out the window, as he observed from the rear-view mirror, there was a tremendous happy and contented aura about her. Surely this had something to do with Mr. Mentuhotep. Even though they parted at the Airport, there seemed a till-we-meet again expectation about her that made even he, the chauffeur, pleased. Soon they pulled into her parent's driveway. He got out, opened the door and she exited saying playfully: "Thanks Sidney, going to meet the man!"

Jamison, the Butler, greeted her at the door. "Hello, Ms. Fantegla. How are you this evening?" "Fine, Jamison! Oh my, your aroma fills the air. What is it?" "It's a surprise, but especially for you." "Thanks," she responded. "Where are they?" she asked. "Your parents are in the Cocktail Room. Dinner will be served in 20 minutes." "Great," she said walking into the Cocktail Room.

Fantegla: "Hello, Mother, Dad. It's always so nice to see you."
Mistress: "Oh, darling, what a beautiful gown you're wearing," as she embraced and kissed her mom.
Mister: "How splendid you look this evening, my dear." He too came in for his embrace and kiss.
Fantegla: "Thank you, dad."
Mistress: "Can I fix you a drink, honey?"
Fantegla: "Oh, just some orange juice, thank you."
Mistress: "So, what's new?"
Fantegla: "Well, Michael went back to Egypt day before yesterday. He said something about finishing some business over there. I'm to join him in ten days for a return cruise. Naturally I will have to take time off from my volunteering at Marcus Garvey Nursing Home in Brooklyn and the Veterans Hospital in Manhattan."
Mistress: "But of course. Besides, Sarlinda will still be there and she can cover for you. Oh, how sweet of Michael to have you join him in Egypt!" Turning to her husband, "We've been putting off that Alaska cruise for some time now."
Mister: "As soon as I clear my desk dear, as soon as I clear my desk."
Fantegla: "So, how's business Dad?"
Mister: "Business is good. President Reagan has been good for business. Investments are high. Oil stocks, are up. Real estate is in

267

a boom. I'm putting up two twenty-four-story buildings for office and residence. The one in New York is nearing completion and we broke ground for one in Aspen, Colorado, last week."

Mistress: "Please, sweetness; let's not bore the beautiful teacup with business talk at dinner. We invited her to enjoy our company and to get the "411" on Michael." Entering the Cocktail Room, Jamison said: "Dinner is served, Madam."

Mistress: "Thank you, Jamison." Grasping her daughter's arm, she walked her to the dining room. "How sweet you look this evening. I'm so happy to see you're so happy. Michael has certainly been good for you."

Fantegla: "He certainly has been a tremendous inspiration and lover, Mother."

Mistress: "Oh, the juicy part."

Entering the dining room and taking their seats at the dinner table, she remarked: "Oh, mother, the aroma is a knockout. What is it?"

Mistress: "Roast veal. It's a Jamison special. He said he prepared it especially for you."

Fantegla: "My favorite," she responded.

Mistress: "So tell me all the good news. I want all the details!"

Fantegla: "I'm pregnant!"

Crash! The sound of glass breaking! Mrs. Somersett dropped her glass.

Mistress: "Oh, my gosh!" Getting up from her chair she moved to hug and embrace Fantegla.

Mister: "Did I hear right?"

Mistress: "Yes sweetness, we're going to be grandparents." Turning to Fantegla she asked: "Are you sure?"

Fantegla: "Yes, about one month."

Mistress: "Does Michael know?"

Fantegla: "No. I only got the results today."

Mistress: "How is he going to take it?"

Fantegla: "I'm sure he's going to be happy."

Mister: "Can they tell the sex at this early age?"

Fantegla: "Not as yet."

Mistress: "I'm hoping for a granddaughter."

Mister: "I'm hoping for a grandson."

Fantegla: "Well, just let me deliver. Then you folks can have all the fun you want."

Mister: "Well, if I don't get what I want you will have to make another."

INTRIGUE THROUGH TIME

Mistress: "You silly old man. This house will be rocked. We have not had such joy on our doorsteps for the longest. This will be a grand celebration."

Mister: "Let me fix a drink. This calls for a celebration right now. My darling daughter needs to be toasted."

Mistress: "Fix me one too. I longed for the day when I would be a grandmother.

Raising their glasses, Mr. Somersett offered the toast.

Mister: "To our wonderful little teacup who has blossomed into a charming and beautiful young woman. Now she has blest us with the wonderful news of a grandchild. This means our line will continue. I'm cleaning out my desk by next week and when she goes to Egypt to meet Michael in ten days, we're going on that Alaska cruise."

Mistress: "You go, my man! Honey, you have certainly brought a lot of happiness and goodwill back to this house. You repay us for all the good we have done with you. Simply continue that tradition of love and caring, and I'm sure and confident you two will make wonderful parents. Now, let's eat up. You're feeding two, or is it three?"

They all burst into laughter. When Jamison came into the room with the serving, he looked at his Mistress in astonishment.

Mistress: "She's pregnant."

Jamison: "The Lord be praised! Hallelujah! This house is going to be rocking again," he said. After that they completed the meal in silent smiles. Main course, desert, coffee, all were mopped up in the quiet excitement that transformed their outlooks. As they ended dinner and she parted for the Plaza, there was a new aura in the home, one of expected joy, happiness and the thought of planning for a big wedding.

All day long, day two, day three, day four and day five, our Hero remained at the grind stone. He painted, enjoyed the view, been observed by people coming over the mountain who stopped to observe, comment and then descend the slopes. When he had mastered the routine of the predictable sunset, last visitors exiting the temple, clanging of the gates being locked, he would remain sitting in the dark enjoying the serenity of the stillness of the temple. He surveyed the entire amphitheater, the surrounding terrain and the

FREDERICK MONDERSON

lights far off in the distance, near the Nile River. Even more important, he kept track of the moon and starlight illuminating the slopes of the mountain. However, as he moved up and down the slope taking Polaroid shots of the temple for his wall display, he had located the precise spot where his treasure lay buried. As such, it was only a matter of time before he made his final move.

Day six his visitors showed up again accompanying Jiusi his Guide. Apparently, the wealthy art dealer in New York telegraphed the authorities and wanted to know how he was coming along. Reassuring Mr. Gray his man was okay, they came to check on him, give him the contact news and also to inspect his progress. By this time his walls were inundated with photographs, trial pieces and in various stages of completion, six finely executed oil canvases painted in photographic depiction of the temple, with the sunset in different phases of its passage.

"This is excellent work you have done here," he was told. Another said: "At first, I thought it rather silly you would spend so much time and money to paint the temple, but now I'm convinced of the value of your time and work. The masterpieces you have produced here are a tribute not simply to your skill, but the goodwill and cooperation between Egypt and America. We will now leave you to your work. I will reply to the telegraph telling Mr. Gray not only are you well and doing fine, but also praise the fine masterpieces you have produced. You are truly a great artist. Good day."
Mentuhotep: "Thank you." By the end of day six he was ready to make his move. So wonderfully convincing had been developments thus far, it was highly unlikely he would have any more visitors.

As the day ended and routine unfolded, he moved umbrella, easel, chair, art supplies, indoors. Then he donned his close-fitting black night gear for stealth and camouflage. With his double backpack in place, he rearranged his easel leg for pick-axe purposes, and took the large pot-spoon for cooking he had brought along. Then he took his usual place of contemplation and sat motionless in the dark.

In the long stillness of the night, he made his move. Like a panther he descended the slope and reached his target spot. Within thirty minutes his pick and spoon had broken ground and scaled away nearly two feet of soil. Then he made contact with a metal object. Working even more quickly he freed one chest, then another. Soon

INTRIGUE THROUGH TIME

he quietly emptied their contents, making sure no clanging sound could be heard and carried in the stillness of the night. Replacing the chests, he then covered them again with the original soil. He smoothed out the area and trod the dust to make everything appear normal. He simply hoped no one would cross over the mountain before the sun began to bleach the soil eliminating, the discolored subsoil. In no time he was back up the slope and in his residence.

Come day seven, he set up his umbrella, easel and chair. Then he took his Polaroid camera and moved down the slope. In the vicinity of his fortune, he paused to take a few shots of the temple, adjusting his camera and seemingly and unobtrusively began kicking and spreading the soil without making a splash. Soon the footprints had restored the area to its normal state, and then he posed and took one more photo of the temple from that position, in the event prying eyes were focused on him. Then he moved back to the summit. Moving back to the residence he pasted more photographs on the walls making the place still more normal. This done, he further secured his backpack, then moved to his perch to continue his work, keep his eye on the spot, looking out for visitors and praying the sun would do its task of restoring the soil to normalcy.

Day seven ended, day eight ended, and so too day nine. By the end of his last day, he packed his belongings. All the food supplies had been used up. In that bag, he made space for the photographs, much of the paint supplies were also used. He made a special effort to leave evidence of orchestrated garbage, to fulfill the impression regarding the work he had done.

There were many pieces of sketches purposely done to be destroyed and trashed. These discarded trial pieces were designed to be examined by officials who may follow up on his visit. The good pieces of his work were neatly stored in the other bag. Parts of the canvas pieces were made to protrude from his bag conveying the impression of the working artist. Everything was set for the next day's early descent from the mountain.

FREDERICK MONDERSON

Coming down the Mountain at Deir el Bahari, the Temple begins to emerge larger and with greater clarity.

That evening as the sun went down, Mentuhotep returned to his perch. He imbibed in the quietude as the night sky reflected against the white limestone of the temple. His mind returned to the age of his former existence. He thought of his job as both architect and Imperial Commander, and his family, friends, lover Nekajai, stables, chariots, and even his Nile boat. The one modern counterbalancing reality is the beautiful Fantegla who has come to play such a stabilizing, and enriching force in his life. The love life she radiates has empowered his vision of the future.

By 7:00 am, Mentuhotep had been awake, dressed and ready. Soon he strapped on his backpack, with bags in hand, he began his descent from the mountain. He knew he had to go all the way, and then some. As he progressed the temple came into clearer view. The closer he came to street level the more his heart began pounding. He knew it ain't over, 'till it's over. Finally, he was on the flats. Normally, most visitors would turn toward the temple, but he headed away from it. An early guard at the outer gate of the temple waved at him without wondering why he was leaving when visitors would be coming. Just then one of the earliest buses that brought tourists to the temple passed him. He wondered; in his day it would be a chariot making its way along the tree-lined Avenue of Sphinxes that led up to the Pylon; while he moved away towards the Valley Temple by the river. Still, he kept moving quickly and methodically as more vehicles passed him heading for the temple, and he for the Nile. By this time, Ra, the Sun God, had risen upon the eastern horizon and was showering the land with golden rays of heat and brightness. On and on he went, and about forty-five minutes from beginning the descent, he reached the Nile. He was now in the homestretch and just kept going.

Crossing his beloved River on a felucca he thought: 'I've made it.' He remembered in days of old, boatmen sang on the journey across as they guided the sails of, as opposed to engine powered, Nile vehicles. 'Now the boats are more colorful,' he thought, 'with more fancy sounding names.' The boatman enquired where he wanted to land. Noticing his Nile Cruiser, he said, "Just behind the Nile Cruiser, African Queen." Just then he remembered the Celestial Ferryman who brought the good souls across the Celestial Ocean, and he handed him a $100.00 US note.

He was so thankful. 'This is a week's wages,' the boatman thought. But for Mentuhotep, he had performed an indispensable service and checking his watch it was now 8:00 am.

On a ruse, he approached the gangplank of the African Queen. At the entrance, he explained he was to board the Cruiser around 2:00 pm, but wanted to use the facilities to wash-up. Noticing his dusty shoes and pants as somewhat rugged, the attendant thought he may have come a long way and welcomed him aboard. Checking the Guest List, he found Mr. Michael Mentuhotep registered as a passenger on the Cruise to Cairo. He was on Deck Three, Room Three-fifteen, and he was shown to his room. He was informed the previous evening his suitcases were delivered from his hotel by a porter, Jiusi Cummerson.

Flopping down on the bed, he slowly relaxed his tensed muscles that had geared up for the rigors of the descent and possible eventualities. After a nice hot shower, he changed his clothes and came down to breakfast. There with a smiling chef named Mohammed, he exchanged pleasantries and had a big breakfast of an omelet of eggs, onions, cheese and parsley. From the buffet tables he chose beef sausage, croissant, Danish, a fruit cocktail, orange juice, cacadaeo juice and coffee with milk and sugar. He smiled as he devoured the first of many meals in his newfound state of luxury.

FREDERICK MONDERSON

One of the remaining figures of Queen Hatshepsut that survived the destruction her temple suffered at the hands of reactionaries who sought to eliminate her name and being from historical recognition.

Smiling Chef Mohammed who graciously served Mentuhotep his breakfast at the Sonesta Hotel in Luxor.

INTRIGUE THROUGH TIME

After breakfast he called Jiusi to tell him not to make the climb to the summit for 11:00 am. He chose to make an early descent. "Thank you for everything," he said. "I have just boarded the African Queen and was happy to find you had delivered my suitcases. If you would meet me instead at the ship's entrance at 11:00 am, I just wish to offer you a token of my appreciation."
"I'll be there, Sir," he answered. "In fact," Mentuhotep said, "There will be an envelope for you at the desk."
"Thank you very much, Sir," he responded.

At the desk he placed three - $100.00 US notes in an envelope and wrote the name Jiusi Cummerson. He returned to his room, locked his door and crashed. Hours later, he was awakened to the swaying of the ship that had set sail for Cairo.

Two days later, after a number of stops along the way, the African Queen docked in Cairo. Mr. Mentuhotep took a cab to Mena House Hotel. Never once did he open his backpack. That night at dinner he reminiscence about the wonderful times he experienced with Fantegla, and looked forward with great anticipation to her coming, in the morning. The transatlantic cruise home should be a wonderful experience. Then he thought about a more long-lasting relationship with the lady. But instantly, his mind shifted to 'What will I do with my newfound wealth?' 'What will be the best strategy to dispose of the antiques pieces?' 'Who would be most useful in that venture?" He instantly thought of Mr. Gray the art dealer, Ghafoor the antiques dealer, and Lord Stanhope, the authenticating expert. He should give Lord Stanhope wide latitude to supply contacts in Europe.

He must consider making a significant offer to Mr. Somersett who purchased his first collection. He must also consider other options of investing the wealth he will acquire from sales of his pieces. However, he must be careful of too rapid an introduction of these rare pieces on the Antiques market. It must be done with great stealth so as not to attract too much attention to him. Feeling a little tired he retired for the evening with instruction for a wake-up call at 6:00 am.

FREDERICK MONDERSON

33.   Going to Meet the Man!

Aboard Egypt Air 811, Fantegla sat pondering her arrival in Cairo. She thought of meeting Michael for the first time on foreign soil, the expectedly exciting time they should have in his home country, the sight-seeing and the relaxing and enjoyable cruise home. Most important, she looked forward to seeing his face when she told him of the expected bundle of joy. The only lingering thought, she pondered, 'When would be the best time to break the news to him?' 'Maybe from down under, his surprise will be more meaningful,' she thought. Just then she heard the 'thud' of the aircraft touching down and the announcement: "Ladies and Gentlemen, welcome to Cairo International Airport. The time is now 8:30 am, and the temperature is eighty-four degrees. Please remain seated with seat belts fastened until the captain turns off the seat belt sign. After completing Immigration and Customs requirements, you must register any video camcorders in your possession with the proper authorities. That completed, have a wonderful stay and thank you for flying Egypt Air."

After completing Immigration requirements and collecting her luggage, a beaming Fantegla Somersett walked out of the terminal into the waiting arms of Mr. Wonderful, Michael Mentuhotep.

"Hello my sweet! How was your flight?" he asked.
Fantegla: "Smooth, but filled with excited anticipation to be in your arms," she responded.
Mentuhotep: "This should be a truly wonderful and exciting time for us as we head back home."
Fantegla: "I agree, wholeheartedly."

Then they were off to his hotel. That afternoon they took a cab to the Ghizeh Pyramids, visited the Pyramid Boat Museum and moved to the desert site for a panoramic view of the Pyramids. There she chose to ride a camel and have photographs taken of her atop one of these "Ships of the desert," with the pyramids as a backdrop in the distance. Clearly Sister Girl was having a whale of a time. After all, she was on vacation in the land of ancient Egypt with the most exciting man she has ever known, in love and pregnant. What more could she ask for?

INTRIGUE THROUGH TIME

The next day they visited the Cairo Museum with cameras in hand. Tutankhamon's treasure really fascinated her. The golden mask, coffins, crook and flail, and other forms of jewelry were quite appealing to her. She took a photo beside the golden mask of the boy king. She confessed to Michael her love for ancient jewelry. She greatly admired the decorated coffins of Psusennes. They visited the room with Papyrus. There is also a room with large clumps of hair, like Afros worn by African Americans. This was not surprising to him. However, Michael was again particularly moved by seeing Thutmose IV's chariot, as well as other chariots in their cases. It brought back the good and bad times of his chariot experiences. They moved on to the Hall of Divinities. She returned to take a picture beside the two black statues of Tutankhamon. Then they took the stairs to the first floor.

They went from Period to Period on the first floor. Old Kingdom, Middle Kingdom, New Kingdom and the statues and sarcophagi continued to fascinate them both. The statue of Mentuhotep interested him because of his temple next to the Queen's at *Deshret* (Deir el Bahari). His father named him after this king. She wanted a photograph beside the kneeling statue and the Sphinx of Queen Hatshepsut. He posed to have a photograph taken beside his Queen, and, while she thought it odd that he would take the photograph, she was happy to see him in her camera lens.

He took her to see the necklace of Princess Nekajai. She was astounded that it looked exactly as the one Michael wore. Not really an expert on ancient jewelry she just thought it a coincidence he had one like it. She was more interested in the happy feeling she was experiencing and thought of the wonderful times that lay ahead.

Soon they finished the tour and stopped in the bookstore on the way out. He bought two Guide Books, she bought postcards to send home to friends and family. Finally, they left the Museum but still took time to take photos alongside the statues on the grounds.

Looking around she enquired about the white memorial off to the corner of the grounds. He obliged her interest and stepped over to

277

view the Auguste Mariette Mausoleum. Mentuhotep was amazed to see the portraits of the individuals who share this sacred space with Mr. Mariette.

Auguste Mariette Memorial housing the busts of the famous pioneers in Egyptological research who made Ancient Egyptian cultural history a professional discipline.

Chabas and Dumichen

Lemans and Goodwin

INTRIGUE THROUGH TIME

De Rouge and Samuel Birch (1815-1884)

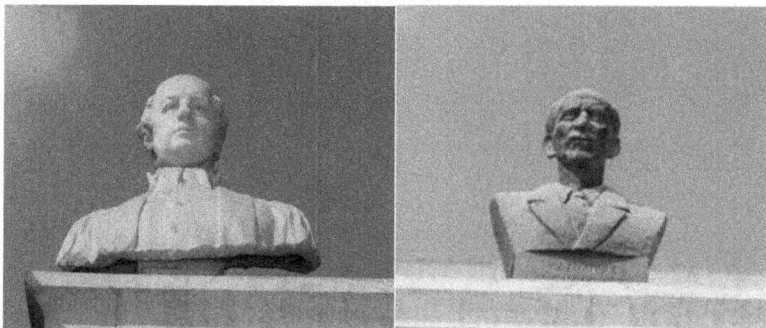

Hincks and Kazimierz Michalowski

Luigi Vassili and Brugsch Pascha

FREDERICK MONDERSON

Richard Lepsius (1810-1884) and Th. De Veira

B.C. Loncherik Hippolito Rosellini

L. Habachi and Sany Galova

INTRIGUE THROUGH TIME

Selim Hasan and Ahmed Kamal

Z. Ghoneim and J.F. Champollion

Amdee Feyron and Pleyte

FREDERICK MONDERSON

Sir Gaston Maspero and Peter Le Page Renouf

Auguste Mariette looks toward the Cairo Museum institution he helped create that has been so instrumental in developing the discipline of Egyptology and preserving the monuments of an ancient culture that continues to fascinate the world about its originality.

INTRIGUE THROUGH TIME

Walking to the other end of the grounds to once more admire this wonderful building holding such memorable artifacts of his country's history, Mentuhotep turned and looked upwards. As an architect himself, our hero was flabbergasted to see the name of the architect, M. Dourgnon listed. In his day, architects did not place their name on monuments and only received any recognition if her majesty thought an individual deserved such an honor. In this case, "to have one's name written in the colonnade" was the honor of the day.

An architect himself, Mentuhotep was pleased to see another get recognition, for in his day architects did not display their names on their work. Then, turning to once more admire the beautifully exquisite upper regions of the entrance portal to the Museum, Mentuhotep smiled, knowing in his day he produced work just as beautiful which was a part of his function of architect and Commander of the Imperial Guard of His Majesty, Herself, Queen Hatshepsut.

FREDERICK MONDERSON

Eventually, they exited the premises and hailed a cab to ride back to Mena House.

On the way, the taxi driver enquired if they had visited a Papyrus or Perfume Factory. He said Lotus Oils had the best perfumes and His Majesty's Papyrus carried the most authentic and best art on papyrus in Cairo. The both liked the names. She bought the sweet-smelling stuff and he, Papyrus with a message, viz., Psychostasia or the Judgment, the King in his Chariot trampling a foe, the Goddess Nuit spanning the sky. He gave a thought to importing papyrus for sale in New York but soon dismissed the idea. His business transactions must be of a more costly nature. Finally, they reached Mena House. He settled accounts with the taxi driver and gave him a big tip for he realized the Perfume Factory stop and purchase brought great joy to Fantegla.

Back at the hotel as they came up for air in the erogenous zone, he told her: "Well, honey, our stay in Egypt is over. Tomorrow morning, we head to the Danish Cutter for the Trans-Atlantic Cruise back home."

"Great," she said smiling, "now the real fun begins," thinking 'I've been away from my man for so long, I have lots to make up. After all, I could not get more pregnant.'

Luckily, she was not saying much out loud. Michael was in deep thought. Having been on military expeditions in his day, he knew you must remain consistently vigilant until the mission is completed. This time it was down to the wire. Before then, anything could go wrong. He simply wanted to board the Danish Cutter Cruiser and leave the Port of Alexandria. In ancient times this place was called *Racotis*. Only after boarding can he really think clearly of giving Fantegla the full treatment.

Come morning on the fateful day. They were up, showered, dressed and down to breakfast. Soon they checked out of the hotel and were in a cab heading to the Port to board their cruise ship. Suddenly, halfway there a police car appeared behind them with lights flashing and siren blazing. The driver said: "I wonder what all the commotion is," and he pulled over to the side. Soon the vehicle passed and continued on its way with siren blazing and lights still flashing. Shortly after they made the Pier and there, she stood the Danish Cutter, the object of their great escape. Fatefully, he thought,

INTRIGUE THROUGH TIME

'a slow boat' home with merriment and 'great expectations for the future.' 'This should be the ride of our lives.'

After he had unloaded their luggage, the taxi driver got a hefty reward for simply pulling over and allowing the police to continue on their way, doing their job. Soon the couple and their luggage were aboard, checked into their lavish cabin and closed the door. After a while they could not tell if it was the motion of their waterbed, or that the ship had unmoored and was heading out to sea.

One evening, two days later they had cleared the Mediterranean and were heading into the Atlantic Ocean. While embraced on deck enjoying the stars between the heavens and the deep blue sea, she said quietly: "I'm pregnant." Without batting an eyelid, still looking straight ahead, he gave her a warm, soft, sensitive hug, something he was famous for. He thought, 'Vizier Puyemre and mother Cheraisha, here is your grandchild finally. Better late than never!' The future never looked brighter!

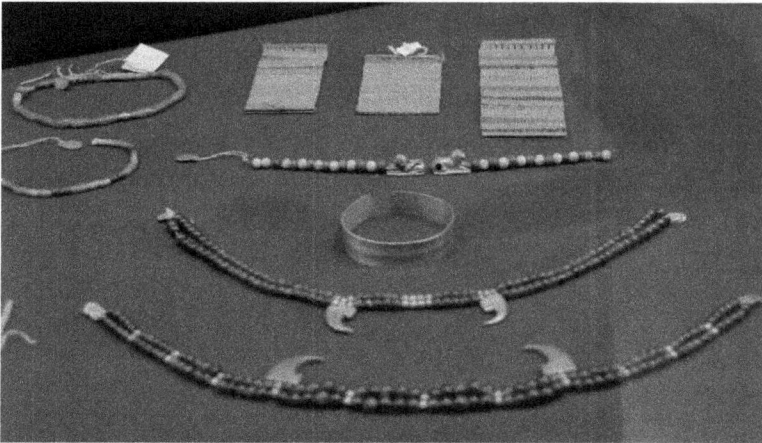

Some jewelry Mentuhotep retrieved from his Deir el Bahari "horde" as displayed at the Cairo Museum of Egyptian Antiquities.

Ankh, symbol of life in pure gold.